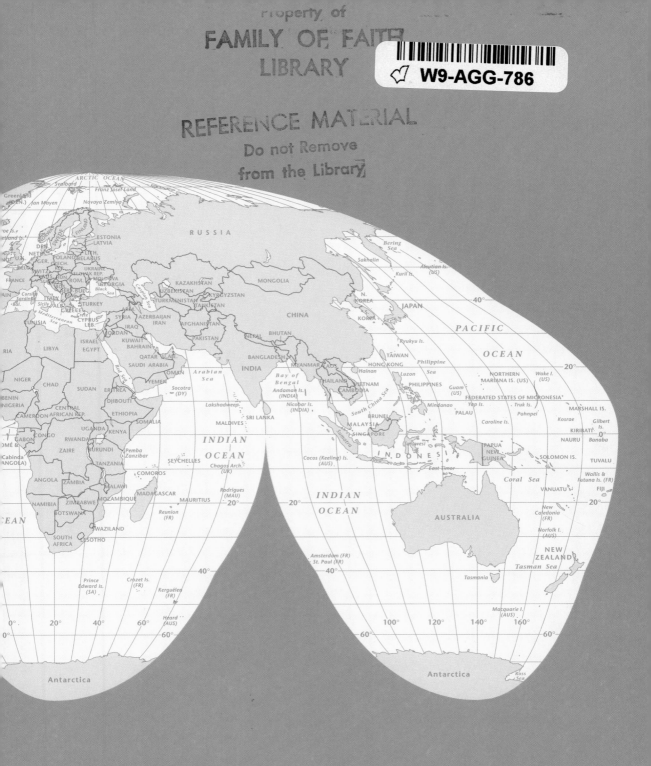

Junior
Worldmark
Encyclopedia
of the

Nations

VOLUME 2

Junior Worldmark Encyclopedia of the

Nations

An imprint of Gale Research
An ITP Information/Reference Group Company

Changing the Way the World Learns

NEW YORK • LONDON • BONN • BOSTON • DETROIT
MADRID • MELBOURNE • MEXICO CITY • PARIS
SINGAPORE • TOKYO • TORONTO • WASHINGTON
ALBANY NY • BELMONT CA • CINCINNATI OH

VOLUME 2

Bulgaria to
Czech Republic

JUNIOR WORLDMARK ENCYCLOPEDIA OF THE NATIONS

Timothy L. Gall and Susan Bevan Gall, *Editors*
Rosalie Wieder, *Senior Editor*
Deborah Baron and Daniel M. Lucas, *Associate Editors*
Brian Rajewski and Deborah Rutti, *Graphics and Layout*
Cordelia R. Heaney, *Editorial Assistant*
Dianne K. Daeg de Mott, Janet Fenn, Matthew Markovich,
    Ariana Ranson, and Craig Strasshofer, *Copy Editors*
Janet Fenn and Matthew Markovich, *Proofreaders*

U•X•L Staff

Jane Hoehner, *U•X•L Developmental Editor*
Sonia Benson and Rob Nagel, *Contributors*
Thomas L. Romig, *U•X•L Publisher*
Mary Beth Trimper, *Production Director*
Evi Seoud, *Assistant Production Manager*
Shanna Heilveil, *Production Associate*
Cynthia Baldwin, *Product Design Manager*
Barbara J. Yarrow, *Graphic Services Supervisor*
Mary Krzewinski, *Cover Designer*
Margaret McAvoy-Amoto, *Permissions Associate (Pictures)*

Library of Congress Cataloging-in-Publication Data
Junior Worldmark encyclopedia of the nations / edited by Timothy Gall
  and Susan Gall.
       p.   cm.
    Includes bibliographical references and index.
    ISBN 0-7876-0741-X (set)
    1. Geography--Encyclopedias, Juvenile. 2. History--Encyclopedias,
Juvenile. 3. Economics--Juvenile literature. 4. Political science--
Encyclopedia, Juvenile. 5. United Nations--Encyclopedias,
Juvenile. I. Gall, Timothy L. II. Gall, Susan B.
G63.J86   1995
910'.3--dc20   95-36739
                                                        CIP

ISBN 0-7876-0741-X (set)
ISBN 0-7876-0742-8 (vol. 1)   ISBN 0-7876-0743-6 (vol. 2)   ISBN 0-7876-0744-4 (vol. 3)
ISBN 0-7876-0745-2 (vol. 4)   ISBN 0-7876-0746-0 (vol. 5)   ISBN 0-7876-0747-9 (vol. 6)
ISBN 0-7876-0748-7 (vol. 7)   ISBN 0-7876-0749-5 (vol. 8)   ISBN 0-7876-0750-9 (vol. 9)

U•X•L is an imprint of Gale Research Inc.,
an International Thomson Publishing Company.
ITP logo is a trademark under license.

CONTENTS

Guide to Country Articles

Every country profile in this encyclopedia includes the same 35 headings. Also included in every profile is a map (showing the country and its location in the world), the country's flag and seal, and a table of data on the country. The country articles are organized alphabetically in nine volumes. A glossary of terms is included in each of the nine volumes. This glossary defines many of the specialized terms used throughout the encyclopedia. A keyword index to all nine volumes appears at the end of Volume 9.

Flag color symbols

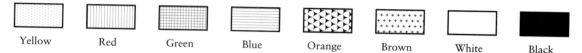

Yellow   Red   Green   Blue   Orange   Brown   White   Black

Alphabetical listing of sections

Section	No.	Section	No.
Agriculture	21	Income	18
Armed Forces	16	Industry	19
Bibliography	35	Judicial System	15
Climate	3	Labor	20
Domesticated Animals	22	Languages	9
Economy	17	Location and Size	1
Education	31	Media	32
Energy and Power	27	Migration	7
Environment	5	Mining	25
Ethnic Groups	8	Plants and Animals	4
Famous People	34	Political Parties	14
Fishing	23	Population	6
Foreign Trade	26	Religions	10
Forestry	24	Social Development	28
Government	13	Topography	2
Health	29	Tourism/Recreation	33
History	12	Transportation	11
Housing	30		

Sections listed numerically

No.	Section	No.	Section
1	Location and Size.	19	Industry
2	Topography	20	Labor
3	Climate	21	Agriculture
4	Plants and Animals	22	Domesticated Animals
5	Environment	23	Fishing
6	Population	24	Forestry
7	Migration	25	Mining
8	Ethnic Groups	26	Foreign Trade
9	Languages	27	Energy and Power
10	Religions	28	Social Development
11	Transportation	29	Health
12	History	30	Housing
13	Government	31	Education
14	Political Parties	32	Media
15	Judicial System	33	Tourism/Recreation
16	Armed Forces	34	Famous People
17	Economy	35	Bibliography
18	Income		

Abbreviations and acronyms to know

GMT= Greenwich mean time. The prime, or Greenwich, meridian passes through Greenwich, England (near London), and marks the center of the initial time zone for the world. The standard time of all 24 time zones relate to Greenwich mean time. Every profile contains a map showing the country and its location in the world.

These abbreviations are used in references to famous people:
b.=born
d.=died
fl.=flourished (lived and worked)
r.=reigned (for kings, queens, and similar monarchs)

A dollar sign ($) stands for US$ unless otherwise indicated.

BULGARIA

Republic of Bulgaria

Republika Bulgaria

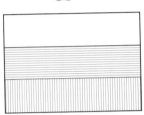

CAPITAL: Sofia (Sofiya).

FLAG: The flag is a tricolor of white, green, and red horizontal stripes.

ANTHEM: *Bulgariya mila, zemya na geroi (Dear Bulgaria, Land of Heroes).*

MONETARY UNIT: The lev (Lv) of 100 stotinki has coins of 1, 2, 5, 10, 20, and 50 stotinki and 1 and 2 leva, and notes of 1, 2, 5, 10, 20, 50, and 100 leva. Lv1 = $1.209 (or $1 = Lv0.827).

WEIGHTS AND MEASURES: The metric system is the legal standard.

HOLIDAYS: New Year's Day, 1 January; Labor Days, 1–2 May; Education and Culture Day, 24 May; Christmas, 24–25 December.

TIME: 2 PM=noon GMT.

1 LOCATION AND SIZE

Part of the Balkan Peninsula, Bulgaria has an area of 110,910 square kilometers (42,823 square miles) with a total boundary length of 2,162 kilometers (1,343 miles). It is slightly larger than the state of Tennessee. Bulgaria's capital city, Sofia, is located in the west central part of the country.

2 TOPOGRAPHY

Bulgaria consists of the Danubian tableland in the north; the Balkan Mountains (Stara Planina) in the center of the country; and the Thracian Plain, drained by the Maritsa River, in the south. The Rhodope, Rila, and Pirin mountains lie in the southwestern part of the country. The highest point in Bulgaria is the Musala peak, at 2,925 meters (9,596 feet). The Danube river forms most of the northern boundary with Romania.

3 CLIMATE

The Danubian tableland is exposed to cold winter winds from the north. The Thracian Plain, protected from the northern frosts by the Balkan Mountains, has a modified Mediterranean climate. January temperatures are between 0° and 2°C (32°–36°F) in the lowlands but colder in the mountains; July temperatures average about 22° to 24°C (72°–75°F). Precipitation amounts to an average of 64 centimeters (25 inches).

4 PLANTS AND ANIMALS

Most trees in the northeast steppe region have been cut down to make room for farm land. The Balkan Mountains are covered by broadleaf forests at lower altitudes and by needle-leaf conifers at higher elevations. The vegetation of the Thracian Plain is a mixture of forest and Mediterranean plants. Clearing of forests has reduced the amount of wildlife, which includes bears, foxes, squirrels, elks, wildcats, and rodents of various types.

5 ENVIRONMENT

Transportation, chemical production, and other industries have polluted Bulgaria's air. Twenty-five percent of Bulgaria's forests have been significantly damaged by air pollution. Bulgaria's rivers and the Black Sea are also seriously affected by industrial and chemical pollutants.

A total of 3 species of mammals, 15 bird species, and 1 species of reptile are endangered. Also threatened as of 1994 are 88 plant species out of a total of 3,650.

6 POPULATION

The population estimate in 1994 is 8,907,799. The projected population for the year 2000 is 8,897,000. The estimated average density in 1994 was about 80 persons per square kilometer (208 persons per square mile). Sofia, the capital and principal city, had an estimated population of 1,141,142 in 1990.

7 MIGRATION

Most emigrants since the 1950s have been Turks bound for Turkey or other Balkan countries. A total of 313,894 emigrated to Turkey in 1989 because of government persecution. In 1991, about 3 million Bulgarians were living abroad, including 1,200,000 in the former Yugoslavia, 800,000 in other Balkan countries, and 500,000 in the former Soviet Union.

8 ETHNIC GROUPS

In the mid-1990s, Bulgarians accounted for an estimated 80–85% of the total population. The Turks number about 900,000–1,250,000 (10–14% of the total). The number of Gypsies is estimated at 450,000–700,000 (5–8%) and the number of Pomaks at 150,000–300,000 (1–3%). Other groups include Macedonians, Romanian-speaking Vlachs, and Greek-speaking Karakatchans (nomadic mountain shepherds of Romanian origin). Bulgaria's cities have small minorities of Russians, Jews, Armenians, Tatars, and Greeks.

9 LANGUAGES

Bulgarian is classified as a Slavic language of the southern group, which also includes Macedonian, Serbo-Croatian, and Slovenian. Bulgarian was the first Slavic language to be written down. In the ninth century, two monks, Cyril and Methodius, created a new alphabet. It is based partly on the Greek alphabet and became known as the Cyrillic alphabet. Today it is used for Russian and other Slavic languages.

10 RELIGIONS

According to recent estimates, about 88% of the population belongs to the Eastern Orthodox Church. An estimated 9% are Muslims and 3% are Jews. The new constitution of 1991 guarantees freedom of religion to all. Diplomatic relations with the Vatican were established in 1990.

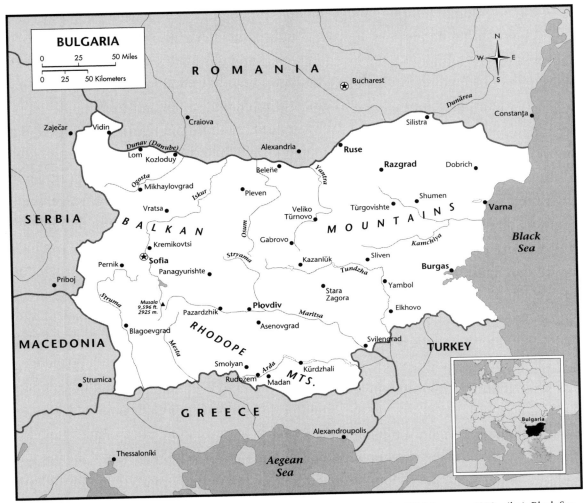

LOCATION: 41°14′ to 44°13′N; 22°22′ to 28°37′E. **BOUNDARY LENGTHS:** Romania, 609 kilometers (378 miles); Black Sea, 378 kilometers (235 miles); Turkey, 259 kilometers (161 miles); Greece, 493 kilometers (306 miles); Yugoslavia, 506 kilometers (315 miles). **TERRITORIAL SEA LIMIT:** 12 miles.

11 TRANSPORTATION

Railroads are still the basic means of freight transportation in Bulgaria. Of the 4,294 kilometers (2,668 miles) of railroad lines in use in 1991, about 94% were standard gauge. In 1991, about 1,450,000 registered vehicles traveled on about 33,535 kilometers (20,839 miles) of hard-surfaced roads, including 242 kilometers (150 miles) of highways.

Water transportation is also significant. At the end of 1991, Bulgaria's maritime fleet totaled 1.2 million gross registered tons, as compared with 97,800 gross regis-

3

Photo credit: George Petrov

A view of downtown Sofia, Bulgaria's capital city. Located in the front of the photo is the Parliament building; behind it is St. Alexander Nevski Cathedral.

tered tons in 1961. The major seaports are Burgas and Varna. Principal river ports are Ruse, Lom, and Vidin. Sofia's Vrazhdebna Airport is the major air center, but there are also international airports at Varna and Burgas. Civilian airlines in Bulgaria performed 1,171 million passenger-kilometers (728 million passenger-miles) of service in 1992.

12 HISTORY

Early History

The Bulgarians have lived in their present homeland for thirteen centuries. They represent a merger of Bulgar invaders and local Slavic tribes which occurred in the seventh century. The Bulgarians' language and cultural roots came from the Slavs; their name and their early political system came from the Bulgars, a Central Asian Turkic tribe.

The early Bulgarian state adopted Christianity in AD 865. However, by the end of the fourteenth century, Bulgaria was overrun by the Ottoman Turks, who ruled the country until 1878.

1878–1944

In 1878, northern Bulgaria became an independent principality under Turkish control, with its capital at Sofia. In 1885, it seized control of the remaining part of the country, then known as Eastern Rumelia. In 1908, Bulgaria declared itself a kingdom completely independent of Turkey. The ruling Bulgarian prince, Ferdinand of Saxe-Coburg-Gotha, assumed the title of tsar.

Bulgaria was on the losing side in World War I and lost its outlet to the Aegean Sea in 1919. By this time, Ferdinand had abdicated in favor of his son, Boris III, who ruled Bulgaria until his death in 1943. After an early period of stability and reform, King Boris's government became more and more dictatorial.

When World War II broke out, Bulgaria moved toward an alliance with Germany in the hope of regaining territories lost in World War I. However, in September 1944, Soviet troops crossed the Danube and took control of the country. A coalition government was established, dominated by the Communist Party.

1946–1981

In September 1946, the Bulgarian people voted to replace the monarchy with the People's Republic of Bulgaria. A new constitution in 1947 gave the government control of industry, banking, public utilities, and agriculture. Each program was modeled on the Soviet system.

The Bulgarian government remained steadfastly loyal to Moscow. However, in the late 1980s and early 1990s, the radical changes that Mikhail Gorbachev was introducing in the Soviet Union encouraged reformist elements within the Bulgarian Communist Party. The reformists eventually won the day and Bulgaria's first non-Communist government since World War II was elected in October 1991. The new government undertook an ambitious program of economic and political transformation.

However, Bulgaria's economy has continued to deteriorate and political and economic problems persist.

13 GOVERNMENT

The Constitution of July 1991 provides for a presidential-parliamentary form of republican government.

The president, who is chief of state, is popularly elected. The president chooses the prime minister, who is then confirmed by the National Assembly. In practice, the president sets the overall direction of policy. The prime minister and his cabinet, presently fourteen people, are responsible for putting that policy to work. The legislative branch of government is the National Assembly, with 240 seats.

Bulgaria is divided into eight counties, plus the city of Sofia.

14 POLITICAL PARTIES

The former Communist Party, renamed the Bulgarian Socialist Party (BSP) in 1990, is committed to a program of economic reform and democratization. There is an internal split between those pushing for fast reform and those wishing to slow it down or prevent it altogether.

The Socialists did surprisingly well in the 1991 elections, gaining 53% of the vote. By 1992, their support had dropped to 33%, making them a minority party by

Photo credit: AP/Wide World Photos

Two Bulgarian women line up to cast their ballots in Bulgaria's first free election since 1932.

four parliamentary seats. The largest vote-getter in 1992 was the Union of Democratic Forces (UDF), an umbrella group of opposition forces.

The third party, the Movement for Rights and Freedoms (MRF), primarily represents the interests of Bulgaria's large Turkish minority (about 11% of the population).

Right-wing parties include the Bulgarian National Radical Party, the Defense of National Interests, and the Revival Movement. The Revival Movement is led by Father Georgi Gelemenov, who makes no secret of his admiration for Nazi ideology.

In practice, however, support for these parties seems to be limited.

In the 1992 elections, the UDF took 110 seats, the BSP took 106 seats, and the MRF took 24 seats, giving this smallest party a powerful voice as the necessary coalition partner.

15 JUDICIAL SYSTEM

Under the 1971 constitution, members of the Supreme Court are elected by, and subordinate to, the National Assembly. The Supreme Court is a court of original as well as appellate jurisdiction and is organized into criminal, civil, and military divisions. Its judges serve five-year terms.

Below the Supreme Court there were, in 1985, 28 provincial courts and 105 regional courts. A law of 2 June 1961 provided for "comrades" courts to be established at all businesses of 50 or more employees to deal with violations of labor discipline, peace, and property. Sentences vary and cannot be appealed.

A Constitutional Court is responsible for judicial review of legislation and for resolving issues of competency of the other branches of government, as well as impeachments and election law.

16 ARMED FORCES

By 1993, the strength of the armed forces was estimated at 107,000 men, including 70,000 draftees. It consists of ground, naval, and air elements. The army numbered 75,000, the navy 10,000, and the air force 22,000, with some 259 combat aircraft.

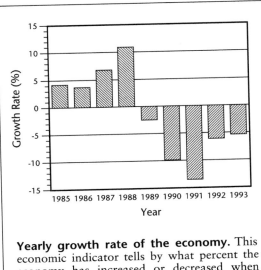

Yearly growth rate of the economy. This economic indicator tells by what percent the economy has increased or decreased when compared with the previous year.

17 ECONOMY

Until 1990, the country had a centrally planned economy, along Soviet lines. Its sequence of five-year economic plans, beginning in 1949, emphasized industrial production. The Bulgarian economy was greatly influenced by the breakup of the Soviet Union, because it relied on the Soviet Union and other CMEA (Council for Mutual Economic Assistance) countries for essential imports and as the major markets for its exports.

Bulgaria began an economic reform program supported by the IBRD (International Bank for Reconstruction and Development) and IMF (International Monetary Fund). However, the economy remained largely state-controlled. The unemployment rate was 16% in 1993; the inflation rate was 73%.

18 INCOME

In 1992, the gross national product (GNP) was $11,906 million at current prices, or $1,140 per capita. For the period 1985–92 the average inflation rate was 30.7%, resulting in a real growth rate in per capita gross national product of –3.6%.

19 INDUSTRY

In the postwar period, the Communist regime emphasized an industrial program that resulted in a large increase in the metalworking and chemical industries. Official statistics indicate that industrial output grew by 1,100% between 1956 and 1980. Ferrous metallurgy (iron-working) was given special emphasis in the 1960s, machine-building and chemicals in the 1970s and early 1980s, and high technology in the mid-1980s.

In 1992, industrial production included cement, 2,132,000 tons; crude steel, 1,551,000 tons; pig iron and ferroalloys, 853,000 tons; sulfuric acid, 404,208 tons; canned fruit and vegetables, 102,148 tons; refined sugar, 97,596 tons; 68,604 washing machines; and 61,380 television sets.

20 LABOR

In 1992, total employment amounted to 3,112,900. Of this total, 40.2% was employed in industry and construction (45.5% in 1985); 18% in agriculture and forestry (20.9% in 1985); 10.6% in trade (8.4% in 1985); 7.8% in transport and communications (6.6% in 1985); and 23.5% in social, cultural, health, and other services (18.5% in 1985).

Women represent about half of all agricultural workers outside the collective farms, where their participation is even greater. They also comprise nearly half the industrial labor force. The 1991 constitution guarantees the right of all to form or join trade unions of their own choosing.

Bulgaria's child labor laws are fairly well enforced. The minimum age for employment is sixteen, or eighteen for dangerous work. Some underage children work on family farms, but abuses appear to be rare.

21 AGRICULTURE

In 1991, the total agricultural land area covered 6,161,000 hectares (15,224,000 acres), of which 4,162,000 hectares (10,284,000 acres) were fields and 1,999,000 hectares (4,940,000 acres) were meadows and pastures. In March 1991, the government adopted a land law which restored ownership rights to former owners of land taken over by the government.

Production of the following crops in 1992 (in thousands of tons) was: wheat, 3,270; corn, 2,300; barley, 1,100; sunflower seeds, 470; tobacco, 90; and soybeans, 16. Bulgaria is a major supplier of grapes, apples, and tomatoes to Europe and the former Soviet Union. Potatoes and paprika are also important crops.

22 DOMESTICATED ANIMALS

Meadows and pastures make up about 18% of the total land area. Bulgaria had 21 million fowl, 6.7 million sheep, 3 million hogs, 329,000 donkeys, and 113,000 horses in 1992. Meat production (in carcass weight) in 1992 amounted to 614,000 tons. In the same year, the country produced 1,550,000 tons of milk and 88,300 tons of eggs.

23 FISHING

Fishing resources in the Black Sea are not very abundant. In 1991, the total catch was 49,915 tons. Whiting account for about 40% of the catch.

24 FORESTRY

Forests cover over 35% of Bulgaria's territory, with about 24% coniferous and 76% deciduous trees. In 1991, Bulgaria produced 3.6 million cubic meters of timber. Intensive cutting and neglect before, during, and after World War II have harmed Bulgaria's forests. The government has planted new trees in many areas. The twenty-year plan (1961–80) called for the planting of 1.4 million hectares (3.5 million acres). During the 1980s, annual reforestation averaged 50,000 hectares (123,500 acres).

25 MINING

Coal is the most important mineral fuel. The principal metallic ores are copper, iron, lead, and zinc. In 1991, more than 90% of total copper ore production (6 million tons) came from the three mining complexes of Elatzite, Medet, and Assarel. That year, more than 80% of total iron ore production (one million tons) came from the open pit mine at Kremikovtsi. Other minerals mined are manganese (45,000 tons in 1991), lead, zinc, uranium, and gold.

26 FOREIGN TRADE

In 1992, the principal exports were rolled sheet metal, cigarettes, industrial trucks, tobacco, urea, wines, zinc, and footwear, in that order. The principal imports were crude oil, natural gas, motor cars, diesel fuel, fuel oil, coal, and pharmaceuticals.

After 1990, trade with Western Europe, Greece, the former Yugoslavia, and Turkey became much more important than before. In 1991, 49.8% of all exports still went to the former Soviet Union and 43.2% of all imports still came from the former Soviet Union.

Excluding the former Soviet Union, Bulgaria's main trade partners in 1992 were Germany, Turkey, France, Italy, the former Yugoslavia, and Greece.

27 ENERGY AND POWER

In the 1980s, Bulgaria produced only about 35% of its energy needs. Of the 38,917 million kilowatt hours produced in 1991, 36,476 million kilowatt hours were produced by thermal stations (including 13,184 million kilowatt hours by nuclear power plants) and 2,441 million kilowatt hours by hydroelectric plants. Lignite and brown coal are major sources (98%) for thermal power plants.

By 1991, nuclear plants supplied about 40% of Bulgaria's power. Continuous problems with the two oldest reactors contributed to the decline of the country's overall electrical production. The reactors were shut down in 1991.

Petroleum output was 500,000 tons in 1991. In September 1974, a Soviet-Bulgar-

Photo credit: George Petrov

A street vendor attracts a customer in the oldtown section of the southern city of Plovdiv.

ian natural gas pipeline was opened with an annual carrying capacity of five million cubic meters. In 1991, Libya doubled its crude oil deliveries to Bulgaria to 160,000 tons per month, in order to offset declining exports from the former Soviet Union.

28 SOCIAL DEVELOPMENT

Social insurance is administered by the trade unions and is comprehensive. A state employee qualifies for sickness benefits after three months of employment. Disability pensions range from 40% to 75% of previous earnings. Benefits also include old age and survivors' pensions.

Selected Social Indicators

These statistics are estimates for the period 1988 to 1993. For comparison purposes, data for the United States, and averages for low-income countries and high-income countries, are also given.

Indicator	Bulgaria	Low-income countries	High-income countries	United States
Per capita gross national product†	**$1,140**	$380	$23,680	$24,740
Population growth rate	**-0.4%**	1.9%	0.6%	1.0%
Population growth rate in urban areas	**0.5%**	3.9%	0.8%	1.3%
Population per square kilometer of land	**80**	78	25	26
Life expectancy in years	**71**	62	77	76
Number of people per physician	**318**	>3,300	453	419
Number of pupils per teacher (primary school)	**14**	39	<18	20
Illiteracy rate (15 years and older)	**7%**	41%	<5%	<3%
Energy consumed per capita (kg of oil equivalent)	**1,954**	364	5,203	7,918

† The gross national product (GNP) is the total dollar value of all goods and services produced by a country in a year. The per capita GNP is calculated by dividing a country's GNP by its population. The World Bank defines low-income countries as those with a per capita GNP of $695 or less. High-income countries have a per capita GNP of $8,626 or more. Less than 14% of the world's 5.5 billion people live in high-income countries, while almost 60% live in low-income countries.

> = greater than   < = less than

Sources: World Bank, Social Indicators of Development 1995, Baltimore: Johns Hopkins University Press, 1995. Central Intelligence Agency, World Fact Book, Washington, D.C.: Government Printing Office, 1994.

Special benefits include a grant upon birth of a child and monthly family allowances for children, the amounts increasing with the number of children. As of 1991, paid maternity leave was 100% of earnings for 10–14 months, depending on the number of other children.

Although women have equal rights under the constitution, they have not had the same employment opportunities as men.

29 HEALTH

The Ministry of Health is the controlling agency for the health system in Bulgaria, spending $1,154 million in 1990. Medical care has never been well funded, and the shift from a centrally planned to a private enterprise system made matters worse. Doctors continue to receive low wages and operate inadequate and outdated machinery. Patients on the whole receive minimal health services.

In 1990, there were 28,497 doctors. From 1988 to 1992, Bulgaria had 3.19 doctors per 1,000 people (in 1990, one physician to 320 people). In 1990, there were 90,000 hospital beds (10 per 1,000).

More people die from strokes in Bulgaria than anywhere else in Europe, and circulatory diseases account for almost 60% of deaths. Smoking is on the increase; alcohol consumption is high; physical activity is low; and obesity is common. Bulgarians have a high intake of fats, sugars, and salt. One out of eight people has high blood pressure. Life expectancy in 1992 was 71 years on the average.

30 HOUSING

Although housing construction during 1976–85 averaged about 60,000 units per year, the housing shortage continues, especially in the larger cities. This is due to the influx into urban areas of new workers and the emphasis placed on nonresidential construction.

At the end of 1985, there were 3,092,000 dwelling units in the country, 24% more than in 1975; by 1991, this figure had risen to 3,406,000. The number of new houses built plummeted from 62,926 in 1988 to 40,154 in 1989, 26,200 in 1990, and 19,423 in 1991.

31 EDUCATION

Illiteracy has been decreasing steadily. The government claims that literacy is universal, but Western sources estimate 7% illiteracy. Education is free and compulsory for eight years between the ages of seven and fifteen. In 1991, there were 2,827 primary level schools with 62,012 teachers and 920,694 students. At the secondary level, there were 28,874 teachers and 383,825 students, 233,528 of them in vocational courses.

There are over 30 higher education institutions, including 4 universities. The most important is the University of Sofia, founded in 1888. The others are: University of Plovdiv, University of Veliko Tarnovo, and American University in Bulgaria (founded in 1991). All higher level institutions had a total of 185,914 students and 23,954 teaching staff in 1991.

32 MEDIA

Postal and telecommunications systems are owned and operated by the state. Telex service to the rest of the world improved markedly in 1982, when a new computerized telegraph exchange was put in service. By the mid-1980s, most communities were connected by telephone; telephones numbered 2.7 million in 1991. In the same year, there were 3,970,000 radio receivers and 2,260,000 TV sets. There are 20 AM and 15 FM stations and 29 TV stations. Television was introduced in 1959; in 1992 there were 2 television channels.

In 1991, Bulgaria published 728 newspapers, with a total annual circulation of 1,079 million; the 13 dailies had an annual circulation of 760,200. The principal Sofia papers, with their estimated daily circulations (1992), are *24 Chasa* (320,000); *Trud* (250,000); *Democraciya* (105,000); *Otechestven Vestnik* (100,000); *Vecherni Novini* (90,000); and *Zemedelsko Zname* (30,000).

33 TOURISM AND RECREATION

Despite the country's economic troubles, tourism in Bulgaria has risen rapidly since the end of Communist rule. The tourist industry is in the process of being turned over to private ownership, a development that is expected to improve the quality of accommodations. Bulgaria is rich in mineral waters and has numerous tourist spas.

Visitors are attracted to the Black Sea resorts and the Balkan mountains. In 1990, tourist receipts totaled approximately $320 million. The number of foreign visitors was estimated at 6.8 million in 1991, of whom 3.2 million came from Europe and 2.7 million from the Middle East and Turkey.

34 FAMOUS BULGARIANS

Kristo Botev (1848–76) was one of Bulgaria's greatest poets. The most significant writer after the liberation of 1878 was Ivan Vazov (1850–1921), whose *Under the Yoke* gives an impressive picture of the struggle against the Turks. Elin Pelin (1878–1949) and Iordan Iovkov (1884–1939) wrote popular short stories on regional themes. Elias Canetti (b.1905), Bulgarian-born but living since 1938 in the United Kingdom, received the Nobel Prize for literature in 1981. Ivan Mrkvicka (1856–1938), a distinguished Czech painter who took up residence in Bulgaria, founded the Academy of Fine Arts in Sofia.

The best-known modern Bulgarian, Georgi Dimitrov (1882–1949), was falsely charged in 1933 with burning the Reichstag building in Berlin. He became general secretary of the Comintern until its dissolution and prime minister of Bulgaria in 1946. Todor Zhivkov (b.1911) was first secretary of the Bulgarian Communist Party between 1954 and 1989, the longest tenure of any Warsaw Pact leader. Zhivkov's daughter Lyudmila Zhivkova (1942–81), a Politburo member since 1979, was regarded by Western observers as second only to her father in power and influence. Todor Zhivkov was replaced by Dimitar Popov as premier of a coalition government headed by the Socialist Party (formerly the Communist Party).

35 BIBLIOGRAPHY

Bulgaria: A Country Study, 2nd ed. Washington, D.C.: Government Printing Office, 1993.

Constant, Stephen. *Foxy Ferdinand, Tsar of Bulgaria*. London: Sidgwick & Jackson, Ltd., 1979.

Crampton, R. *A Short History of Modern Bulgaria*. Cambridge, England: Cambridge University Press, 1987.

Resnick, A. *Bulgaria*. Chicago: Children's Press, 1995.

Welsh, William A. *Bulgaria*. Boulder, Colo.: Westview, 1986.

BURKINA FASO

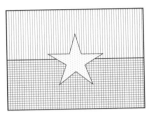

Republic of Burkina Faso

Burkina Faso Jamahiriya

CAPITAL: Ouagadougou.

FLAG: The flag consists of two equal horizontal stripes of red and green divided by a narrow gold band. A five-point gold star is at the center.

ANTHEM: The national anthem begins "Contre le férule humiliante il y a déjà mille ans" ("Against the humiliating bondage of a thousand years").

MONETARY UNIT: The Communauté Financière Africaine franc (CFA Fr) is a paper currency with one basic official rate based on the French franc (100 CFA Fr = Fr1). There are coins of 1, 2, 5, 10, 25, 50, 100, and 500 CFA francs, and notes of 50, 100, 500, 1,000, 5,000, and 10,000 CFA francs. CFA Fr1 = $0.0018 (or $1 = CFA Fr571).

WEIGHTS AND MEASURES: The metric system is the legal standard.

HOLIDAYS: New Year's Day, 1 January; Anniversary of the 1966 Revolution, 3 January; Labor Day, 1 May; Independence Day, 5 August; Assumption, 15 August; All Saints' Day, 1 November; Christmas, 25 December. Movable religious holidays include Id al-Fitr, 'Id al-'adha', Milad an-Nabi, Easter Monday, Ascension, and Pentecost Monday.

TIME: GMT.

1 LOCATION AND SIZE

Burkina Faso (formerly Upper Volta), a landlocked country in West Africa, has an area of 274,200 square kilometers (105,869 square miles). Comparatively, the area occupied by Burkina Faso is slightly larger than the state of Colorado. Burkina Faso has a total boundary length of 3,192 kilometers (1,983 miles). The capital city of Burkina Faso, Ouagadougou, is located in the center of the country.

2 TOPOGRAPHY

Burkina Faso consists for the most part of a vast plateau approximately 180–300 meters (600–1,000 feet) above sea level.

The highest point (749 meters/2,457 feet) is near the Mali border, northwest of Orodara.

3 CLIMATE

The climate is characterized by high temperatures, especially at the end of the dry season. The harmattan, a dry east wind, brings hot spells from March to May, when maximum temperatures range from 40°C to 48°C (104° to 119°F); from May to October, the climate is hot and wet, and from November to March, comfortable and dry. January temperatures range from 7°C to 13°C (44° to 55°F). Average annual rainfall varies from 115 centimeters (45 inches) is the southwest to less than 25 centimeters (10 inches) in the extreme north and northeast.

4 PLANTS AND ANIMALS

The area is largely wild bush country with a mixture of grass and small trees. The savanna, or plains, region is mainly grassland in the rainy season and semidesert during the harmattan period. Animal life, possibly the widest variety in West Africa, includes the elephant, hippopotamus, buffalo, monkey, crocodile, giraffe, various types of antelope, and a wide variety of bird and insect life.

5 ENVIRONMENT

The major environmental problems facing Burkina Faso are drought and the advance of the northern desert into the savanna, or plains. The frequent droughts in Burkina Faso and its location in the Sahara desert contribute to the nation's water supply problems. According to the World Health Organization, 80% of all disease in Burkina Faso is caused by unsafe water. Of 147 species of mammals, 10 are considered endangered.

6 POPULATION

The 1994 population was estimated at 10,278,771, with an average annual growth rate of about 2.9%. The projected population for the year 2000 is 11,833,000. Most people live in the south and center of the country, and over 80% of the population is rural.

7 MIGRATION

Seasonal labor migration in Burkina Faso began in the colonial period as a means of obtaining money for taxes and continues today as a way of increasing income. According to some estimates, as many as 2 million Burkinabe (citizens of Burkina Faso) live abroad at any one time, about half in Côte d'Ivoire and the rest throughout West Africa, where many are employed on coffee and cocoa plantations.

8 ETHNIC GROUPS

The main ethnic group in Burkina Faso is the Mossi, who make up about 55% of the total population. They are mainly farmers and live in the central portions of the country. The Bobo, the second-largest ethnic group (about 1 million), are mostly farmers, artisans, and metalworkers living in the southwest around Bobo-Dioulasso.

9 LANGUAGES

French is the official language of Burkina Faso, and Moré, spoken by 55% of the population, is the most important native language. The various ethnic groups speak their own languages.

10 RELIGIONS

An estimated 65% of the population presently follows traditional religions. Of the remainder, 25% are Muslim, and 10% are Christian, mostly Roman Catholic, who comprise 9.2% of the entire population.

11 TRANSPORTATION

In 1991, Burkina Faso had 16,500 kilometers (10,253 miles) of roads and tracks, of which 1,300 kilometers (808 miles) were paved. Many of the secondary roads are not open all year.

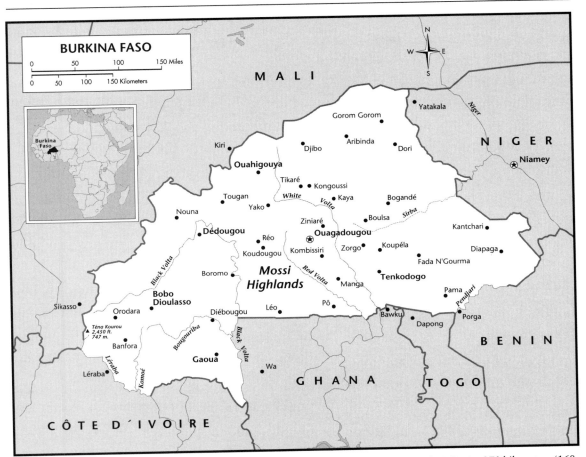

BURKINA FASO

```
0        50       100      150 Miles
0     50    100    150 Kilometers
```

MALI

NIGER

Burkina
Faso

Yatakala

Niger

Gorom Gorom

Kiri

Djibo

Aribinda

Dori

Niamey

Ouahigouya

Tikaré

Kongoussi

Bogandé

Kantchari

Tougan

White Volta

Kaya

Yako

Boulsa

Sirba

Nouna

Ziniaré

Dédougou

Réo

Ouagadougou

Koupéla

Diapaga

Koudougou

Kombissiri

Zorgo

Mossi
Highlands

Fada N'Gourma

Boromo

Red Volta

Manga

Bobo
Dioulasso

Tenkodogo

Pama

Sikasso

Orodara

Diébougou

Léo

Pô

Bawku

Porga

Pendjari

Téna Kourou
2,450 ft.
747 m.

Bougouriba

Dapong

BENIN

Banfora

Black Volta

Gaoua

Black Volta

Wa

Léraba

Komoé

Léraba

GHANA

TOGO

CÔTE D´IVOIRE

LOCATION: 9°30′ to 15°N; 2° to 5°W. **BOUNDARY LENGTHS:** Niger, 628 kilometers (390 miles); Benin, 270 kilometers (168 miles); Togo, 126 kilometers (78 miles); Ghana, 544 kilometers, (338 miles); Côte d'Ivoire, 531 kilometers (330 miles); Mali, 1,202 kilometers (747 miles).

The 510 kilometer (317 mile) Mossi Railroad in Burkina Faso is part of the line that begins at Abidjan, Côte d'Ivoire, and ends in Niger, some 1,145 kilometers (710 miles) away. There are international airports at Ouagadougou and Bobo Dioulasso, and many smaller airfields.

12 HISTORY

Until the end of the 19th century, the history of Burkina Faso is the history of the empire-building Mossi. According to legend and tradition, the Mossi entered the region from the 11th to the 13th century.

Beginning in the 14th century, the Mossi were engaged in repeated wars with the neighboring empires of Mali and Songhai, and they occupied Timbuktu (now in Mali) at various times. They were defeated by Askia Daoud of Songhai in the 16th century and thereafter stopped fighting their powerful neighbors. Their warrior

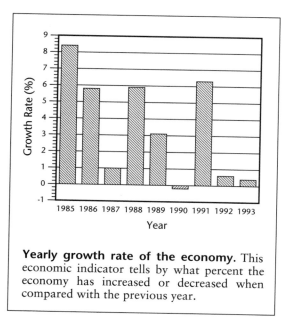

Yearly growth rate of the economy. This economic indicator tells by what percent the economy has increased or decreased when compared with the previous year.

tradition and their internal unity continued, however. When the first known European arrivals occurred, late in the 19th century, internal fighting made the Mossi prey to the invaders. The Mossi accepted French domination as a form of protection from their hostile neighbors.

In 1919, the French created a separate colony called Upper Volta (now Burkina Faso), but in 1932, Upper Volta's territory was divided among Niger, French Sudan (now Mali), and Côte d'Ivoire. Throughout the colonial period, the traditional political structure of the Mossi was unchanged, and the moro naba of Ouagadougou was regarded by the French as the emperor of the Mossi.

In 1958, Upper Volta's territorial assembly voted to make the country a self-governed state within the French Commu-

nity. The republic achieved independence on 5 August 1960. Maurice Yaméogo, leader of the Volta Democratic Union, became president, and his government banned all opposition parties. In 1965, a single election list was offered to the people, and the opposition—joined by civil servants, trade unionists, and students—started riots. Yaméogo was replaced in January 1966 by Lieutenant Colonel (later General) Sangoulé Lamizana, a former army chief of staff, who suspended the 1960 constitution, dissolved the National Assembly, and formed a military-civilian cabinet.

During the 1970s and early 1980s, Upper Volta suffered from severe political unrest, with military takeovers in 1980, 1982, and 1983, and 1987. In 1984 the nation was renamed Burkina Faso, meaning roughly "Land of Upright Men."

13 GOVERNMENT

A new constitution, establishing the Fourth Republic, was adopted on 2 June 1991 and called for an Assembly of People's Deputies with 107 seats. Captain Compaoré is Chief of State and Head of Government and he chairs a Council of Ministers. Current law calls for a second, consulting council, and proposals to formally constitute it have been set in motion by the Assembly.

14 POLITICAL PARTIES

Following the military takeover of 25 November 1980, all political parties were banned. The Compaoré government legalized parties before holding elections on 24 May 1992. Compaoré's Popular Democratic Organization—Worker's Movement (ODP-MT) gained 78 seats. The National Convention of Progressive Patriots—Social Democratic Party (CNPP-PSD) won 12 seats, and the African Democratic Assembly (ADA) won 6. Eight other parties are represented in the Assembly of People's Deputies.

15 JUDICIAL SYSTEM

At the top of the judicial system are the courts of appeal at Ouagadougou and Bobo-Dioulasso. District courts deal with cases involving civil, criminal, and commercial law, and a court at Ouagadougou specializes in common law. The courts of appeal are in the capital. In addition to the courts described above, traditional courts at the village level apply customary law in cases involving divorce and inheritance.

16 ARMED FORCES

In 1993, Burkina Faso had an army of 7,000 personnel. The army consisted of five small infantry regiments, one airborne regiment, one artillery battalion, one tank battalion, and one engineering battalion. The 200-member air force had 18 combat aircraft. Paramilitary forces totaled 1,750, and 45,000 men and women serve in a "people's militia."

17 ECONOMY

Burkina Faso is an agricultural country where about 85% of the labor force produces food, mostly for domestic consumption. Food staples—millet and sorghum, maize and rice—are the main crops. Cotton is the principal export crop.

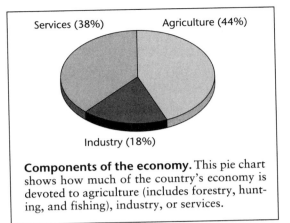

Components of the economy. This pie chart shows how much of the country's economy is devoted to agriculture (includes forestry, hunting, and fishing), industry, or services.

18 INCOME

Burkina Faso's gross national product (GNP) is about $2,908 million at current prices, or about $300 per person. For the period 1985–92 the average inflation rate was 1.8%, resulting in a real growth rate in GNP of 0.9%.

19 INDUSTRY

Industry accounts for 18% of Burkina's gross domestic product (GDP). The principal centers for economic activity are Bobo-Dioulasso, Ouagadougou, Banfora, and Koudougou, cities on the rail line to Abidjan, Côte d'Ivoire.

20 LABOR

Over 85% of the population was working in agriculture and animal husbandry in 1992, mostly at a subsistence level.

According to Burkina Faso's Labor Code, the minimum age for employment is 14. However, most children actually begin work at an earlier age, either on small

Photo credit: Corel Corporation.

A straw merchant in Burkina Faso.

family farms or within the traditional apprenticeship system.

21 AGRICULTURE

Agriculture employs the majority of the work force and accounts for an estimated 44% of the gross domestic product (GDP). In 1991, however, only an estimated 13% of the total land area was being farmed.

22 DOMESTICATED ANIMALS

In 1992 there were an estimated 6,860,000 goats, 5,350,000 sheep, 427,000 asses, 530,000 pigs, and 22,000 horses. About 120,000 head of cattle were exported in 1992, many to Côte d'Ivoire.

23 FISHING

The country has no access to the sea, and freshwater areas are limited. Fish are still caught by traditional methods, and production amounted to 7,012 tons in 1991.

24 FORESTRY

Almost all of Burkina Faso's primitive forest have been cut down for fuel or to make way for farmland. Reforestation did not begin until 1973.

25 MINING

Burkina's mineral sector is largely undeveloped. Long underestimated, the Poura gold reserves (southwest of Ouagadougou) have proven to be capable of producing

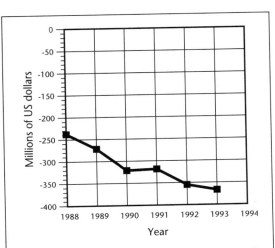

Yearly balance of trade measured in millions of US dollars. The balance of trade is the difference between what a country sells to other countries (its exports) and what it buys (its imports). If a country imports more than it exports, it has a negative balance of trade (a trade deficit). If exports exceed imports, there is a positive balance of trade (a trade surplus).

export earnings in excess of US$30 million annually.

26 FOREIGN TRADE

The main imports in 1989 were miscellaneous manufactured articles (24.8%), cereals (12.3%), chemicals (12.2%), and non-electrical machinery (10.8%).

France is Burkina Faso's most important single trading partner, with 29.2% of Burkina's exports going to France and 28.8% of imports coming from France. After France, imports came from Côte d'Ivoire and Thailand.

27 ENERGY AND POWER

The burning of wood accounts for about 92% of energy requirements. All petroleum products are imported. Total installed electrical capacity in 1991 was 59,000 kilowatts, all of it thermal.

28 SOCIAL DEVELOPMENT

The very nature of tribal organization carries with it a type of social welfare, in that the basic needs of the individual are cared for by the group.

29 HEALTH

In 1992, there were three hospital beds per 10,000 inhabitants. Average life expectancy in 1992 was estimated at 47 years. In the same year, 70% of the population had access to health care. In 1993, the government of Burkina Faso took on the project of upgrading facilities and skills, achieving control of many diseases.

30 HOUSING

Many African people, especially the Mossi, live in round huts with cone-shaped straw roofs or in rectangular huts with flat roofs.

31 EDUCATION

Though education is listed as compulsory for all children aged 6 to 15, attendance is not enforced. All public education is free. The language of instruction is French. Primary education lasts for six years and secondary for seven years. The Center for Higher Education was established in 1969, and in 1974 it became the University of Ouagadougou.

32 MEDIA

Radio, telephone, and telegraph service is available to Paris and to neighboring

Selected Social Indicators

These statistics are estimates for the period 1988 to 1993. For comparison purposes, data for the United States and averages for low-income countries and high-income countries are also given.

Indicator	Burkina Faso	Low-income countries	High-income countries	United States
Per capita gross national product†	$300	$380	$23,680	$24,740
Population growth rate	2.9%	1.9%	0.6%	1.0%
Population growth rate in urban areas	11%	3.9%	0.8%	1.3%
Population per square kilometer of land	35	78	25	26
Life expectancy in years	47	62	77	76
Number of people per physician	57,213	>3,300	453	419
Number of pupils per teacher (primary school)	60	39	<18	20
Illiteracy rate (15 years and older)	82%	41%	<5%	<3%
Energy consumed per capita (kg of oil equivalent)	16	364	5,203	7,918

† The gross national product (GNP) is the total dollar value of all goods and services produced by a country in a year. The per capita GNP is calculated by dividing a country's GNP by its population. The World Bank defines low-income countries as those with a per capita GNP of $695 or less. High-income countries have a per capita GNP of $8,626 or more. Less than 14% of the world's 5.5 billion people live in high-income countries, while almost 60% live in low-income countries.

> = greater than   < = less than

Sources: World Bank, Social Indicators of Development 1995, Baltimore: Johns Hopkins University Press, 1995. Central Intelligence Agency, World Fact Book, Washington, D.C.: Government Printing Office, 1994.

countries. Two radio stations are run by Radiodiffusion Nationale, the government radio corporation.

Burkina Faso had four daily newspapers in 1991, all published in Ouagadougou, with a total circulation of 19,500. L'Observateur Paalya had the highest circulation (8,000).

33 TOURISM AND RECREATION

Tourist attractions include the Nazinga, Arly, and "W" park game preserves, the National Museum and artisan centers in Ouagadougou, and market towns such as Gorom-Gorom.

34 FAMOUS BURKINABE

The best-known Burkinabe are Maurice Yaméogo (b.1921), a former president of Upper Volta during 1960–66; Moro Naba Kougri (1930–82), the traditional sovereign of the Mossi; and Sangoulé Lamizana (b.1916), who was president of Upper Volta from 1966 to 1980.

35 BIBLIOGRAPHY

Skinner, Elliott P. African Urban Life: The Transformation of Ouagadougou. Princeton, N.J.: Princeton University Press, 1974.

———. The Mossi of Burkina Faso: Chiefs, Politicians and Soldiers. Prospect Heights, Ill.: Waveland Press, 1989.

BURUNDI

Republic of Burundi
République du Burundi
Republika yu Burundi

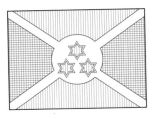

CAPITAL: Bujumbura.

FLAG: The national flag consists of a white circle in the center with arms extending to the four corners. The circle contains three red stars with green borders. Upper and lower fields formed by the circle and its arms are red; the fields on the sides are green.

ANTHEM: *Burundi Bwacu (Our Burundi)*, beginning "Burundi bwacu, Burundi buhire" ("Our Burundi, O blessed land").

MONETARY UNIT: The Burundi franc (BFr) is a paper currency. There are coins of 1, 5, and 10 francs, and notes of 10, 20, 50, 100, 500, 1,000, and 5,000 francs. BFr1 = $0.0039 (or $1 = BFr257.26).

WEIGHTS AND MEASURES: The metric system is the legal standard.

HOLIDAYS: New Year's Day, 1 January; Labor Day, 1 May; Independence Day, 1 July; Assumption, 15 August; Victory of UPRONA, 18 September; 13 October; All Saints' Day, 1 November; Christmas, 25 December. Movable religious holidays include Easter Monday, Ascension, and Pentecost Monday.

TIME: 2 PM = noon GMT.

1 LOCATION AND SIZE

Burundi is a landlocked country in east-central Africa with an area of 27,830 square kilometers (10,745 square miles). About 7% of Burundi's land area is made up of lakes. Comparatively, the area occupied by Burundi is slightly larger than the state of Maryland. Burundi's capital city, Bujumbura, is located in the western part of the country.

2 TOPOGRAPHY

Burundi is a country mainly of mountains and plateaus. A western range of mountains runs north–south and continues into Rwanda. The highest point is 2,760 meters (9,055 feet).

3 CLIMATE

Burundi in general has a tropical highland climate, with a wide daily temperature range in many areas. Temperature also varies considerably from one region to another, mostly as a result of differences in altitude. The central plateau enjoys pleasantly cool weather, with an average temperature of 20°C (68°F). The area around Lake Tanganyika is warmer, averaging 23°C (73°F). The highest mountain areas are cooler, averaging 14°C (57°F).

4 PLANTS AND ANIMALS

Burundi is one of the most eroded and deforested countries in all of tropical Africa. Of the remaining trees, the most common are eucalyptus, acacia, fig, and oil palms along the lake shores.

Photo credit: Cynthia Bassett

Burundi girls along the roadside.

Wildlife was plentiful before the region became agricultural. Still found are the elephant, hippopotamus, crocodile, wild boar, lion, antelope, and flying lemur, as well as such game birds as guinea fowl, partridge, duck, geese, quail, and snipe. All in all, some 633 bird species have been reported. In Lake Tanganyika there is a great variety of fish, including the Nile perch, freshwater sardines, and rare tropical specimens.

5 ENVIRONMENT

There are no national parks in Burundi, and laws against hunting and poaching are not enforced. The cutting of forests for fuel is uncontrolled despite legislation requiring permits. Soil erosion due to deforestation and improper terracing (ridging in the hillside) is also a serious problem. Burundi also has a problem with maintaining the purity of its water supply.

6 POPULATION

One of the most densely populated countries in Africa, Burundi in mid-1994 had an estimated total of 6,417,932 inhabitants, for an average of 231 persons per square kilometer (597 per square mile). A population of 7,237,000 is projected for the year 2000. Bujumbura, the capital, had a population of about 240,000 in 1990. Other urban areas are small and serve mainly as commercial and administrative centers.

7 MIGRATION

At the end of 1992 there were about 271,700 refugees in Burundi. Some 25,800 were from Zaire and 245,600 from Rwanda. Most of the refugees from Rwanda were members of the Tutsi tribe escaping from Hutu-ruled Rwanda.

8 ETHNIC GROUPS

The population is made up mainly of Hutu (also known as Bahutu), a Bantu people, traditionally farmers, who constitute about 85% of the inhabitants. A tall warrior people, the Tutsi (Watutsi, Watusi, Batutsi) make up less than 15% of the population but dominate the government and military.

9 LANGUAGES

The main language is Kirundi, a Bantu language. Kirundi and French are the official languages. In all the larger centers, Swahili is used as an international language.

10 RELIGIONS

In 1992, it was estimated that over 85% of the population was Christian. In 1993, 59.9% of this number was Roman Catholic. Many inhabitants follow African traditional practices, centered around belief in spirits.

11 TRANSPORTATION

Lack of adequate transportation has slowed Burundi's development. The country is landlocked, and there are no rail-

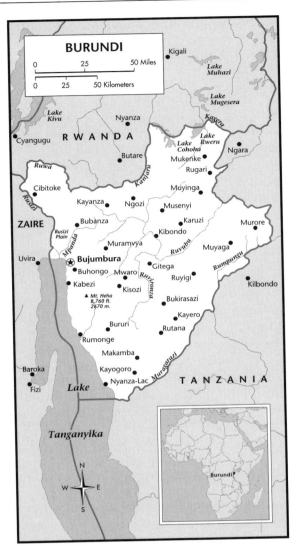

LOCATION: 2°20′ to 4°28′s; 29° to 30°50′E. **BOUNDARY LENGTHS:** Rwanda, 290 kilometers (180 miles); Tanzania, 451 kilometers (280 miles); Zaire, 233 kilometers (145 miles).

roads. Roads total 5,900 kilomters (3,666 miles). In 1991 there were 8,500 passenger cars and 11,000 commercial vehicles. Air service is maintained by Air Burundi, which operates domestic service and flies to Rwanda, Tanzania, and Zaire. International service is provided by Air Zaïre, Sabena, and other airlines.

12 HISTORY

The first known inhabitants of what is now Burundi were the Twa, a Pygmy tribe of hunters. Between the 7th and 10th centuries AD, the Hutu, a Bantu agricultural people, occupied the region, probably coming from the Congo Basin. In the 15th and 16th centuries, tall warriors, the Tutsi, who were believed to have come originally from Ethiopia, entered the area.

The Tutsi, a wandering pastoral people, gradually enslaved the Hutu and other inhabitants of the region. A social system based on castes, or classes—the conquering Tutsi and the subject Hutu—became the dominant feature of social relations. The Hutu did the farming and grew the food in return for cattle, but generally had no part in government. The Tutsi were the ruling caste and did no manual labor. The ownership of land was gradually transferred from the Hutu tribes to the king of the Tutsi, called the "mwami."

Foreign Exploration

In 1871, The British explorers Stanley and Livingstone landed at Bujumbura and explored the Rusizi River region. Later, other explorers, mostly German, visited Burundi. After the Berlin Conference of 1884–85, the German zone of influence in East Africa was extended to include Rwanda and Burundi.

The history of Burundi under German control was marked by constant struggles and rivalry, in contrast to the peaceful state of affairs in Rwanda. In 1923, the League of Nations gave Belgium control of the region, which was known as Ruanda-Urundi (present-day Rwanda and Burundi). The Belgians adopted the same policy of indirect government employed by the Germans, retaining the entire established structure. In 1946, Ruanda-Urundi became a United Nations trust territory under Belgian control.

Burundi Independence

On 1 July 1962, Burundi became an independent kingdom headed by Mwami (King) Mwambutsa IV. He was removed from office in July 1966 and was replaced in September by his heir, Mwami Ntare V. On 29 November 1966, Mwami Ntare V in turn was overthrown by a military takeover headed by Premier Michel Micombero, and Burundi was declared a republic with Micombero as president. In 1969 and 1972, the Micombero government was threatened by Hutu-led takeover attempts, the second of which resulted in widespread civil war and 100,000 deaths. By the end of 1973, however, the government was fully in control.

On 1 November 1976, President Micombero was stripped of all powers by a military takeover led by Colonel Jean-Baptiste Bagaza. Bagaza was then named president. The new government, like the old one, was dominated by Tutsi. A new constitution was adopted in 1981, and a National Assembly was elected in 1982. Bagaza was reelected unopposed to a new five-year term in 1984, but in September 1987, he was overthrown by the military while he was attending a conference in Canada. Major Pierre Buyoyo became president.

Ethnic Violence

After an eruption of ethnic violence in 1988, in which between 5,000 and 25,000 Hutu were massacred, Major Buyoyo agreed to the restoration of multiparty politics in 1991. A new constitution was approved in March 1992. In the elections of June, 1993, Buyoyo was defeated by Melchior Ndadaye. Ndadaye's government was broad based, with nine Tutsis (including the prime minister) among the 23 ministers. However, on 21 October 1993, Burundi's first elected president—also its first Hutu president—and several cabinet members were assassinated by Tutsi soldiers in an unsuccessful military takeover attempt. In the resulting violence, as many as 100,000 people may have been killed.

In February 1994, Ndadaye's successor, Cyprien Ntaryamira, was inaugurated. But his liberal government was unable to restore order. In an effort to negotiate peace, he went to Tanzania for meetings. On his flight home, the plane in which he was returning, along with Rwanda's President Habyarimana, was shot down near Kigali, Rwanda's airport. Two other members of his cabinet also died in the attack.

13 GOVERNMENT

A new constitution which recognized "democracy, human rights and development" was adopted on 13 March 1992. It provides for a directly elected president, a

Photo credit: Cynthia Bassett

The traditional Sunday market attracts all the Tutsi tribe villagers.

prime minister, and an 81-seat National Assembly.

14 POLITICAL PARTIES

Until 1993, Burundi's Party for Unity and National Progress (UPRONA) controlled the country. But in the 1993 elections, President Ndadaye's party, the Burundi Democratic Front (FRODEBU) received 72% of the vote and 65 of parliament's 81 seats. UPRONA won the remaining seats with 21% of the ballots cast. Other parties include the Burundi People's Party (RPB), the Party for the Reconciliation of the People (PRP), and the People's Party (PP).

15 JUDICIAL SYSTEM

The Court of Appeals and the Supreme Court are located in Bujumbura. The constitution provides for a state security court. The 1992 constitution establishes a number of new courts including a constitutional court to review all new laws to make sure they are constitutional. Under the new constitution, the judiciary is declared independent. In practice, however, the system remains dominated by the Tutsi tribal group.

16 ARMED FORCES

In 1993, Burundi had an army with about 5,500 soldiers. The troops include two infantry battalions, a battalion of commandos, and a battalion of paratroopers. The naval force had 50 members and 3 patrol boats. The air force had 150 members with three counterinsurgency (those fighting against the revolt) aircraft and 14 support aircraft and helicopters.

17 ECONOMY

Burundi's economy is based on agriculture and livestock. Bananas, plantains, sweet potatoes, and manioc are Burundi's staple crops, followed by beans, taro, and maize. Coffee and tea are the main export crops, and cotton is emerging as an important export (5.7% of export earnings in 1987).

18 INCOME

In 1992 Burundi's gross national product (GNP) was $1,193 million at current prices, or $180 per person. For the period 1985–92 the average inflation rate was 4.3%, resulting in a real growth rate in per capita GNP of 1.0%.

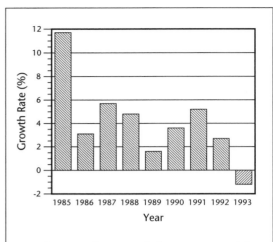

Yearly growth rate of the economy. This economic indicator tells by what percent the economy has increased or decreased when compared with the previous year.

19 INDUSTRY

Industrial activities are mostly concentrated in Bujumbura. The industrial sector primarily transforms agricultural and forestry products like cotton, coffee, tea, vegetable oil, and woods into finished products. The future of industrial development is largely linked to the development of electric power and transportation, as well as improved commercial relations with neighboring countries.

20 LABOR

The total labor force in 1990 was 2,779,777, mostly working on small farms. Of the total labor force, over 90% was engaged in agriculture in 1992.

The current Labor Code states that children under the age of 16 are not

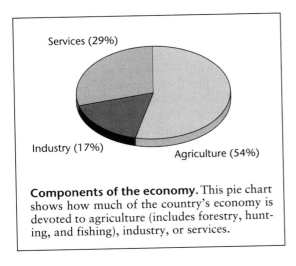

Components of the economy. This pie chart shows how much of the country's economy is devoted to agriculture (includes forestry, hunting, and fishing), industry, or services.

Services (29%)

Industry (17%)

Agriculture (54%)

allowed to be employed by a formal business, although it also states that they may do part-time work that does not damage their health or interfere with their schooling. In fact, young children are often seen doing heavy manual labor, including transporting bricks on their heads, in rural areas during the school year. Children are legally not allowed to work at night, though many still do on an unofficial basis. In everyday life, children are expected to help support their families by participating in family businesses and working on family farms.

21 AGRICULTURE

About 90% of the population depends on agriculture for a living. Most agriculture consists of subsistence farming, with only about 15% of the total production marketed. Principal crops for local consumption are manioc, beans, bananas, sweet potatoes, corn, and sorghum. The primary export crop is coffee. In 1992, coffee pro-

duction was 34,000 tons. Other export crops are cotton and tea.

Much of the land has suffered a loss of fertility because of soil erosion from poor agricultural practices, irregular rainfall, lack of fertilizer, and shortened fallow (plowed but unfertilized) periods.

22 DOMESTICATED ANIMALS

Livestock in 1992 included some 440,000 head of cattle, 932,000 goats, 370,000 sheep, and 105,000 pigs. There are also large numbers of beehives. Honey production was estimated at 1,010 tons in 1992. Social prestige has traditionally come from ownership of cattle, resulting in the accumulation of large herds of poor-quality stock which slow economic development by cutting down the amount of land available for food growing and destroying pasture land by overgrazing.

23 FISHING

There are three main methods of fishing in Lake Tanganyika: industrial, native, and traditional. The total for native and traditional fishing was 23,094 tons in 1991.

24 FORESTRY

Erosion and cutting, chiefly for fuel, have almost entirely eliminated Burundi's forests. The harvesting of wood has increased only slightly since the late 1970s, and the emphasis has now shifted to reforestation. Natural forest covered 67,000 hectares (165,600 acres) in 1991, up 8% from 1981 as a result of reforestation efforts.

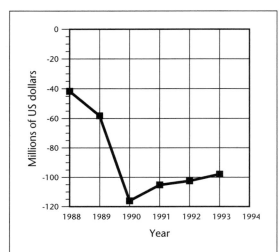

Yearly balance of trade measured in millions of US dollars. The balance of trade is the difference between what a country sells to other countries (its exports) and what it buys (its imports). If a country imports more than it exports, it has a negative balance of trade (a trade deficit). If exports exceed imports, there is a positive balance of trade (a trade surplus).

25 MINING

Tin production has significantly increased in recent years from five tons in 1987 to 124 tons in 1991. Peat offers an alternative to increasingly scarce firewood and charcoal as a domestic energy source. The most significant mineral deposits in Burundi include gold, kaolin (china clay), limestone for cement, nickel, phosphate, platinum-group metals, rare-earth metals, and vanadium.

26 FOREIGN TRADE

Burundi's export income is highly unstable. Since 1987 it has varied widely with shifts in world coffee prices, Burundi's major export. Other export items include tea, hides and skins, and minerals. Imports consist mainly of processed foods, textiles, foodstuffs, vehicles, and fuel.

In 1991, the United States bought 38.5% of Burundi's exports while Germany bought 34.8%, almost all in coffee. Belgium accounted for 14.1% of imports, followed by France and Germany (9.8% and 8.8%, respectively).

27 ENERGY AND POWER

Bujumbura and Gitega are the only two cities in Burundi that have municipal electricity service. Burundi's total installed capacity was 43,000 kilowatts in 1991. In 1991, recorded production was about 136 million kilowatt hours, 99% of which was hydroelectric. Burundi imports all of its petroleum products from Kenya and Tanzania. Wood and peat account for 94% of all energy consumption in Burundi.

28 SOCIAL DEVELOPMENT

Under the tribal system, the individual's basic welfare needs have traditionally been the responsibility of the group. Even now, the family remains the most important social welfare institution. There are social centers for women and youth. Missions help to look after orphans and the aged. For the relatively small number of wage earners, a government social security system insures against accidents and occupational diseases and provides pensions.

29 HEALTH

Many of Burundi's people do not eat enough animal protein and fat, so almost all diseases associated with malnutrition

Selected Social Indicators

These statistics are estimates for the period 1988 to 1993. For comparison purposes, data for the United States and averages for low-income countries and high-income countries are also given.

Indicator	Burundi	Low-income countries	High-income countries	United States
Per capita gross national product†	$180	$380	$23,680	$24,740
Population growth rate	3.1%	1.9%	0.6%	1.0%
Population growth rate in urban areas	6.6%	3.9%	0.8%	1.3%
Population per square kilometer of land	231	78	25	26
Life expectancy in years	50	62	77	76
Number of people per physician	17,236	>3,300	453	419
Number of pupils per teacher (primary school)	63	39	<18	20
Illiteracy rate (15 years and older)	50%	41%	<5%	<3%
Energy consumed per capita (kg of oil equivalent)	24	364	5,203	7,918

† The gross national product (GNP) is the total dollar value of all goods and services produced by a country in a year. The per capita GNP is calculated by dividing a country's GNP by its population. The World Bank defines low-income countries as those with a per capita GNP of $695 or less. High-income countries have a per capita GNP of $8,626 or more. Less than 14% of the world's 5.5 billion people live in high-income countries, while almost 60% live in low-income countries.

> = greater than   < = less than

Sources: World Bank, *Social Indicators of Development 1995,* Baltimore: Johns Hopkins University Press, 1995. Central Intelligence Agency, *World Fact Book,* Washington, D.C.: Government Printing Office, 1994.

are found in Burundi. In 1991, 80% of the population had access to health care. In 1992, the infant mortality rate was 108 per 1,000 live births. Average life expectancy is estimated at 50 years.

30 HOUSING

The basic type of housing in the rural areas is the hut, most commonly beehive shaped, made of strips of wood woven around poles (wattle), and now covered with tin (thatch has become scarce). The huts are generally not grouped into villages but are organized in groups on a family basis.

31 EDUCATION

Education is now compulsory for children between the ages of 7 and 13. Primary education lasts for six years and secondary education for seven. The languages of instruction in schools are Kisundi and French. Only about 4% of the eligible young people attend secondary or technical schools. The shortage of trained teachers and administrators is a major problem. The University of Burundi in Bujumbura (founded in 1960) is the country's only institution of higher learning.

32 MEDIA

Burundi has a radio broadcasting station, the government-run Voice of the Revolution. A television service, Télévision Nationale du Burundi, was established in 1984. In 1991 Burundi had 340,000 radios and 5,000 television sets, and there were 9,600 telephones. The government issues a French-language daily, *Le Renouveau de Burundi,* with a circulation of 20,000, and a weekly newspaper, *Ubumwe,* published in Kirundi, with a circulation of 2,000.

33 TOURISM AND RECREATION

The tourist industry is still in its infancy, but there is ample opportunity for development. Lake Tanganyika is internationally famous for its scenic beauty. Points of interest include Bujumbura, the capital, on Lake Tanganyika; Gitega, the former capital, with its museum and traditional handicraft center; and the Mosso area in the southeast, with its fairly abundant wildlife. The northeast has a great variety of tropical birds. Burundi is also rich in folk art. The dancers and drummers of the Tutsi are particularly well known.

34 FAMOUS BURUNDIANS

Mwami Ntare I Rushatsi (c. 1500), a warrior and administrator, succeeded in unifying the country under Tutsi rule.

35 BIBLIOGRAPHY

Daniels, Morn. *Burundi.* Santa Barbara, Calif.: Clio Press, 1992.

Foster, F. Blanche. *East Central Africa: Kenya, Uganda, Tanzania, Rwanda, and Burundi.* New York: Watts [1981], 1980.

CAMBODIA

Cambodia

CAPITAL: Phnom Penh

NOTE: Cambodia (formerly known as Kampuchea and the Khmer Republic) was known as Cambodia until 1976 and again since 1989. As of 1994, there are two rival claimants for legitimate government authority. One of these, the People's Republic of Kampuchea (PRK), was established in January 1979 in the wake of a Vietnamese invasion; it maintained control of the capital by means of an occupation force of Vietnamese troops. The other, Democratic Kampuchea (DK; Kampuchea Pracheathipateyy), is represented by a coalition government-in-exile, but with considerable following in the Cambodian countryside; it continues to hold Cambodia's seat in the UN.

FLAG: The flag has a red center field with a white silhouette of the temple complex at Angkor Wat. The center field is bordered top and bottom by blue bands.

MONETARY UNIT: Money was officially abolished in 1975, and for nearly five years the domestic economy operated almost exclusively on a system of barter (trade) and government rationing. In March 1980, the PRK reintroduced the riel (R) of 100 sen, equal in value to 1 kilogram (2.2 lb) of rice and with an approximate exchange value of R1 = $0.0004 (or $1 = R2,500).

WEIGHTS AND MEASURES: Both the metric system and traditional weights and measures are in general use.

HOLIDAYS: National Day, 9 January; New Year, April; Victory over American Imperialism Day, 17 April; Labor Day, 1 May; Day of Hatred, 20 May; Feast of the Ancestors, 22 September.

TIME: 7 PM = noon GMT.

1 LOCATION AND SIZE

Situated in the southeast corner of Indochina, Cambodia has an area of 181,040 square kilometers (69,900 square miles), slightly smaller than the state of Oklahoma, with a total boundary length of 3,015 kilometers (1,873 miles).

Cambodia's capital city, Phnom Penh, is located in the southcentral part of the country.

2 TOPOGRAPHY

Cambodia is a country of forested mountains and well-watered plains. The central part of the country forms a gigantic basin for the Tonle Sap, or Great Lake, and the Mekong River. Between the Tonle Sap and the Gulf of Thailand lie the Cardamom Mountains and the Elephant Range. In the north, the Dangrek Mountains, 320 kilometers (200 miles) long and 300 to 750 meters (1,000–2,500 feet) high, mark the

Thailand frontier. The short coastline has an important natural harbor, Kampong Som Bay.

3 CLIMATE

The climate is tropical, with a wet season from June through November and a dry season from December to June. Temperatures range from 20° to 36°C (68–97°F), and humidity is consistently high. The lowlands, which are often flooded during the rainy season, receive about 200 centimeters (80 inches) of rainfall annually, but there is less precipitation in the western and northern portions of the country.

4 PLANTS AND ANIMALS

Cambodia, with its densely covered mountains, has a wide variety of plant and animal life. There are palm, rubber, coconut, kapok, mango, banana, and orange trees, as well as high sharp grasses.

Birds, including cranes, pheasants, and wild ducks, and mammals such as elephants, wild oxen, panthers, and bears abound throughout the country. Fish, snakes, and insects are also abundant (plentiful).

5 ENVIRONMENT

By 1985, the clearing of the land for agricultural purposes and the damage from the Vietnam war resulted in the destruction of 116 square miles of forest land. The nation has 21.1 cubic miles of water with 94% used for farming activity and 1% used for industrial purposes. Cambodia's cities produce 0.2 million tons of solid waste per year. Three-fourths of Cambodia's wildlife areas have been lost

through the destruction of its forests. As of 1994, 21 of Cambodia's mammal species and 13 of its bird species were endangered, and 11 of its plant species were also threatened.

6 POPULATION

According to the official estimate, the population was 9,054,000 in 1992, but the United States Bureau of the Census estimated a population of only 7,612,332 in 1994. On the basis of the official estimate, Cambodia had an overall population density of 50 per square kilometer (130 per square mile). A population of 10,580,000 was forecasted by the United Nations for the year 2000.

In 1991, the population of Phnom Penh, the capital, was estimated at 900,000.

7 MIGRATION

After the People's Republic of Kampuchea came to power in January 1979, continued fighting and political instability resulted in a new exodus of refugees. About 630,000 Cambodians left the country between 1979 and 1981, of which about 208,000 were able to resettle in other countries, including 136,000 in the United States. Most of the rest remained in camps on the border with Thailand, but they were allowed back into Cambodia in 1993.

Between 1979 and 1987 there was a new migration of ethnic Vietnamese into Cambodia. Official sources insisted that the total number was under 60,000, but opposition groups contended that the number totaled over 500,000, and was

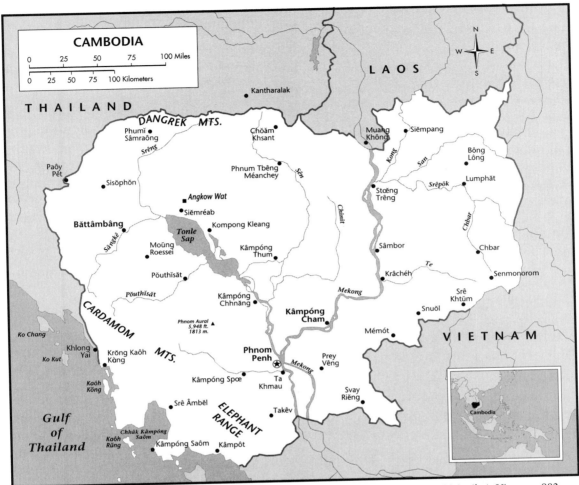

CAMBODIA

0	25	50	75	100 Miles
0	25	50	75	100 Kilometers

LOCATION: 102°31′ to 108°E; 10° to 15°N. **BOUNDARY LENGTHS:** Laos, 541 kilometers (336 miles); Vietnam, 982 kilometers (610 miles); Gulf of Thailand, 389 kilometers (242 miles); Thailand, 803 kilometers (499 miles). **TERRITORIAL SEA LIMIT:** 12 miles.

intended to consolidate Vietnamese control over the country.

8 ETHNIC GROUPS

Over 90% of the population are ethnic Khmers, descendants of the original population in the area. The largest minority groups were the Chinese (about 61,000) and Vietnamese (estimated at 56,000). National minorities are the Cham and a number of small tribal groups.

9 LANGUAGES

Khmer, the national language, is spoken by most inhabitants. French, the second language, is often used in commerce and government. The Vietnamese and the Chinese use their own languages, as do other minorities.

10 RELIGIONS

Although Theravada Buddhism is the religion of some 90% of the inhabitants (1992) and has been the state religion since 1989, traditional native religions are followed by most persons as well. The Chinese and most Vietnamese in Cambodia practice a traditional mixture of Mahayana Buddhism, Taoism, Confucianism, ancestor worship, and traditional religions. Before 1975 there were some 100,000 Muslims (mostly Cham-Malays), 50,000 Roman Catholics (Europeans and Vietnamese), and a few Protestants. The mountain tribes are animists; in the post–World War II years, Christian missionaries made some converts among them.

The government that took power in 1975 practically abolished Buddhism, defrocking some 70,000 monks and turning pagodas (religious buildings) into warehouses. Islamic spokesmen have claimed that 90% of Cambodian Muslims were massacred after 1975. All mosques and Catholic churches were destroyed. The PRK regime that came to power in 1979 permitted the return of religious practice, and hundreds of pagodas were reopened.

11 TRANSPORTATION

As of 1991, Cambodia had an estimated 13,351 kilometers (8,234 miles) of main roads; most are in poor condition. The Mekong River is the most important inland waterway. The opening of the deepwater port of Kampong So in 1975 made Cambodia largely independent of Vietnam for oceangoing shipping. Cambodia's main airport is at Phnom Penh; there are regular flights between Phnom Penh, Hanoi, Vientiane, and Ho Chi Minh City.

12 HISTORY

The Cambodians are descendants of the Khmers, who in the 6th century established the Indian-influenced Angkor Empire. For the next 900 years they ruled the area of present-day Cambodia. According to legend, the founder of the Khmer dynasty was Kampu Svayambhuva, from whose name "Kampuchea" comes. By the 14th century, after years of military expansion, the Khmer empire extended over most of Southeast Asia. Angkor, the capital city, was a complex of great temples, palaces, and shrines. In the following centuries, however, continuing attacks by the Thai and the Vietnamese weakened the empire. By the end of the 18th century much of Cambodia had become Thai and Vietnamese territory. In 1863, the king of Cambodia placed the country under French protection. The French joined Cambodia to Laos and Vietnam to form French Indochina. The French ruled this protectorate until the end of World War II.

Cambodia became a constitutional monarchy on 6 May 1947, and was officially granted independence within the French Union on 9 November 1949. On 17 October 1953, during the height of the French-Indochinese war, Prince Norodom Sihanouk, who had ascended the throne in 1941, was granted full military and con-

Photo credit: AP/Wide World Photos

A family of four squeezes onto a small motorcycle during an outing in Cambodia's capital city, Phnom Penh. Motorcycles and bicycles are a common mode of transportation in the Cambodian capitol.

trol of his country by France. During the next 15 years, Sihanouk sought to keep Cambodia neutral in the deepening conflict that was taking place in neighboring Vietnam between Vietnam and the United States. This proved increasingly difficult, however, as the National Liberation Front (also known as the Viet-Cong) used Cambodian border areas as bases from which to launch attacks on the Republic of Vietnam (RVN, or South Vietnam). In 1969, the United States launched an undeclared air war against these guerrilla sanctuaries.

End of Khmer Monarchs

On 18 March 1970, Marshal Lon Nol, prime minister and army chief, overthrew the chief of state, Prince Sihanouk; the coup ended 1,168 years of rule by Khmer monarchs. Sihanouk fled to Beijing, where, on 5 May, he announced formation of the Royal Government of National Union of Kampuchea (GRUNK). Meanwhile, on 30 April, United States President Richard M. Nixon announced an "incursion" into Cambodia of 30,000 United States and 40,000 RVN troops. Their object was to destroy Vietnamise strongholds in Cambodia. The operation, which incited mass protests in the United States, was terminated on 30 June without having gained its military objectives, but bombing of the region continued with devastating effects on Cambodia's economy.

The Khmer Republic

On 9 October, the Lon Nol government in Phnom Penh abolished the monarchy and changed Cambodia's name to the Khmer Republic. Lon Nol was elected president of the republic. However, the GRUNK forces continued their fight and eventually took control of the government on 5 January 1976. The new rulers renamed the country Democratic Kampuchea (DK). Pol Pot was named prime minister. The GRUNK government immediately undertook a massive reorganization of the country's economic and social life. The new government ordered the evacuation of Phnom Penh and plunged the country into near-total isolation. Currency was abolished, social relations completely overhauled, religion almost eradicated, education suspended, and families divided. From 2 million to 3 million people may have died of starvation, exhaustion, disease, or massacre under the Pol Pot regime.

In December 1978, Vietnam invaded Cambodia with a force of more than 100,000 troops. They took control of the country and installed a pro-Vietnamese government. Khmer Rouge rebels fled to the jungles and began a guerilla war against the new government. The following years saw further fighting and competition for political power.

Finally, on 23 October 1991 an end to thirteen years of war in Cambodia was achieved with the signing of the Comprehensive Political Settlement for Cambodia. In 1993 the first multiparty election in more than 20 years was held. A 120 members national assembly was elected and a new constitution was ratified. After the elections, Cambodia maintained a fragile peace. However, on 11 June 1994 the Khmer Rouge announced it had formed a parallel government with headquarters in northern Cambodia. In response, the National Assembly voted to outlaw the Khmer Rouge. Once again the country was in turmoil. In July of 1994, it was estimated that 55,000 Cambodians were again fleeing Khmer Rouge attacks in the western provinces.

The war in Cambodia has been called "The Coward's War" by the human rights group Asia Watch. Because of the war, Cambodia today has the world's highest percentage of physically disabled persons, and mines may have inflicted more wounds than any other weapon.

13 GOVERNMENT

On 23 October 1991 a United Nations peace accord was signed by Cambodia's political factions; the agreement provided for elections with proportional representation. The country was divided into 20 provinces. In 1993 a National Assembly was elected and a new constitution was ratified. The monarchy was reestablished and commitments to liberal democracy, the rule of law, and women's rights were included. Prince Norodom Sihanouk ratified the constitution and again became King of Cambodia. The government of the State of Cambodia has survived as a shaky coalition since the elections. On 11 June 1994 the Khmer Rouge announced that it had formed a parallel government headquartered in northern Cambodia with Khieu Samphan as president.

14 POLITICAL PARTIES

The main political parties include FUNC-INPEC (National Front for an Independent, Neutral, Peaceful and Cooperative Cambodia), Prince Sihanouk's main political organization formed in 1981; the KPNLF (Khmer People's National Liberation Front); and the Khmer Rouge.

15 JUDICIAL SYSTEM

The 1993 constitution of the Kingdom of Cambodia provides legal guarantees such as presumption of innocence until proven guilty and also guarantees an independent judiciary. The structure of the new judicial system will be defined by laws yet to be enacted.

16 ARMED FORCES

The restored Cambodian government has a regular army of 80,000, an air force of 1,000, and a navy of 4,000, armed with Russian and Chinese equipment, some left by the departed Vietnamese army. Another 270,000 Khmer and minorities make up provincial and village militia. Russia provides 500 advisors while 29 nations support 10,200 United Nations peacekeepers.

17 ECONOMY

Twenty years of civil war and rule by the Khmer Rouge placed heavy economic burdens on Cambodia. Serious damage to industry and agriculture required massive rehabilitation and reconstruction. Sources note that 50–60% of basic transport and

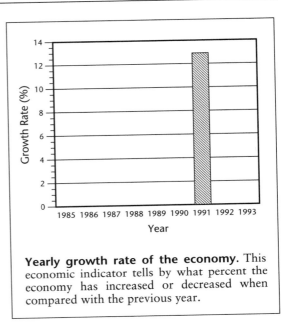

Yearly growth rate of the economy. This economic indicator tells by what percent the economy has increased or decreased when compared with the previous year.

communications facilities have been destroyed. Market-oriented reforms have been introduced to dismantle the socialist-style economy. Since 1989 Cambodia has passed legislation to restore the right to own and inherit property, free prices, and open up the country to increased trade and foreign investment.

In the early 1990s Cambodia remained mainly agricultural with more than 85% of workers employed in farm work. Inexpensive, unskilled Cambodian labor is plentiful, but there is a severe shortage of educated and trained personnel. In addition, the nation still must overcome corruption and mismanagement, and the widening gap between the urban rich and the rural poor.

Realization of Cambodia's tourism potential awaits the achievement of a sustained peace, as does development of

Cambodia's significant natural resources, which include timber, rubber, gems, and oil and natural gas.

18 INCOME

In 1992, Cambodia's gross national product (GNP) was $2 billion at current prices, or $280 per person. For the period 1985–92 the average inflation rate was 250-300%.

19 INDUSTRY

Industrial activity has traditionally centered on the processing of agricultural and forestry products and on the small-scale manufacture of consumer goods. Rice milling has been the main food-processing industry. Industrial expansion came to a virtual halt in 1970 with the outbreak of war. The Pol Pot government placed all industries under state control in 1975. When the PRK took over in 1979, industrial plants began to reopen. By late 1985 there were a reported 60 government-run factories producing household goods, textiles, soft drinks, pharmaceutical products, and other light consumer goods.

Major industries include rice milling, fishing, wood and timber products, rubber (largely abandoned since 1975), cement, and gem mining. Cambodia has significant mineral deposits of gold, silver, iron, copper, marble, limestone and phosphate, and a gem industry.

20 LABOR

In 1992, the working population was officially estimated at 3,964,011, of which 56% were female, due in large part to killings by the Khmer Rouge. The vast major-

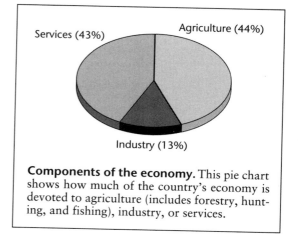

Components of the economy. This pie chart shows how much of the country's economy is devoted to agriculture (includes forestry, hunting, and fishing), industry, or services.

ity of Cambodia's population engages in farming, forestry, or fishing. In August 1992, a new labor law was passed which allowed workers to form unions, prohibited forced labor, set a minimum wage, and set the legal working age at 16. By necessity, however, many youths under 16 engage in street trading, construction, and light manufacturing.

21 AGRICULTURE

Because of the lack of natural resources and the primitive industrial base in Cambodia, agriculture is the key area in the economy. Rice provides the staple diet and prior to 1970 was Cambodia's major export, along with rubber. By 1974 production had declined to 635,000 tons, but it rose to 2,2545,000 tons in 1992, two-thirds greater than in the years immediately following the Vietnamese invasion.

Rubber has traditionally been the second most important agricultural crop. However, rubber plantings were almost completely destroyed by the end of 1971.

A Cambodian boy gets the scare of his life riding a cart being pulled by a trained monkey at a public market. An enterprising Cambodian, trying to promote his products, uses the monkey to attract customers. The boy, plucked from the audience, was paid about $.04 for the ride.

The Pol Pot and Khmer Rouge governments made efforts to revive the rubber industry. Recovery has been uneven and slow, and has reached only 35,000 tons in 1992.

22 DOMESTICATED ANIMALS

Livestock, raised primarily by private households, traditionally supplied an important supplement to the Cambodian diet. The Pol Pot regime stressed cattle and poultry breeding, but thousands died during the chaotic years of the late 1970s. According to official sources, livestock levels in 1992 were cattle, 2.2 million (as compared with 700,000 in 1979), and pigs, 1.7 million (as compared with 100,000 in 1979).

23 FISHING

Production of freshwater fish, the main protein element in the Cambodian diet, traditionally ranked next to rice and rubber in the national economy. About half of Cambodia's freshwater catch came from the Tonle Sap.

Ocean fishing developed significantly during the 1980s; the saltwater catch totaled 3,015 tons in 1982 and 36,400 tons in 1991. In 1991, inland fishing amounted to 74,700 tons, up from 65,700 tons in 1982.

24 FORESTRY

About 76% of Cambodia is forested, but taking advantage of its natural resources has been difficult because of limited transportation and damage caused by war. The main products of the forest industry are timber, resins, wood oil, fuel, and charcoal. Production of roundwood, averaging about 4 million cubic meters in the late 1960s, fell off sharply during the 1970–75 war, but increased to 6.4 million cubic meters in 1991.

25 MINING

Cambodia's known mineral resources are limited. Substantial deposits of bauxite, discovered in the early 1960s north of Battambang and southeast of Phnom Penh, have yet to be worked. Potter's clay is common, and deposits of phosphates, used for fertilizer, exist in southern Kampot province, as well as near Phnom Sampou. Precious gems are mined in Pallin, near the Thai border. High quality cornflower-blue sapphires have been the most value gemstone produced to date, and high quality rubies have also been found. It is unlikely that exploitation of the nation's limited mineral resources can be undertaken, however, until the many explosive mines planted throughout the country can be safely removed.

26 FOREIGN TRADE

In 1986 major export trading partners with Cambodia were Vietnam, the former USSR, Eastern Europe, Japan, and India. For imports, major trading partners were the same countries. The United States trade embargo against Cambodia was lifted in January 1992 by President Bush. As of 1992 Cambodian exports were mostly agricultural, comprised mainly of timber and rubber. Logging is a ready source of badly needed export revenues for both the government and the other political factions. In 1992 imports to Cambodia were capital goods, raw materials, and, in recent years vehicles, motorcycles, and consumer products.

27 ENERGY AND POWER

Wood is the most widely used fuel for transportation, industrial, and domestic purposes. Most of the few existing electric power plants must use imported diesel oil and natural gas.

28 SOCIAL DEVELOPMENT

During the Pol Pot period, the social fabric of the country was severely damaged. Overall social conditions in Cambodia remain among the worst in southeast Asia. Political violence peaked in the period before the United Nations-sponsored elections of May 1993 and then fell sharply. Cambodia's new constitution provides equal rights for women in areas including work and marriage.

29 HEALTH

Life expectancy in Cambodia is 52 years. Dysentery, malaria, tuberculosis, trachoma, and yaws are widespread. The 1970–75 war and the 1975–79 upheaval aggravated many health problems. Malnutrition became widespread among the millions driven to Phnom Penh in the wake of the fighting and who were driven out of that city when the Khmer Rouge took

Selected Social Indicators

These statistics are estimates for the period 1988 to 1993. For comparison purposes, data for the United States and averages for low-income countries and high-income countries are also given.

Indicator	Cambodia	Low-income countries	High-income countries	United States
Per capita gross national product†	$280	$380	$23,680	$24,740
Population growth rate	3.2%	1.9%	0.6%	1.0%
Population growth rate in urban areas	6.4%	3.9%	0.8%	1.3%
Population per square kilometer of land	50	78	25	26
Life expectancy in years	52	62	77	76
Number of people per physician	9,523	>3,300	453	419
Number of pupils per teacher (primary school)	n.a.	39	<18	20
Illiteracy rate (15 years and older)	38%	41%	<5%	<3%
Energy consumed per capita (kg of oil equivalent)	52	364	5,203	7,918

† The gross national product (GNP) is the total dollar value of all goods and services produced by a country in a year. The per capita GNP is calculated by dividing a country's GNP by its population. The World Bank defines low-income countries as those with a per capita GNP of $695 or less. High-income countries have a per capita GNP of $8,626 or more. Less than 14% of the world's 5.5 billion people live in high-income countries, while almost 60% live in low-income countries.

n.a. = data not available.   > = greater than   < = less than

Sources: World Bank, *Social Indicators of Development 1995,* Baltimore: Johns Hopkins University Press, 1995. Central Intelligence Agency, *World Fact Book,* Washington, D.C.: Government Printing Office, 1994.

over. In 1991, only 36% of the population had access to safe water and a mere 14% had adequate sanitation. In 1991, 53% of the population had access to health care services.

30 HOUSING

Cambodia's housing traditionally compared favorably with that of other countries in Southeast Asia. The most common type of dwelling consists of one or more rooms raised on mangrove piles some 3 meters (10 feet) above the ground.

Mass emigration from the cities during 1975–76 resulted in many dwellings being left vacant, in contrast to the dire over-crowding that occurred in the last years of the war. In the countryside, meanwhile, much of the transplanted population was forced to reside in improvised shelters.

31 EDUCATION

Under the Pol Pot regime, education was limited to political instruction. Most of the educated class had been killed by 1979. According to PRK sources, only 50 of 725 university instructors and 307 of 2,300 secondary-school teachers survived the Pol Pot era. Under the PRK, education was gradually recovering. Adult literacy was estimated to be 62% in 1993. Total school enrollment increased from about 1 million in 1979 to more than 1.7 million in 1985, and the number of teachers more than doubled, from 21,000 to 46,500. All schooling is public, and six years of primary education (ages 6–12) are compulsory. Most students continue their higher education at foreign universities.

32 MEDIA

Cambodia's communications network was almost totally destroyed by the Khmer Rouge. There are two radio networks, the Voice of the Kampuchean People and the Voice of the Phnom Penh People. TV-Kampuchean began color transmissions in 1986. There were an estimated 955,000 radios and 70,000 television sets in 1991. There is one daily newspaper, *Pracheachun* (1991 circulation 25,000). In early 1994, over 40 Khmer-language newspapers were available.

33 TOURISM AND RECREATION

Until the intrusion of war in the late 1960s, Angkor Wat and other remains of the ancient Khmer Empire were the major attractions for visitors to Cambodia. Under the Pol Pot regime, tourism was nonexistent, and it was not revived under the PRK. However, since the 1992 United Nations peace plan, tourism has rebounded, spurred by the opening of hundreds of new facilities and many new diplomatic missions. In 1993, over 120,000 tourists visited Cambodia, and a 50% increase was expected for 1994.

34 FAMOUS CAMBODIANS

Foremost among ancient heroes were Fan Shihman, greatest ruler of the Funan Empire (150–550), and Jayavarman II and Jayavarman VII, monarchs of the Khmer Empire who ruled between the 10th and 13th centuries. Prince Norodom Sihanouk (b.1922) is the best-known living Kampuchean. Khieu Samphan (b.1931) replaced Sihanouk as chief of state. The actual head of the GRUNK regime during 1975–79 was Pol Pot, the assumed name of Saloth Sar (b.1925), who presided over a drastic restructuring of society that left as many as 2–3 million dead.

35 BIBLIOGRAPHY

Chandler, David P. *The Land and People of Cambodia.* New York: HarperCollins, 1991.

Greenblatt, M. *Cambodia.* Children's Press, 1995.

Ross, Russell R. (ed.). *Cambodia: A Country Study.* 3rd ed. Washington, D.C.: Library of Congress, 1990.

Shawcross, William. *Sideshow: Kissinger, Nixon, and the Destruction of Cambodia.* New York: Simon & Schuster, 1987.

Welaratna, Usha. *Beyond the Killing Fields: Voices of Nine Cambodian Survivors in America.* Stanford, Calif.: Stanford University Press, 1993.

CAMEROON

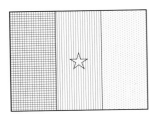

Republic of Cameroon
République du Cameroun

CAPITAL: Yaoundé.

FLAG: The flag is a tricolor of green, red, and yellow vertical stripes with one gold star imprinted in the center of the red stripe.

ANTHEM: The national anthem begins "O Cameroun, berceau de nos ancêtres" ("O Cameroon, cradle of our ancestors").

MONETARY UNIT: The Communauté Financière Africaine franc (CFA Fr) is a paper currency. There are coins of 1, 2, 5, 10, 25, 50, 100, and 500 CFA francs, and notes of 50, 100, 500, 1,000, 5,000, and 10,000 CFA francs. CFA Fr1 = $0.0018 (or $1 = CFA Fr571).

WEIGHTS AND MEASURES: The metric system is the legal standard.

HOLIDAYS: New Year's Day, 1 January; Youth Day, 11 February; Labor Day, 1 May; National Day, 20 May; Christmas, 25 December. Movable religious holidays include Ascension, Good Friday, Easter Monday, End of Ramadan (Djoulde Soumae), and Festival of the Lamb ('Id al-Kabir or Djoulde Laihadji).

TIME: 1 PM = noon GMT.

1 LOCATION AND SIZE

Situated in West Africa, Cameroon, shaped like an elongated triangle, contains an area of 475,440 square kilometers (183,568 square miles), extending 1,206 kilometers (749 miles) north–south and 717 kilometers (446 miles) east–west. Comparatively, the area occupied by Cameroon is slightly larger than the state of California. Cameroon's capital city, Yaoundé, is located in the southern part of the country.

2 TOPOGRAPHY

There are four geographical regions: the western lowlands, which extend along the Gulf of Guinea coast; the northwestern highlands, which consist of forested volcanic mountains, including Mt. Cameroon, the nation's only active volcano and the highest peak in West Africa; the central region, which extends eastward to the border with the Central African Republic; and the northern region, which is essentially a vast tropical plain that slopes down to the Chad Basin.

3 CLIMATE

The southern and northern regions of the country are two distinct climatic areas. In the south there are two dry seasons, December to February, and July to September. The northern part of the country has a more comfortable climate. The temperature ranges from 22° to 29°C (72° to 84°F) along the coast. The dry season in the north is from October to April.

4 PLANTS AND ANIMALS

Cameroon possesses practically every variety of plants and animals found in tropical

Africa. Dense rain forest grows along the coast and in the south. This gives way northward and eastward to open woodland and plains. Major game animals include buffalo, elephant, hippopotamus, antelope, Derby eland, and kudu.

5 ENVIRONMENT

Cameroon has 14 national parks and equivalent reserves covering about 2.5 million hectares (6.2 million acres), more than 5% of the country. Nevertheless, poaching is a major problem because of insufficient guards. Destruction of the remaining forests is heavy, even within reserved lands. Fires and commercial exploitation of the forests result in the elimination of 200,000 hectares per year. Overgrazing is degrading the semi-arid northern range lands. Air pollution is a significant environmental problem in Cameroon. The country also has a problem with volcanic activity, flooding, and insect infestation.

6 POPULATION

The 1994 population was estimated at 12,333,904, as compared with a 1987 census report of 10,483,655. However the United Nations estimated a population of 13,275,000 for 1995. A population of 15,293,000 was projected by the United Nations for the year 2000. In 1990, the capital, Yaoundé, had about 823,000 inhabitants.

7 MIGRATION

There is some migration to and from Nigeria and other neighboring states, but there are no statistics on the volume. At the end of 1992 there were an estimated 41,700 Chadian refugees in Cameroon.

8 ETHNIC GROUPS

Cameroon has an extremely heterogeneous (mixed) population, consisting of approximately 200 ethnic groups. The principal groups are Bantus, including the Duala, Bassa, Fang, Bulu, and Eton. The Bantu peoples generally are in the south, and the Fulani in the north.

9 LANGUAGES

French and English are the official languages. Many African languages and dialects are spoken; most belong to the Bantu and Sudanic language groups.

10 RELIGIONS

Freedom of conscience and freedom of religion are guaranteed by the constitution. The Fulani people in the north are mainly Muslim, but Christian missionaries have been particularly active in other areas. Some 53% of the population identifies itself as Christian, of whom 28.1% are Roman Catholics. As many as 22% are Muslims, 18.8% tribal religionists, and 18% Protestants.

11 TRANSPORTATION:

In 1991, Cameroon had 65,000 kilometers (40,400 miles) of roads, of which 50% were unpaved. In 1991 there were 94,000 automobiles and 82,000 other vehicles in use. There are 1,003 kilometers (623 miles) of railways.

Of the operating maritime ports in Cameroon, Douala is the busiest and most

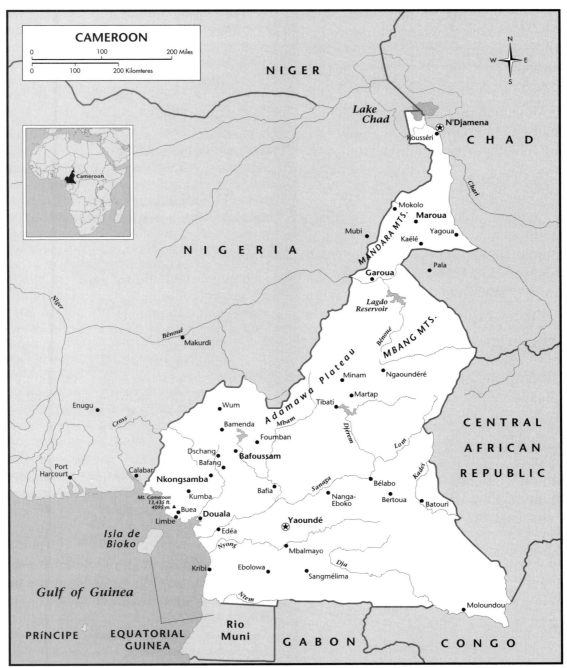

CAMEROON

0 — 100 — 200 Miles
0 — 100 — 200 Kilomteres

Cameroon

N I G E R

Lake Chad

C H A D

N'Djamena

Kousséri

Chari

Mokolo
Maroua
Mubi
MANDARA MTS.
Kaélé
Yagoua

N I G E R I A

Pala

Garoua

Niger

Lagdo Reservoir

Bénoué

MBANG MTS.

Makurdi

Minam
Ngaoundéré

Adamawa Plateau

Martap

Enugu

Wum
Tibati

Djérem

Cross

Bamenda
Mbam
Foumban

C E N T R A L

A F R I C A N

R E P U B L I C

Port Harcourt

Calabar

Dschang
Bafang

Bafoussam

Lom

Kadéi

Sanaga

Nkongsamba

Bafia
Bélabo

Kumba

Nanga-Eboko
Bertoua
Batouri

Mt. Cameroon
13,435 ft.
4095 m.
Buea
Douala

Limbe
Edéa

Yaoundé

Isla de Bioko

Nyong

Mbalmayo

Kribi
Ebolowa
Dja

Sangmélima

Gulf of Guinea

Ntem

Moloundou

PRÍNCIPE

EQUATORIAL GUINEA

Rio Muni

G A B O N

C O N G O

LOCATION: 1°40′ to 13°5′N; 8°30′ to 16°11′E. **BOUNDARY LENGTHS:** Chad, 1,047 kilometers (651 miles); Central African Republic, 822 kilometers (511 miles); Congo, 520 kilometers (323 miles); Gabon, 302 kilometers (188 miles); Equatorial Guinea, 183 kilometers (114 miles); Gulf of Guinea coastline, 364 kilometers (226 miles); Nigeria, 1,921 kilometers (1,194 miles). **TERRITORIAL SEA LIMIT:** 50 miles.

important. Garoua, on the Bénoué River, is the main river port, but it is active only from July to September. Cameroon Shipping Lines, which is 67% government owned, had a fleet of two freighters, totaling 24 gross registered tons as of January 1992. The main international airport is at Douala. In 1991, Cameroon Airlines carried 260,700 passengers.

12 HISTORY

The area now known as Cameroon and eastern Nigeria was the place of origin of the Bantu peoples. After the 12th century AD, the organized Islamic states of the Sudanic belt at times ruled the grasslands of northern Cameroon.

The modern history of Cameroon began in 1884, when the territory came under German rule. During their occupation from 1884 to 1914, the Germans advanced into the interior, cultivated large plantations, laid roads, and began constructing a railroad and the port of Douala. When World War I broke out, the territory was invaded by French and British forces. After the war, one-fifth of the former German Kamerun, which was next to eastern Nigeria, was assigned to the United Kingdom, and the remaining four-fifths was assigned to France under League of Nations mandates.

During the period 1919–39, France made notable contributions to the development of the territory, but political liberty was restricted, and a system of compulsory labor introduced by the Germans continued. When France fell to the Germans in World War II, the territory again came under German control. How-

ever, the French government (called the Free French) went into exile and continued to fight the Germans. In August 1940, Colonel Philippe Leclerc, an envoy of French General Charles de Gaulle, landed at Douala and seized the territory for the Free French. After the defeat of the Germans in World War II, French Cameroon was granted representation in the French National Assembly. An elected territorial assembly was instituted and political parties were recognized, thus establishing a basis for Cameroonian nationalism.

Immediately, many political parties began to emerge, but only one had effective organization and strength, the Union of Cameroon Peoples (Union des Populations du Cameroun—UPC). The UPC demanded immediate reunification of the British Cameroons and French Cameroon and eventual independence. In 1955, the UPC, accused of being under extreme left-wing influence, launched a campaign of sabotage, violence, and terror that continued sporadically until 1971.

Finally, a proposal to unify British Cameroons and French Cameroon was ratified by popular referendum on 20 May 1972; the vote was reportedly 99.97% in favor of unification. A new constitution went into effect on 2 June and the country was renamed the United Republic of Cameroon. Ahmadou Ahidjo became president of the republic; running unopposed, he was reelected for a fourth five-year term on 5 April 1975. In June, by constitutional amendment, the office of prime minister was created, and Paul Biya was appointed to the post. Ahidjo, reelected unopposed, began his fifth five-year term as president

Photo credit: AP/Wide World Photos

Housing in a jungle village is basic. Most of these buildings in Edéa are made of wood cut locally from trees cleared to make the space. No electricity, no plumbing, and no sanitation services are installed. A woman sits outside her home with most of her possessions—pots for cooking and washing.

in May 1980. In November 1982 he resigned and was succeeded by Biya. However, Biya's own presidential guard turned against him and attempted to overthrow the government in April. The plot failed and the rebellion was stamped out by the army. In retaliation, 46 of the plotters were executed. A state of emergency was declared, and remained in effect for over five years.

Late in 1984, the name of the country was changed to the Republic of Cameroon. Democratic reforms were begun in 1990, but political power remains firmly in the hands of President Biya. Biya was reelected on 11 October 1992 in elections that were disputed by international observers. The constitution places few checks on the power of the president. Consequently, the Biya government is widely unpopular. The government is weak and the opposition is divided.

13 GOVERNMENT

Under the 1972 constitution, as amended in 1984, Cameroon is a republic headed by a president who is elected by universal suffrage (vote) to successive five-year terms. The president appoints the ministers and vice-ministers and can dismiss them. He is also the head of the armed forces and can make the laws. The legislative branch is composed of a National Assembly of 180 members.

14 POLITICAL PARTIES

The Cameroon National Union (Union Nationale Camerounaise—UNC) was Cameroon's sole legal political party until opposition parties were legalized in 1990. In 1985, it was renamed the Cameroon People's Democratic Movement (CPDM or Rassemblement Démocratique du Peuple Camerounaise—RDPC).

15 JUDICIAL SYSTEM

The legal system includes magistrates' courts in the provinces and a 15-member High Court of Justice, appointed by the National Assembly. The Supreme Court gives final judgment on appeals from the judgments of the provincial courts of appeal. A Court of Impeachment has the right to try the president for high treason and cabinet ministers for conspiracy against the security of the state. State Security Court established in 1990 hears cases involving internal or external state security.

16 ARMED FORCES

Cameroon's armed forces totaled 7,700 in 1993. The army had 6,600 personnel organized in five infantry battalions, one paratroop commando battalion, one artillery battalion, one engineering battalion, a presidential guard of infantry and armored car battalions, and various support units. The navy had 800 personnel, two small ships, and 34 patrol boats. The air force had 300 personnel and 16 combat aircraft. Paramilitary police forces totaled 4,000.

17 ECONOMY

A rising economic star among African nations, Cameroon has nonetheless seen its economy suffer since the mid-1980s. The causes of this about-face were the simultaneous sharp declines in petroleum, coffee, and cacao prices and the rise of the United States dollar relative to the French franc.

However, Cameroon's economy retains a number of fundamental strong points. It is based on a diversified and self-sufficient agriculture supplemented by substantial petroleum production and a sizable manufacturing sector. Livestock and fishing subsectors are both significant contributors to the domestic economy.

18 INCOME

In 1992 Cameroon's gross national product (GNP) was $10,003 million at current prices, or $820 per person.

19 INDUSTRY

Since independence, Cameroon has had a favorable attitude toward industry. The government, once a large shareholder in many industries, including aluminum, wood pulp, and oil refining, now advocates increased privatization (from public to private control). In 1986, Cameroon announced its intention of giving up its shares in 62 companies.

Cameroon's first oil refinery opened at Limbé in May 1981. It has a capacity of about 50,000 barrels a day and produced about 3,241,000 metric tons of motor and heating fuels in 1984. Another major industrial enterprise is the aluminum plant at Edéa, which began operations in 1957 with ore imported from Guinea. Output was 87,500 metric tons in 1990. There are also about 20 large sawmills and 5 plywood factories. In 1988, cement production was 586,000 tons; beer and soft drinks, 6,277,000 hectoliters; soap, 23,400 tons; and footwear, 1,733,000 pairs. In 1990, raw sugar production was at 81,000 tons and cigarettes at 4,300 million units.

20 LABOR

There were 4,200,000 people in the labor force in 1992, most of whom were in agriculture. In 1992, the estimated national unemployment rate was 15–20%. In August 1992, the National Assembly passed a new labor code, permitting workers to form and join unions of their choosing. Under the new rules, groups of at least 20 workers may organize a union provided they register with the Ministry of Labor.

21 AGRICULTURE

Agriculture remains the principal occupation of the vast majority of the population, although only about 15% of the land is arable (fit for cultivation). The most important cash crops are cocoa, coffee, cotton, bananas, rubber, palm oil and kernels, and peanuts. The main food crops are plantains, cassava, corn, millet, and sugarcane.

Cameroon is among the world's largest cocoa producers; 94,000 tons of cocoa were produced in 1992. Two types of coffee, robusta and arabica, are grown; production was 85,000 tons in 1992. About 85,000 hectares (210,000 acres) are allocated to cotton plantations. Some cotton is exported, while the remainder is processed by local textile plants. A total of 108,000 tons of seed cotton was produced in 1992; ginned cotton output was 48,000 tons. Bananas are grown mainly in the southwest; 1992 estimated production was 520,000 tons. The output of rubber, also grown in the southwest, was 42,000 tons in 1992. Estimated production in 1992 of palm kernels and oil was 53,000 and 107,000 tons, respectively. For peanuts (in the shell) the figure was 100,000 tons. Small amounts of tobacco, tea, and pineapples are also grown.

22 DOMESTICATED ANIMALS

In 1992 there were 4,730,000 head of cattle, 3,560,000 each of goats and sheep, and 1,380,000 hogs. Most stock breeding is carried out in the north. Livestock products in 1992 included 73,000 tons of beef and about 12,400 tons of eggs. Attempts to improve livestock and hides and skins have been hindered by the social system, in which livestock constitutes a source of prestige, security, and wealth.

23 FISHING

The fishing industry is not highly developed. Most fish are caught by artisan (craftsman) fishermen in small motorized boats. The total catch was an estimated 78,000 tons in 1991.

[24] FORESTRY

In 1991, the forest area of 24.4 million hectares (60.2 million acres) included about 52% of the land area. The principal types of trees felled (cut down) are assié, azobe, dussil, eloorba, mahogany, sapele, sipo, illomba, ayus, iroko, dibetu, and silk cotton. Timber exports in 1991 were about 728,000 cubic meters of logs and 253,000 cubic meters of sawn timber. In 1991, roundwood production was estimated at 14,637,000 cubic meters.

[25] MINERAL PRODUCTION

While Cameroon has steadily increased its oil production, the discovery and exploitation of other mineral resources have been slow. Bauxite deposits, in the Minam and Martap region, are estimated at one billion tons. Iron deposits containing an estimated 200 million tons have been discovered south of Kribi. There is a large variety of other mineral deposits, including diamonds, tin, gold, and mica, but only gold is commercially exploited.

[26] FOREIGN TRADE

Coffee and cocoa are Cameroon's principal agricultural exports, accounting for 32.1% of export earnings (1989). Cork, wood, and cotton account for an additional 16.4%. Petroleum provided 18.0% of exports in 1989, while basic manufactures (19.0%) and machinery and transport equipment (5.2%) provided additional export revenues. The leading imports are machinery and transportation equipment, basic manufactures (textiles and paper), chemicals (medicines and insecticides), and food.

France is by far Cameroon's leading trade partner. It received 23.5% of Cameroon's exports and shipped 36.5% of Cameroon's imports in 1989. Cameroon sent 19.3% of its exports to Belgium, 10% to the United States, and 8.8% to Germany. After France, the Netherlands was Cameroon's next leading supplier of imports (9.1%).

[27] ENERGY AND POWER

Electric power reached 2,702 kilowatt hours in 1990, of which 50% was used to process aluminum. Hydropower supplies 85% of the total. As of 1993, oil exploration had resumed. If new discoveries of oil are not found soon, Cameroon may cease being a net petroleum exporter by 2000, and production would stop by 2005.

Hydroelectric resources remain the most readily exploitable form of energy in Cameroon. Electrical energy is produced primarily by two hydroelectric stations on the Sanaga River.

[28] SOCIAL DEVELOPMENT

Social centers concern themselves with child care, hygiene, and juvenile delinquency, and they maintain kindergartens, orphanages, and classes in homemaking. There are no welfare services covering the whole population. However, a 1969 law established an employees' old age, invalid, and survivors' pension plan, financed by employee and employer contributions. Benefits are also paid for occupational diseases and accidents. The Public Health Service is supposed to provide free medical, surgical, and pharmaceutical services to those unable to pay.

Selected Social Indicators

These statistics are estimates for the period 1988 to 1993. For comparison purposes, data for the United States and averages for low-income countries and high-income countries are also given.

Indicator	Cameroon	Low-income countries	High-income countries	United States
Per capita gross national product†	$820	$380	$23,680	$24,740
Population growth rate	2.8%	1.9%	0.6%	1.0%
Population growth rate in urban areas	4.9%	3.9%	0.8%	1.3%
Population per square kilometer of land	26	78	25	26
Life expectancy in years	56	62	77	76
Number of people per physician	12,001	>3,300	453	419
Number of pupils per teacher (primary school)	51	39	<18	20
Illiteracy rate (15 years and older)	46%	41%	<5%	<3%
Energy consumed per capita (kg of oil equivalent)	87	364	5,203	7,918

† The gross national product (GNP) is the total dollar value of all goods and services produced by a country in a year. The per capita GNP is calculated by dividing a country's GNP by its population. The World Bank defines low-income countries as those with a per capita GNP of $695 or less. High-income countries have a per capita GNP of $8,626 or more. Less than 14% of the world's 5.5 billion people live in high-income countries, while almost 60% live in low-income countries.

> = greater than   < = less than

Sources: World Bank, *Social Indicators of Development 1995*, Baltimore: Johns Hopkins University Press, 1995. Central Intelligence Agency, *World Fact Book*, Washington, D.C.: Government Printing Office, 1994.

29 HEALTH

Many missionaries maintain health and leprosy centers. The government is pursuing a vigorous policy of public health improvement, with considerable success in reducing sleeping sickness, leprosy, and other diseases.

The need for modern equipment is especially urgent, with many clinics using outdated equipment, some of which is imported illegally from Nigeria. In 1993, there was only one physician per 12,001 people, and one nursing professional per 1,690 people. In 1992, only 41% of the population had access to health care services. Life expectancy is 56 years.

30 HOUSING

Differences in climate, building materials, and patterns of living have resulted in a variety of traditional structures in rural areas. There is a housing shortage, and many people live in thatched hovels of mud and wood, with no running water or modern facilities. The Cameroonian government has engaged in housing improvement and construction programs in urban and rural areas.

31 EDUCATION

Education is free in state schools and compulsory between ages 6 and 13. Most secondary schools have been made bilingual, with instruction in both French and English. Working alongside the public schools are the missionary schools, which have been extremely important in the history of Cameroonian education. Children go through six years of primary schooling followed by three years of secondary at the first stage and two years at the second.

At Yaoundé University (founded in 1962) and other equivalent institutions, there were 31,360 students and 761 instructors in 1990. There are faculties of science, law and economics, and arts at Yaoundé, which maintains four regional campuses.

32 MEDIA

An automatic telephone exchange system links all important cities and towns. As of 1991, some 61,567 telephones were in use.

There are broadcasting stations at Yaoundé and other cities offering programs in French, English, and many African languages. About 1,725,000 radios and 279,000 television sets were in use in 1991.

Most Cameroonian publications are issued irregularly and have small circulations. The majority are published in French, but some appear in Bulu, Duala, and other native languages of Cameroon. The major daily is the *Cameroon Tribune,* published in French in Yaoundé, with a weekly English-language edition; circulation was 70,000 in French and 25,000 in English during 1991.

33 TOURISM AND RECREATION

Cameroon's chief tourist attractions are its forests, savanna, jungle, and wild game. The 16 national parks and game reserves are equipped with camps for tourists. The diverse ethnic groups and their cultures and Cameroonian art have also proved of interest to visitors. There are several good hotels in the major cities.

34 FAMOUS CAMEROONIANS

Ahmadou Ahidjo (b.1924) was president of Cameroon from 1960 until 1982. Paul Biya (b.1933) became president in 1982 after having served as prime minister since 1975. The best-known literary figures are the novelists Ferdinand Oyono (b.1928) and Mongo Beti (b.1932).

35 BIBLIOGRAPHY

Bjornson, Richard. *The African Quest for Freedom and Identity: Cameroonian Writing and the National Experience.* Bloomington: Indiana University Press, 1991.

DeLancey, Mark. *Cameroon.* Oxford: Clio, 1986.

———. *Cameroon: Dependence and Independence.* Boulder, Colo.: Westview Press; London: Dartmouth, 1989.

Stager, Curt. "Cameroon's Killer Lake." *National Geographic,* September 1987, 404–420.

CANADA

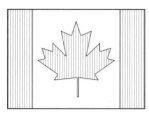

CAPITAL: Ottawa.

FLAG: The national flag, adopted in 1964, consists of a red maple leaf on a white field, flanked by a red vertical field on each end.

ANTHEM: Since 1 July 1980, *O Canada* has been the official anthem.

MONETARY UNIT: The Canadian dollar (c$) is a paper currency of 100 cents. There are coins of 1, 5, 10, 25, and 50 cents and 1 dollar, and notes of 2, 5, 10, 20, 50, 100, and 1,000 Canadian dollars. Silver coins of 5 and 10 dollars, commemorating the Olympics, were issued during 1973–76. c$1 = us$0.7227 (or us$1 = c$1.3837). US currency is usually accepted, especially in major cities and along the border.

WEIGHTS AND MEASURES: The metric system is the legal standard.

HOLIDAYS: New Year's Day, 1 January; Good Friday; Easter Monday; Victoria Day, the Monday preceding 25 May; Canada Day, 1 July; Labor Day, 1st Monday in September; Thanksgiving Day, 2d Monday in October; Remembrance Day, 11 November; Christmas Day, 25 December; Boxing Day, 26 December. Other holidays are observed in some provinces.

TIME: Newfoundland, 8:30 AM = noon GMT; New Brunswick, Nova Scotia, Prince Edward Island, and Quebec, 8 AM = noon GMT; Ontario east of 90° and western Quebec, 7 AM = noon GMT; western Ontario and Manitoba, 6 AM = noon GMT; Alberta and Saskatchewan, 5 AM = noon GMT; British Columbia and Yukon Territory, 4 AM = noon GMT.

1 LOCATION AND SIZE

Canada consists of all of the North American continent north of the United States, except Alaska and the small French islands of St. Pierre and Miquelon. Its total land area of 9,976,140 square kilometers (3,851,808 square miles) makes it slightly larger than China and the United States. The country's total boundary length is 252,684 kilometers (157,602 miles). Canada's capital city, Ottawa, is located in the southeastern part of the country.

2 TOPOGRAPHY

Canada's topography is dominated by the Canadian Shield, an area of Precambrian rocks surrounding the Hudson Bay and covering half the country. East of the Shield is the Maritime area, separated from the rest of Canada by low mountain ranges, and including the island of Newfoundland and Prince Edward Island. South and southeast of the Shield are the Great Lakes–St. Lawrence lowlands, a fertile plain in the triangle bounded by the St. Lawrence River, Lake Ontario, and Georgian Bay.

West of the Shield are the farmlands and ranching areas of the great central plains. Toward the north of this section is a series of rich mining areas, and still farther north is the Mackenzie lowland, traversed (crossed) by many lakes and rivers. The westernmost region of Canada, extending from western Alberta to the Pacific Ocean, includes the Rocky Mountains, a plateau region, the coastal mountain range, and an inner sea passage separating the outer island groups from the fjord-lined (narrow sea inlet) coast. Mt. Logan, the highest peak in Canada, in the St. Elias Range near the Alaska border, is 5,951 meters (19,524 feet) high. The Arctic islands constitute a large group extending north of the Canadian mainland to within 885 kilometers (550 miles) of the North Pole. They vary greatly in size and topography, with mountains, plateaus, fjords, and low coastal plains.

The Nelson-Saskatchewan, Churchill, Severn, and Albany rivers flow into Hudson Bay. The 4,241-kilometers (2,635-miles) Mackenzie River drains an area of almost 2.6 million square kilometers (1 million square miles) into the Arctic Ocean. The Great Lakes drain into the broad St. Lawrence River, which flows into the Gulf of St. Lawrence.

3 CLIMATE

Most of northern Canada has subarctic or arctic climates, with long cold winters lasting 8 to 11 months, short sunny summers, and little precipitation. In contrast, the populated south has a variety of climates.

Cool summers and mild winters prevail along the Pacific coast of British Columbia. Mean temperatures range from about 4°C (39°F) in January to 16°C (61°F) in July, the smallest range in the country. In Ontario and Quebec, especially near the Great Lakes and along the St. Lawrence River, the climate is less severe than in western Canada.

The northwest and the prairies are the driest areas. The windward mountain slopes are exceptionally wet; the protected slopes are very dry. Thus, the west coast gets about 150–300 centimeters (60–120 inches) of rain annually; the central prairie area, less than 50 centimeters (20 inches); the flat area east of Winnipeg, 50–100 centimeters (20–40 inches); and the Maritime provinces, 115–150 centimeters (45–60 inches). The annual average number of days of precipitation ranges from 252 along coastal British Columbia, to 100 in the interior of the province.

4 PLANTS AND ANIMALS

A great range of plant and animal life characterizes the vast area of Canada, with its varied geographic and climatic zones. The flora of the Great Lakes–St. Lawrence region include white pine, sugar and red maples, and beech trees. Coniferous trees (evergreens) abound in the Maritime region, and black spruce in the eastern Laurentian zone.

From the prairie grassland to the Arctic tundra there are aspen, bur oak, cottonwood, and other deciduous (those that shed leaves seasonally) trees. Conifers dominate the northern section. Many types of grasses grow on the interior plains. The wet area along the west coast is famous for its tall, hard conifers. In the Rocky Mountain area are alpine fir, Engelmann spruce, and lodgepole pine. The great Arctic region is covered with low-growing grasses, mosses, and bushes.

Animals range from deer, black bear, and opossum in the Great Lakes–St. Lawrence region to moose, caribou, and

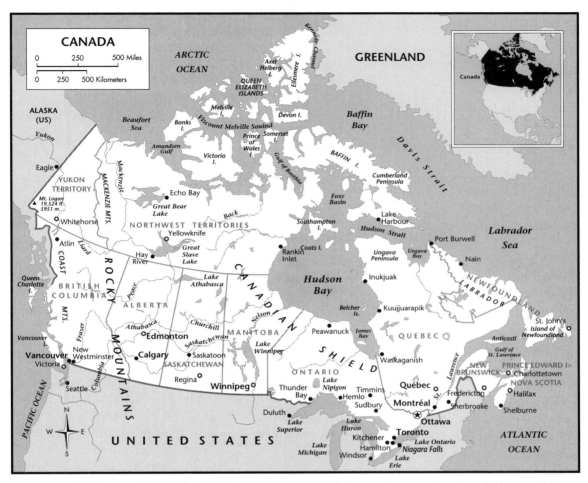

LOCATION: 41°41' to 83°7'N; 52°37' to 141°w. **BOUNDARY LENGTHS:** Arctic Ocean coastline, 9,286 kilometers (5,770 miles); Atlantic coastline, including Kennedy Channel, Baffin Bay, Davis Strait, 9,833 kilometers (6,110 miles); US, 6,416 kilometers (3,987 miles); Pacific coastline, 2,543 kilometers (1,580 miles); Alaska, 2,477 kilometers (1,539 miles); Hudson Strait and Hudson Bay shoreline, 7,081 kilometers (4,400 miles). **TERRITORIAL SEA LIMIT:** 12 miles.

timber wolf in the northern forests, and grizzly bear, mountain goat, and moose in the Rocky Mountain area. Birds include the robin, wood thrush, woodpecker, northern Pigmy-owl, band-tailed pigeon, snowy owl, ptarmigan, and arctic tern. Walrus, seals, and whales inhabit Canada's coastal waters.

5 ENVIRONMENT

Among Canada's most pressing environmental problems in the mid-1980s was acid rain, which poses a threat to natural resources in about 2.6 million square kilometers (1 million square miles) of eastern Canada. As of 1994, acid rain has affected

Photo credit: Susan D. Rock.

Pristine wilderness in Canada's Pacific Northwest.

150,000 lakes in total throughout Canada. About half the acid rain comes from emissions from Canadian smokestacks, but Canada has blamed United States industry for 75% of Ontario pollution.

Canada's rivers have been polluted by agriculture and industry. As of 1994, 50% of Canada's coastal shellfish areas are closed because of dangerous pollutant levels. Canada ranks 12th in the world for hydrocarbon emissions with a total of 2,486.1 metric tons.

Canada has more than 90 bird sanctuaries and 44 National Wildlife Areas, including reserves in the western Arctic to protect waterfowl nesting grounds. The annual Newfoundland seal hunt, producing seals for pelts and meat, drew the anger of environmentalists, chiefly because of the practice of clubbing baby seals to death (adult seals are shot). In 1987, Canada banned the offshore hunting of baby seals, as well as blueback hooded seals.

In 1987, endangered species in Canada included the wood bison, sea otter, right whale, Acadian whitefish, spotted owl, leatherback turtle, American peregrine falcon, whooping crane, and the southern bald eagle. As of 1991, the brown bear, the gray wolf, and the California Condor were also endangered. Of a total of 197 mammals, 5 are endangered, as are 6 bird species. Out of a total of 3,220 plant species nationwide, 13 are endangered.

6 POPULATION

The total population according to the census of 1991 was 27,296,859. In late 1993, the population was estimated at over 28 million. Of the 1991 population, 13.5 million (51%) were female. A population of 30,425,000 was forecasted for the year 2000.

The average population density in 1991 was three per square kilometers (7.7 per square miles). The population is unevenly distributed, ranging from 0.02 per square kilometers (0.045 per square miles) in the Northwest Territories, to 22.8 per square kilometers (59 per square miles) on Prince Edward Island. Nearly two-thirds of the people live within 160 kilometers (100 miles) of the United States boundary. The population movement has long been from rural to urban areas.

The Toronto metropolitan area had a population of 3,893,046 in 1991; Montreal, 3,127,242. Other large metropolitan areas are Vancouver, 1,602,502; Ottawa-Hull (Ottawa is the federal capital), 920,857; Edmonton, 839,924; Calgary, 754,033; Winnipeg, 652,354; and Quebec City, 645,550.

7 MIGRATION

Of a total of 252,042 immigrants in 1993, those from Asia numbered 134,532; Europe accounted for 50,050; Africa, 19,033; the Caribbean, 19,028; the United States, 6,565; and South America, 11,327. Emigration is mainly to the United States. In 1990 there were 871,000 Canadian-born people living in the US.

Canada is a major source of asylum for persecuted refugees. At the end of 1992 Canada harbored 568,200 such persons.

Interprovincial migration is generally from east to west. During 1990–91 British Columbia gained 37,620 more people from other provinces than it lost, and Alberta 7,502, while Ontario lost 22,301 more than it gained, as did Saskatchewan (9,941) and Quebec (7,690).

8 ETHNIC GROUPS

According to the 1991 census, 83.5% of the population was Canadian-born. Persons wholly or partially of British origin (including Irish) made up 44.6% of the total population in 1991; those of total or partial French origin (centered mainly in Quebec, where they constitute 80% of the population), 31.1%. Other European groups included Germans (3.3%), Italians (2.8%), Ukrainians (1.5%), Dutch (1.3%), and Poles (1%). Nearly 28.9% of the total population claimed multiple ethnic origin.

Amerindians numbered 365,375 (1.4%) in 1991 and formed the sixth-largest ethnic group. As of 1992/93 there were 604 Indian bands living on 2,364 reserves. These Indians were classified into 10 major groups by language. There were also 75,150 métis, of mixed European and Indian descent.

Most of the 30,090 Inuit (Eskimos) live in the Northwest Territories, with smaller numbers in northern Quebec and northern Newfoundland (Labrador).

9 LANGUAGES

English and French are the official languages of Canada and have equal status and equal rights and privileges as to their use in all governmental institutions. The federal constitution also gives English and French speakers the right to publicly funded education in their own language at the primary and secondary levels, wherever the number of children justifies it.

The constitution provides for the use of both English and French in the legislature and courts of Quebec, New Brunswick, and Manitoba. Although there are no similar constitutional rights in Ontario and Saskatchewan, these provinces have made English and French the official languages of the courts. In 1984, the Northwest Territories Council adopted an ordinance providing for the use of aboriginal languages and establishing English and French as official languages.

Although Canada is frequently referred to as a bilingual country, in 1991 only 16.3% of the people were able to speak both English and French. In Quebec, 82.3% of the people spoke French as a native language in 1991; in the other provinces, most of the people spoke only English.

Native speakers of Italian numbered 510,980; German, 466,240; Chinese, 498,845; Ukrainian, 187,015; Portuguese, 212,090; and Polish, 189,815. There were 73,870 native speakers of Cree, the most common Indian language; there are at least 58 different Indian languages and dialects.

10 RELIGIONS

In 1990, the principal religious denominations and their memberships in Canada were the Roman Catholic Church, 11,582,350; United Church of Canada, 2,013,258; Anglican Church of Canada, 848,256; Presbyterian Church of Canada, 245,883; Lutherans, 78,566; and Baptists, 201,218. Also represented were Greek Orthodox, Russian Orthodox, Greek Catholic, Mennonite, Pentecostal, and other groups. The estimated Jewish population in 1990 was 310,000.

11 TRANSPORTATION

In spite of the rapid growth of road, air, and pipeline services since 1945, railways are still important because they can supply all-weather transportation in large volume over continental distances. There were 93,544 kilometers (58,134 miles) of railways in 1991. About 90% of the railway facilities are operated by two great conti-

nental systems, the government-owned Canadian National Railways (CNR), with 51,745 kilometers (32,153 miles) of tracks, and the privately owned Canadian Pacific Ltd. (CP), with 34,016 kilometers (21,137 miles). CNR and CP also maintain steamships and ferries, nationwide telegraph services, highway transport services, and hotel chains.

Because of difficult winter weather conditions, road maintenance is a continual and expensive task. There are about 884,272 kilometers (549,487 miles) of roads, including 250,023 kilometers (155,364 miles) of paved highway. Canada ranks next to the United States in per capita use of motor transport, with one passenger car for every 2 persons. Motor vehicles in use in 1991 totaled 16,805,096, including 13,061,084 passenger cars, 3,679,804 trucks, and 64,208 buses. Plans to construct a bridge from Prince Edward Island to the mainland were underway in 1992.

Canada makes heavy use of water transport in domestic as well as foreign commerce. The major part of Canada's merchant fleet—480,000 gross registered tons in 1991—consists of tankers. Montreal is Canada's largest port and the world's largest grain port. Other well-equipped ports are Toronto, Hamilton, Port Arthur, and Fort William on the Great Lakes, and Vancouver on the Pacific Coast.

The St. Lawrence Seaway and Power Project, constructed jointly by Canada and the United States provides an 8-meter (27-feet) navigation channel from Montreal to

Lake Superior. The Athabasca and Slave rivers and the Mackenzie, into which they flow, provide an inland, seasonal water transportation system from Alberta to the Arctic Ocean. The Yukon River is also navigable.

International air service is provided by government-owned Air Canada and Canadian Airlines. Regional service is provided by some 570 smaller carriers. Canada has 1,400 airports, with 1,155 of them usable. The Lester Pearson airport in Toronto is by far the busiest, with 17,278,000 passengers handled in 1991.

12 HISTORY

The first inhabitants of what is now Canada were the ancient ancestors of the Inuit, who probably entered the region between 15,000 and 10,000 BC. Although most Inuit lived near the coast, some followed the caribou herds to the interior and developed a culture based on hunting and inland fishing.

The first recorded arrival of Europeans was in 1497 by the Italian-born John Cabot, who led an English expedition to the shore of a "new found land" (Newfoundland) and claimed the area in the name of Henry VII. In 1534, the French, under Jacques Cartier, claimed the Gaspé Peninsula and discovered the St. Lawrence River the following year.

By 1604, the first permanent French colony, Port Royal (now Annapolis Royal, Nova Scotia), had been founded. Four years later, Samuel de Champlain established the town of Quebec. With the discovery of the Great Lakes, missionaries

Photo credit: Susan D. Rock.

Chateau Frontenac.

and fur traders arrived, and an enormous French territory was established. Between 1608 and 1756, about 10,000 French settlers arrived in Canada. In 1663, New France became a royal province of the French crown.

The movement of exploration, discovery, commercial exploitation, and missionary activity which had begun with the coming of Champlain, was extended by such men as Jacques Marquette, reaching its climax in the last three decades of the 17th century. At that time, French trade and empire stretched north to the shores of Hudson Bay, west to the head of the Great Lakes, and south to the Gulf of

Mexico. Meanwhile, a British enterprise, the Hudson's Bay Company, founded in 1670, began to compete for the fur trade.

The European wars between England and France were paralleled in North America by a series of French and Indian wars. The imperial contest ended after British troops, commanded by James Wolfe, defeated Marquis Louis Joseph de Montcalm on the Plains of Abraham, bringing the fall of Quebec in 1759. The French army surrendered at Montreal in 1760, and the Treaty of Paris in 1763 established British rule over what had been New France.

The Quebec Act of 1774 instituted the separateness of French-speaking Canada that has become a distinctive feature of the country. It also secured the loyalty of the French clergy and aristocracy to the British crown during the American Revolution. Some 40,000 Loyalists from the colonies fled in revolt northward to eastern Canada.

Alexander Mackenzie reached the Arctic Ocean in 1789 and journeyed to the Pacific Ocean in 1793. British mariners secured for Britain a firm hold on what is now British Columbia. The War of 1812, in which United States forces attempting to invade Canada were repulsed by Canadian and British soldiers, did not change either the general situation or the United States-Canadian boundary. In 1846, the United States–Canadian border in the west was resolved at 49°N, and since then, except for minor disputes, the long border has been a line of peace.

The movement for Canadian confederation—political union of the colonies—was spurred in the 1860s by the need for common defense and the desire for a common government to sponsor railroads and other transportation. In 1864 Upper Canada (present-day Ontario) and Lower Canada (Quebec) were united under a common dominion (authority) government.

In 1867, the British North America Act created a larger dominion that was a confederation of Nova Scotia, New Brunswick, and the two provinces of Canada. Since the name Canada was chosen for the entire country, Lower Canada and Upper Canada assumed their present-day names of Quebec and Ontario.

In 1870, the province of Manitoba was established and admitted to the confederation, and the Northwest Territories were transferred to the federal government. British Columbia, on the Pacific shore, joined the confederation in 1871, and Prince Edward Island joined in 1873.

By the turn of the century, immigration to the western provinces had risen swiftly, and the prairie agricultural empire bloomed. Large-scale development of mines and of hydroelectric resources helped spur the growth of industry and urbanization. Alberta and Saskatchewan were made provinces in 1905.

In 1921, Manitoba, Ontario, and Quebec were greatly enlarged to take in all territory west of Hudson Bay and south of 60°N and all territory east of Ungava Bay. In February 1931, Norway formally recognized the Canadian title to the Sverdrup group of Arctic islands (now the Queen Elizabeth Islands). Newfoundland remained apart from the confederation until after World War II; it became Canada's tenth province in March 1949.

More than 600,000 Canadians served with the Allies in World War I, and over 60,000 were killed. The war contributions of Canada and other dominions helped bring about the declaration of equality of the members of the British Commonwealth in the Statute of Westminster of 1931. After the war, the development of air transportation and roads helped weld Canada together, and the nation had sufficient strength to withstand the depression that began in 1929, and the droughts that brought ruin to wheat fields.

Canada was vitally important again in World War II. More than one million Canadians took part in the Allied war effort, and over 32,000 were killed. The nation emerged from the war with enhanced prestige, actively concerned with world affairs and fully committed to the Atlantic alliance.

Domestically, a far-reaching postwar development was the resurgence in the 1960s of French Canadian separatism. Although administrative reforms—including the establishment of French as Quebec's official language in 1974—helped meet the demands of cultural nationalists, separatism continued to be an important force in Canadian politics. In the 1976 provincial elections, the separatist Parti Québécois came to power in Quebec, and its leader, Premier René Lévesque, proposed that Quebec become politically independent from Canada. However, his proposal was defeated, 59.5% to 40.5%, in a 1980 referendum.

Meanwhile, other provinces had their own grievances, especially over oil revenues. The failure of Newfoundland and the federal government to agree on development and revenue sharing stalled the exploitation of the vast Hibernia offshore oil and gas field in the early 1980s.

In the 1980s, Liberal Prime Minister Pierre Elliott Trudeau worked for "patriation" of the constitution (revoking the British North America Act so that Canada could reclaim authority over its own constitution from the United Kingdom). The Constitution Act, passed in December 1981 and proclaimed by Queen Elizabeth II on 17 April 1982, thus replaced the British North America Act as the basic document of Canadian government. However, Quebec, New Brunswick, and Manitoba failed to ratify it due to inter-provincial tensions and other problems.

Canada joined with the United States and Mexico to negotiate the North American Free Trade Agreement (NAFTA), which was built upon the United States–Canada Free Trade Agreement (FTA). The three nations came to an agreement in August 1992 and signed the text on 17 December 1992. NAFTA, which seeks to create a single common market of 370 million consumers, was implemented in 1994.

13 GOVERNMENT

Canada is a federation of ten provinces and two northern territories. In 1982 the

British North America Act of 1867—which effectively served, together with a series of subsequent British statutes, as Canada's constitution—was superseded by the Constitution Act (or Canada Act). Its principal innovations are the Charter of Rights and Freedoms and the provision for amendment.

Under the Constitution Act, the British sovereign remains sovereign of Canada and head of state; for the most part, the personal participation of Queen Elizabeth II in the function of the crown for Canada is reserved for such occasions as a royal visit. The queen's personal representative in the federal government is the governor-general, appointed by the crown on the advice of the prime minister of Canada.

The federal Parliament is made up of the House of Commons and the Senate. A new House of Commons, with 295 members as of 1993, is elected at least once every five years. The leader of the party that wins the largest number of seats in a newly elected House of Commons becomes prime minister and is asked to form the government. The governor-in-council (cabinet) is chosen by the prime minister.

The 104 members of the Senate, or upper house, are appointed for life, or until age 75, by the governor-general on the nomination of the prime minister, with equality of representation for regional divisions. In October 1992, Canadian voters declined a constitutional amendment that would have made the Senate an elected body.

14 POLITICAL PARTIES

Throughout most of the 20th century, national unity has been the primary aim of every Canadian government: leaders of both the English-speaking majority and the French-speaking minority have cooperated to develop a united Canada to which differences arising from national origin were subordinate (of an inferior rank). Canadian nationalism has been fueled partially by reaction against being too closely identified with either the United Kingdom or the United States. In the 1970s, this unity was challenged by a growing demand for French Canadian autonomy.

The Liberal Party (LP), which held office from 1935 to 1957 and again (except for part of 1979) from 1968 to 1984, traditionally emphasized trade and cultural relationships with the United States, while its principal rival, the Progressive Conservative Party (PC), which held power from 1957 to 1968, from May to December 1979, stresses Canada's relationships with the United Kingdom. In economic policy, the Liberals generally champion free trade, while the Conservatives favor a degree of government protection.

The New Democratic Party (NDP) is a labor-oriented party formed in 1961 by the merger of The Cooperative Commonwealth Federation (CCF) and the Canadian Labour Congress.

Brian Mulroney became prime minister following a landslide PC victory in the September 1984 elections. In 1993, the PC fell from power, primarily due to one of the worst Canadian recessions in nearly 60 years and the failure of the PC government to implement constitutional reforms.

Brian Mulroney resigned, and was succeeded by Kim Campbell. Liberals soundly defeated the PC in the October 1993 election. The Liberal party named Jean Chrétien as the new prime minister

15 JUDICIAL SYSTEM

Civil and criminal courts exist on county, district, and superior levels. The Supreme Court in Ottawa has appeals, civil, and criminal jurisdiction throughout Canada; its chief justice and eight associate justices are appointed by the governor-general. The Federal Court of Canada (formerly the Exchequer Court) hears cases having to do with taxation, claims involving the federal government, copyrights, and admiralty (maritime) law. The death penalty in Canada was abolished in 1976; that decision was upheld in a vote by the House of Commons in June 1987.

16 ARMED FORCES

All service in the armed forces is voluntary. Total forces as of 1993 were 84,000; there were 29,700 reserves. The Land Forces had 22,000 troops in 1993; the Maritime Forces had 17,000; and the air force had a strength of 22,400, with eight fighter squadrons (some 300 aircraft).

In 1993, Canadian armed forces were deployed in Cyprus, Syria, Israel, the Sinai, Cambodia, Croatia, Iraq, and Angola, as well as elsewhere in Africa on peacekeeping operations. Defense expenditures in 1992 totaled $10.4 billion.

The Royal Canadian Mounted Police (RCMP) is a civil force maintained by the federal government, originally to police federal territories. However, all the provinces except Ontario and Quebec, which have their own police forces, have entered into contracts with the "mounties" to enforce provincial laws (under the direction of the provincial authorities).

17 ECONOMY

The Canadian economy is the seventh largest among the western industrialized nations. The postwar period has seen a steady shift from the production of goods toward increased emphasis on services. Although no longer the foremost sector of the economy, agriculture is of major importance to the economy. Canada accounts for approximately 20% of the world's wheat trade. Canada is also the world's leading producer of newsprint and ranks among the leaders in other forestry products.

Differences in prosperity among the provinces increased during the 1980s, with the central provinces relatively robust, the western provinces suffering declines in growth because of lower prices for oil and other natural resources, and the Atlantic provinces depressed. By the second quarter of 1990, the economy had begun to decline, affected by a recession and the central bank's monetary policy. Recovery began in the second half of 1991, although the early 1990s were marked by continuing unemployment.

18 INCOME

In 1992, Canada's gross national product (GNP) was $565,787 million at current prices, or $19,970 per person. For the period 1985–92 the average inflation rate was 3.7%, resulting in a real growth rate in GNP of 0.3% per person.

19 INDUSTRY

The leading industrial areas are foods and beverages, transport equipment, petroleum and coal products, paper and paper products, primary metals, chemicals, fabricated metals, electrical products, and wood products. The value of industrial production in 1990 amounted to c$91.3 billion.

Of the total manufacturing output, about half is concentrated in Ontario, which not only is the center of Canadian industry but also has the greatest industrial diversification. Some important industries operate there exclusively. Quebec ranks second in manufacturing production, accounting for more than 25% of the value of Canadian manufactured goods. British Columbia ranks third.

20 LABOR

Employment in 1992 was 12,240,000. There were 13,797,000 in the total civilian labor force in 1992. Of those in civilian employment in 1992, 27.7% were in industry; 3.5% in agriculture; and 73% in services. In 1992, unemployment stood at 11.3%. Payments of c$19.3 billion went to the unemployed in 1992, a record high.

Cold weather and consumer buying habits cause some regular seasonal unem-

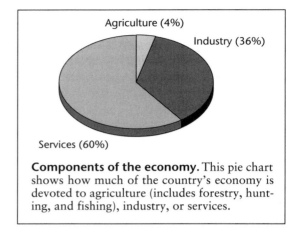

Agriculture (4%)

Industry (36%)

Services (60%)

Components of the economy. This pie chart shows how much of the country's economy is devoted to agriculture (includes forestry, hunting, and fishing), industry, or services.

ployment, but new techniques and materials are making winter construction work more possible, and both government and many industrial firms plan as much work as possible during the winter months.

At the beginning of 1992, labor organizations active in Canada reported a total membership of 4,089,000. Federal and provincial laws set minimum standards for hours of work, wages, and other conditions of employment. Safety and health regulations and workers' disability compensation have been established by federal, provincial, and municipal legislation.

21 AGRICULTURE

Until the beginning of the 1900s, agriculture was the most common Canadian occupation. Since then, however, the farm population has been shrinking. Even in Saskatchewan, the province with the highest proportion of farmers, farm families account for no more than 25% of the total population. For Canada as a whole, agriculture engaged only 3.4% of the economically active population in 1992.

However, Canada is still one of the major food-exporting countries of the world. Farm production continues to increase, as do the size of holdings, crop quantity, quality and variety, and cash income. Canada generates about $23 billion in cash farm receipts annually.

More than 90% of Canada's cultivated area is in the three prairie provinces of Alberta, Saskatchewan, and Manitoba. The trend is toward fewer and larger farms, increased use of machinery, and more specialization.

The estimated output of principal field crops in 1992 (in 1,000 tons) was wheat, 29,870,000; barley, 10,919,000; corn, 4,531,000; rapeseed, 3,689,000; potatoes, 3,529,000; and oats, 2,823,000.

During 1989–90, Canada was the second largest exporter of wheat through the International Wheat Agreement (after the United States); over 9.9 million tons were exported, mostly to Japan, Pakistan, and Iran.

22 DOMESTICATED ANIMALS

Canada traditionally exports livestock products, producing more than the domestic market can use. Animal production (livestock, dairy products, and eggs) now brings in about half of total farm cash income.

Livestock on farms in 1992 numbered 13,002,000 head of cattle; 10,395,000 pigs and hogs; 914,000 sheep and lambs; and 118,000,000 hens and chickens. In 1992, livestock slaughtered included 3,339,000 head of cattle, and calves, 15,285,000 hogs, and 538,000 sheep. Chicken and turkey production totaled 733,000 tons. Milk production in 1992 was 7.3 million tons; butter production amounted to about 100,000 tons, and cheese production to 291,139 tons. Most dairy products are consumed within Canada. In 1992, 317,060 tons of eggs were produced.

23 FISHING

With a coastline of nearly 29,000 kilometers (18,000 miles) and a lake-and-river system containing more than half the world's fresh water, Canada ranks among the world's major fish producers. In 1991 Canada was the world's third-leading exporter of fresh, chilled, and frozen fish. Exports of dried, salted, and smoked fish in 1991 amounted to $338.5 million, more than any other nation except Norway.

More than one billion pounds of cod, haddock, halibut, pollock, and other fish are caught every year along the Atlantic in deep-sea and shore operations. Vast numbers of lobsters and herring are caught in the Gulf of St. Lawrence and the Bay of Fundy. Salmon, the specialty of the Pacific fisheries, is canned for export and constitutes the most valuable item of Canadian fish production. Also exported are fresh halibut and canned and processed herring. Other important export items are whitefish, lake trout, pickerel, and other freshwater fish caught in the Great Lakes and some of the larger inland lakes. Feed and fertilizer are important by-products.

Export sales in 1991 amounted to $2.17 billion. The United States imported more than $1.45 billion of Canada's fish product exports in 1992.

The government protects and develops the resources of both ocean and inland waters and helps expand the domestic market for fish.

24 FORESTRY

In 1991, forests covered 360 million hectares (890 million acres) or 39% of Canada's total land area. Canada ranks as the third-largest producer of coniferous (evergreens) wood products (after the United States and Russia), and is the leading supplier of softwood products for export.

Chief forest products in eastern Canada are pulp and paper products, especially newsprint, three-fourths of which goes to the United States. In the west, the chief product is sawn timber. In 1991, an estimated 52 million cubic meters (1.8 billion cubic feet) of sawn wood was cut. In addition, 52,040,000 cubic meters of pulp wood, and 8,977,000 tons of newsprint were produced.

25 MINING

Some 52 minerals are currently being commercially produced in Canada. Canada is the world's largest producer of mine zinc and uranium and is among the leaders in silver, nickel, aluminum (from imported bauxite), potash, gold, copper, lead, salt, sulfur, and nitrogen in ammonia. Yet the country has only just begun to fully develop many of its most important mineral resources. Beginning in 1981, large

new deposits of gold ore were discovered at Hemlo, Ontario, north of Lake Superior; by 1991, more than 50% of Ontario's gold production came from the three mines in the Helmo district.

Output totals for principal Canadian metals in 1991 (in metric tons) was: iron ore, 35,961,000; copper, 797,603,000; zinc, 1,148,189; uranium, 9,124; nickel, 196,868; molybdenum, 11,333; and lead, 278,141. Gold production was 178,712 kilograms, and silver was 1,338 kilograms.

What are believed to be the world's largest deposits of asbestos are located in the eastern townships of Quebec. Asbestos production in 1991 amounted to 670,000 tons, and was valued at US$240 million. Other nonmetallic mineral production included salt (11,585,000 tons), sand and gravel (200,497,000 tons), peat (762,116 tons), and potash (7,012,000 tons).

26 FOREIGN TRADE

Canada's exports are highly diversified; the principal export groups are industrial goods, forestry products, mineral resources (with crude petroleum and natural gas increasingly important), and agricultural commodities.

Imports are heavily concentrated in the industrial sector, including machinery, transport equipment, basic manufactures, and consumer goods. In 1990, exports were at c$120,521 million and imports c$146,057 million.

The United States is by far Canada's leading trade partner. Canada exchanges raw materials such as crude petroleum and

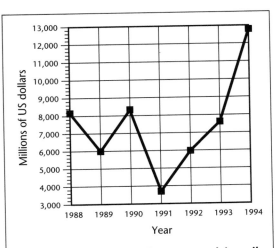

Yearly balance of trade measured in millions of US dollars. The balance of trade is the difference between what a country sells to other countries (its exports) and what it buys (its imports). If a country imports more than it exports, it has a negative balance of trade (a trade deficit). If exports exceed imports, there is a positive balance of trade (a trade surplus).

27 ENERGY AND POWER

Canada's fossil fuels and hydroelectric resources are abundant. Coal production reached 71.1 million metric tons in 1991.

Output of crude oil in 1992 was 98.2 million tons, at a rate of 2,065,000 barrels per day. Natural gas production rose to 116,600 million cubic meters (4,117 billion cubic feet) in 1992, third in the world after Russia and the United States. In 1992, proved crude oil reserves were estimated at 7.6 billion barrels, and natural gas reserves at more than 95.7 trillion cubic feet. Crude oil pipelines totaled 23,564 kilometers (14,642 miles) in length in 1991.

Canada ranks sixth in the production of electric power in the world and first in the production of hydroelectricity. In 1991, Canada's total net installed capacity reached 104.6 million kilowatts. Total electric power generation in Canada in 1991 was 507,913 million kilowatt hours; 61% of it was hydroelectric, 23% was conventional thermal, and 16% was nuclear. Canada's hydroelectric power totaled 284.1 billion kilowatt hours in 1992, more than any other nation.

28 SOCIAL DEVELOPMENT

Welfare needs are met by federal, provincial, and municipal governments as well as by voluntary agencies. Federal programs include family allowances, old age security, and earning-related disability and survivors' pensions. In general, families with children under 16 (and youths aged 16 or 17 who attend school full time), regardless of means, are eligible for small

processed items such as paper for United States machinery, transportation and communications equipment, and agricultural items, such as citrus fruits.

In 1992, the United States accounted for 77% of Canada's exports and 69% of imports. In 1992, the United States, Canada, and Mexico signed the North American Free Trade Agreement (NAFTA), which was ratified by all three countries the following year.

Besides the United States, Canada traded principally with European Community countries, Japan, and the United Kingdom in 1990.

Selected Social Indicators

These statistics are estimates for the period 1988 to 1993. For comparison purposes, data for the United States and averages for low-income countries and high-income countries are also given.

Indicator	Canada	Low-income countries	High-income countries	United States
Per capita gross national product†	**$19,970**	$380	$23,680	$24,740
Population growth rate	**1.2%**	1.9%	0.6%	1.0%
Population growth rate in urban areas	**1.2%**	3.9%	0.8%	1.3%
Population per square kilometer of land	**3**	78	25	26
Life expectancy in years	**78**	62	77	76
Number of people per physician	**469**	>3,300	453	419
Number of pupils per teacher (primary school)	**17**	39	<18	20
Illiteracy rate (15 years and older)	**<1%**	41%	<5%	<3%
Energy consumed per capita (kg of oil equivalent)	**7,821**	364	5,203	7,918

† The gross national product (GNP) is the total dollar value of all goods and services produced by a country in a year. The per capita GNP is calculated by dividing a country's GNP by its population. The World Bank defines low-income countries as those with a per capita GNP of $695 or less. High-income countries have a per capita GNP of $8,626 or more. Less than 14% of the world's 5.5 billion people live in high-income countries, while almost 60% live in low-income countries.

> = greater than   < = less than

Sources: World Bank, Social Indicators of Development 1995, Baltimore: Johns Hopkins University Press, 1995. Central Intelligence Agency, World Fact Book, Washington, D.C.: Government Printing Office, 1994.

monthly allowances (the average was c$33.93 per child in 1991).

Persons aged 65 and over receive monthly pensions, supplemented in some provinces on a means-test basis. Under federal-provincial programs, monthly allowances are paid to needy persons aged 65 to 69, and to needy persons aged 18 or over who are blind or totally and permanently disabled.

The provinces provide services of their own, including allowances to needy mothers and their dependent children, widows, and mothers whose husbands have deserted them, are disabled, or are in mental hospitals. Municipalities, provinces, and voluntary agencies finance child welfare services. Homes for the aged are generally maintained by municipalities and voluntary organizations. Since 1941, an unemployment insurance system and a nationwide free employment service have been in operation.

Liberalization of divorce and abortion laws since the 1960s, coupled with the increased participation of women in the labor force, have brought significant changes to Canadian family life. Since

1968, the crude divorce rate (per 100,000 population) has risen by more than 400%.

Women participate fully in the Canadian labor force, including business and the professions, although government reports show that their average earnings are still less than those of men.

29 HEALTH

Canada adopted a national health insurance scheme in 1971. It is administered regionally, with each province running a public insurance plan and the government contributing about 40% of the cost. Access to health care and cost containment are good, but there are strains on the budget, increased by the demands of an aging population.

Diseases of the heart and arteries account for more than 40% of all deaths, and cancer accounts for just under one-third; the proportion of deaths from causes related to old age is rising. Accidents are the leading cause of death in childhood and among young adult males, and rank high for other population groups. In 1993, life expectancy was estimated at 78 years.

30 HOUSING

There were slightly more than 10 million occupied private dwellings in Canada in 1991. Housing starts were estimated at just over 156,000 during 1991, a 14% drop from 1990 due to the recession. Single homes are the most common type of dwelling, although their relative numbers have gradually fallen in favor of multiple dwellings.

31 EDUCATION

Practically the entire adult population is literate. The age limits of compulsory school attendance are roughly from age 6 to age 15. Primary school lasts for eight years and secondary or high school another three to five years. In 1990, primary schools numbered 12,220. There were 154,698 teachers and 2,371,558 students in primary schools. The same year, secondary schools had 164,125 teachers and 2,292,735 students.

Each province is responsible for its own system of education. While the systems differ in some details, the general plan is the same for all provinces except Quebec, which has two parallel systems: one mainly for Roman Catholics and speakers of French, the other primarily for non-Catholics and speakers of English.

During 1992 there were 69 degree-granting colleges and universities in Canada. In 1991, full-time enrollment in all higher level institutions, colleges and universities was 1,942,814.

Among the oldest Canadian institutions of higher education are the Collège des Jésuites in Quebec City, founded in 1635; the Collège St. Boniface in Manitoba (1827); the University of Ottawa (1848); and St. Joseph's University in New Brunswick (1864). Most university-level instruction is conducted in English. Two private universities on the Scottish model are Dalhousie University in Halifax (1818), and McGill University in Montreal (1821). The first state-supported institution was King's College at York in Upper Canada, which became the Univer-

Canada Place pier in Vancouver.

Photo credit: Susan D. Rock.

sity of Toronto, the largest and one of the most distinguished of Canadian institutions.

32 MEDIA

The ten public and private companies in Telecom Canada provide a major share of the nation's telecommunications services, including all long-distance service, and link regional networks across Canada. There were 20,126,490 telephones in Canada in 1991.

The publicly owned Canadian Broadcasting Corporation (CBC) provides the national broadcasting service in Canada. Privately owned local stations form part of the networks and provide alternative programs. As of 1991, there were 900 AM broadcasting stations, 800 FM stations, and 2,039 television stations. In the same year there were 27,776,000 radios and 17,252,000 television sets. As of May 1987, radio and television services reached 99% of Canadian homes.

In 1991 there were 107 daily newspapers. Although some newspapers in Montreal, Quebec, Toronto, Winnipeg, and Vancouver have more than local influence, most circulate only on a regional basis and have a limited number of readers. Rural areas are served by some 1,100 monthly and weekly publications. There are many consumer magazines, but only *Maclean's* is truly national.

Canada's leading newspapers (with their 1991 daily circulations) include the following: *Toronto Star* (494,681); *Globe and Mail* (330,000); *Le Journal de Montréal* (281,686); *Toronto Sun* (252,895); *Vancouver Sun* (193,749); and *La Presse* (186,590).

33 TOURISM AND RECREATION

From the polar ice cap to the mountains, fjords, and rainforests of the west coast, Canada offers a remarkable range of scenic wonders. Among the most spectacular parks are the Kluane National Park in the Yukon Territory and the Banff (with Lake Louise) and Jasper national parks in the mountains of Alberta. Norse artifacts and reconstructed dwellings can be viewed at the excavation of L'Anse aux Meadows in Newfoundland.

Other attractions include Dinosaur Park in Alberta's Red Deer Badlands; the Cabot Trail in Nova Scotia; and the Laurentians and the Gaspé Peninsula in Quebec. The arts and crafts of the Dene Indians and the Inuit may be seen in cooperative workshops in the Northwest Territories.

Quebec City is the only walled city in North America. Montreal, the second-largest French-speaking city in the world (after Paris), is famous for its fine French cuisine, its vast underground shopping network, and its excellent subway system. Toronto is known for commerce, culture, modern architecture, and an outstanding zoo. One of the world's foremost summer theatrical events is the Shakespeare Festival at Stratford, Ontario.

Fishing and hunting attract many sportsmen to Canada, and ice hockey attracts many sports fans, particularly to the Forum in Montreal. Major league baseball teams play in Montreal and Toronto. In 1992, the Toronto major league baseball team, the Blue Jays, became the first non-American team to both play in and win the World Series. Toronto again won the World Series in 1993.

In 1991, Canada was the world's tenth most popular tourist destination. In that year, 14,988,600 tourists arrived from abroad, 80% of them from the United States and 11% from Europe. Gross receipts from tourism were US$5.5 billion.

34 FAMOUS CANADIANS

Political Figures

Because of their exploits in establishing and developing early Canada, then known as New France, a number of eminent Frenchmen are prominent in Canadian history, among them the explorers Jacques Cartier (1491–1557), Samuel de Champlain (1567?–1635), and Jacques Marquette (1637–75).

Artists

Highly regarded Canadian painters include James Edward Hervey MacDonald (1873–1932), Frederick Horsman Varley (1881–1969), and Emily Carr (1871–1945). Two other artists of distinction were James W. G. MacDonald (1897–1960) and Harold Barling Town (b.1924). The portrait photographer Yousuf Karsh (b.Turkish Armenia, 1908) is a long-time Canadian resident.

Musicians

Well-known Canadian musicians include the pianist Glenn Gould (1932–82); the singers Jon Vickers (b.1926) and Maureen Forrester (b.1931); the bandleader Guy Lombardo (1902–77); and, among recent popular singers and songwriters, Gordon Lightfoot (b.1938), Joni Mitchell (b.1943), and Neil Young (b.1945).

Actors

Canadian-born actors who are known for their association with Hollywood include Mary Pickford (Gladys Mary Smith, 1893–1979), Walter Huston (Houghston, 1884–1950), Lorne Greene (1915–87), Raymond Burr (1917–94), William Shatner (b.1931), and Donald Sutherland (b.1935).

Sports

Notable in the world of sports are ice-hockey stars Maurice ("Rocket") Richard (b.1921), Gordon ("Gordie") Howe (b.1928), Robert Marvin ("Bobby") Hull, Jr. (b.1939), Robert ("Bobby") Orr (b.1948), and Wayne Gretzky (b.1961).

Authors

The *Anne of Green Gables* novels of Lucy Maud Montgomery (1874–1942) have been popular with readers of several generations. Louis Hémon (1880–1913), a French journalist who came to Canada in 1910 and spent only 18 months there, wrote the classic French Canadian novel *Maria Chapdelaine* (1914).

Scientists and Inventors

Among the famous Canadian scientists and inventors are Sir Sanford Fleming (1827–1915), inventor of standard time, and Sir William Osler (1849–1919), the father of psychosomatic medicine. The codiscoverers of insulin, Sir Frederick Grant Banting (1891–1941) and John James Richard Macleod (1876–1935), were awarded the Nobel Prize for medicine in 1923.

35 BIBLIOGRAPHY

Bumsted, J. M. *The Peoples of Canada.* New York: Oxford University Press, 1992.

Canada in Pictures. Minneapolis: Lerner, 1993.

Ingles, Ernest B. *Canada.* Santa Barbara, Calif.: Clio, 1990.

Lee, Douglas B. "Montreal—Heart of French Canada." *National Geographic,* March 1991, 60–85.

Lipset, Seymour Martin. *Continental Divide: The Values and Institutions of the United States and Canada.* New York: Routledge, 1990.

Malcolm, A. H. *The Canadians.* New York: Times Books, 1985.

Nagel, Rob and Anne Commire. "Samuel de Champlain." In *World Leaders, People Who Shaped the World.* Volume III: North and South America. Detroit: U*X*L, 1994.

Shepherd, J. *Canada.* Chicago: Children's Press, 1987.

The Canadian Encyclopedia. 2d ed. Edmonton: Hurtig Publishers, 1988.

CAPE VERDE

Republic of Cape Verde
República de Cabo Verde

CAPITAL: Praia.

FLAG: The flag consists of two white horizontal stripes above and below a red horizontal stripe in the lower half of a blue field. A circle of ten gold stars (representing major islands) is centered around the red stripe on the hoist side.

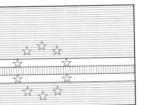

ANTHEM: *É Patria Amada (This Is Our Beloved Country).*

MONETARY UNIT: The Cape Verde escudo (CVE) is a paper currency of 100 centavos. There are coins of 20 and 50 centavos and 1, 2 ½, 10, 20, and 50 Cape Verde escudos, and notes of 100, 500, and 1,000 Cape Verde escudos. CVE 1 = $0.0118 (or $1 = CVE 84.415).

WEIGHTS AND MEASURES: The metric system is used.

HOLIDAYS: New Year's Day, 1 January; National Heroes' Day, 20 January; Women's Day, 8 March; Labor Day, 1 May; Children's Day, 1 June; Independence Day, 5 July; Assumption, 15 August; Day of the Nation, 12 September; All Saints' Day, 1 November; Immaculate Conception, 8 December; Christmas Day, 25 December.

TIME: 10 AM = noon GMT.

1 LOCATION AND SIZE

Cape Verde, containing an area of 4,030 square kilometers (1,555 square miles), is situated in the Atlantic Ocean about 595 kilometers (370 miles) west of Dakar, Senegal. The total coastline is 965 kilometers (600 miles). Cape Verde's capital city, Praia, is located on the southeastern coast of São Tiago Island.

2 TOPOGRAPHY

The island chain is of volcanic origin. Fogo has the only active volcano, Pico do Cano, which reaches 2,829 meters (9,281 feet) above sea level. All but three of the islands are quite mountainous, with prominent cliffs and deep ravines.

3 CLIMATE

A cold Atlantic current produces an arid atmosphere around the archipelago. There are two seasons: December–June is cool and dry, with temperatures at sea level averaging 21°C (70°F); July–November is warmer, with temperatures averaging 27°C (81°F). Although some rain comes during the later season, rainfall is sparse overall.

4 PLANTS AND ANIMALS

There are trees typical of both temperate and tropical climates, depending on elevation. The only native mammal is the long-eared bat.

Photo credit: AP/Wide World Photos

A young boy watches lava flow from an erupting volcano in the African archipelago of Cape Verde's island of Fogo. The lava was flowing at a rate of five to seven meters (5.5–7.7 yards) an hour.

5 ENVIRONMENT

Drought contributes to Cape Verde's land problems along with cyclones, volcanic activity, and insect infestation. The intense demand for wood as fuel has led to the virtual elimination of native vegetation.

6 POPULATION

The population of Cape Verde was 341,491 in 1990, as compared with a 1980 census population of 296,063. It was estimated at 423,372 in 1994. A total of 479,000 was projected for the year 2000.

The annual population growth rate for 1990–95 was 2.9%. More than half of the population lives on the island of São Tiago. In 1990, Praia, the capital city, on São Tiago, was the largest town, with a population of about 62,000.

7 MIGRATION

Slow economic development, combined with a prolonged drought, has produced a sizable outflow of emigrants. By the early 1990s there were some 600,000 Cape Verdean emigrants in the United States, Europe, Latin America, and other African countries.

8 ETHNIC GROUPS

About 70% of the inhabitants of Cape Verde are descendants of Portuguese colonists and their African slaves, who came, most often, from what is today Guinea-Bissau. Another 28% of the inhabitants are entirely African.

9 LANGUAGES

Portuguese is the official language, but Crioulo, an archaic Portuguese dialect with a pronunciation revealing African influences, is the spoken language of Cape Verde.

10 RELIGIONS

Up to 97% of the population of Cape Verde is at least nominally Roman Catholic. Protestant churches, particularly the Church of the Nazarene, account for another 3%.

11 TRANSPORTATION

There are about 2,250 kilometers (1,400 miles) of all types of roadway on the islands. About 15,000 motor vehicles were in use in 1991. Commercial transportation is largely by coastal craft and domestic airlines. In 1986 (the latest year available), the ports handled 394,000 tons of freight. The Amilcar Cabral International Airport is an important refueling point on many African flights.

12 HISTORY

Cape Verde was probably discovered in 1456 by Luigi da Cadamosto. The islands showed no signs of any previous human settlement. Plantation agriculture was established by the Portuguese community and worked by African slaves, who were brought in from the adjacent Guinea coast.

The islands produced trade goods which were used to purchase slaves and consumer items from slavers seeking goods marketable in the African interior. The phaseout of the Atlantic slave trade and the abolition of slavery in the Portuguese Empire brought an end to Cape Verde's importance as a slave-trading center. However, the islands' historical role as a port of call became important again in the mid-twentieth century, when they were used by Portuguese troops in their African campaigns.

After the 1974 military coup in Portugal, an independence agreement was signed leading to the establishment of the independent Republic of Cape Verde on 5 July 1975. Cape Verde and Guinea-

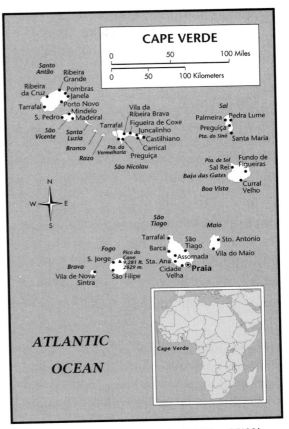

LOCATION: 14°48′ to 17°12′N; 22°40′ to 25°22′W.
TERRITORIAL SEA LIMIT: 12 miles.

Bissau—where Luis de Almeida Cabral, a Cape Verdean, was president—were supposed to work toward unification. But a military coup in Guinea-Bissau toppled Cabral in November 1980. Diplomatic relations with Guinea-Bissau, severed at the time of the coup, were resumed in June 1982.

In 1990, after 15 years of single-party rule by the African Party for the Independence of Cape Verde (PAICV), the constitution was amended to legalize opposition groups.

13 GOVERNMENT

The constitution was amended on 28 September 1990 to legalize opposition parties and revised again in 1992. The People's Assembly now has 79 members and the president is elected directly by popular vote.

14 POLITICAL PARTIES

The African Party for the Independence of Cape Verde (Partido Africano da Independência do Cabo Verde—PAICV) was the sole legal political party from 1975 until 1990. On 28 September 1990, the constitution was amended to legalize opposition parties.

15 JUDICIAL SYSTEM

In the preindependence period, Cape Verde was subject to Portuguese civil and criminal codes. Most provisions of these codes remain in effect. A Supreme Tribunal of Justice hears appeals from subregional and regional tribunals.

16 ARMED FORCES

The Popular Revolutionary Armed Forces numbered 1,300 in 1993. Of these, 1,000 were in a two-battalion people's militia with Russian arms. The navy numbered 200, and the air force numbered about 100.

17 ECONOMY

Agriculture, forestry, and fishing are the leading economic activities of the people of Cape Verde. Cape Verde is drought-prone, and less than 10% of food requirements are met by local producers. Perhaps Cape Verde's most important asset is its strategic economic location, which makes it an important refueling location for international air and ocean traffic

18 INCOME

In 1992 Cape Verde's gross national product (GNP) was $330 million at current prices, or $850 per person. For the period 1985–92 the average inflation rate was 8.6%, resulting in a real growth rate in GNP of 1.8% per person.

19 INDUSTRY

The manufacturing sector employs about 1,700 Cape Verdeans. Besides the salt refining, Cape Verde manufactures frozen and canned fish, tobacco, bread and biscuits, soft drinks, and clothing.

20 LABOR

In 1990, the economically active population numbered 120,565, of whom 25% were engaged in services and agriculture. All workers are free to form and join unions of their choosing.

21 AGRICULTURE

The most widespread agricultural activity of the islands is gardening for domestic consumption. Garden crops include corn, cassava, sweet potatoes, and bananas. Frequent droughts often exacerbate (aggravate) an ongoing water shortage. Agriculture employs about one-quarter of the active population. Estimated 1992 production figures were coconuts, 10,000 tons; sugarcane, 18,000 tons; potatoes, 3,000 tons; bananas, 6,000 tons; sweet potatoes, 3,000 tons; and corn, 6,000 tons.

Selected Social Indicators

These statistics are estimates for the period 1988 to 1993. For comparison purposes, data for the United States and averages for low-income countries and high-income countries are also given.

Indicator	Cape Verde	Low-income countries	High-income countries	United States
Per capita gross national product†	$850	$380	$23,680	$24,740
Population growth rate	2.6%	1.9%	0.6%	1.0%
Population growth rate in urban areas	6.7%	3.9%	0.8%	1.3%
Population per square kilometer of land	89	78	25	26
Life expectancy in years	68	62	77	76
Number of people per physician	5,024	>3,300	453	419
Number of pupils per teacher (primary school)	33	39	<18	20
Illiteracy rate (15 years and older)	53%	41%	<5%	<3%
Energy consumed per capita (kg of oil equivalent)	305	364	5,203	7,918

† The gross national product (GNP) is the total dollar value of all goods and services produced by a country in a year. The per capita GNP is calculated by dividing a country's GNP by its population. The World Bank defines low-income countries as those with a per capita GNP of $695 or less. High-income countries have a per capita GNP of $8,626 or more. Less than 14% of the world's 5.5 billion people live in high-income countries, while almost 60% live in low-income countries.

> = greater than   < = less than

Sources: World Bank, *Social Indicators of Development 1995,* Baltimore: Johns Hopkins University Press, 1995. Central Intelligence Agency, *World Fact Book,* Washington, D.C.: Government Printing Office, 1994.

22 DOMESTICATED ANIMALS

Periodic droughts have significantly lowered the capacity of the islands to pasture livestock. In 1992 there were an estimated 110,000 goats, 19,000 head of cattle, 6,000 sheep, 11,000 asses, 2,000 mules, 1,000 horses, and 86,000 pigs.

23 FISHING

The cold Canary Current, running adjacent to the islands, is an ideal environment for many kinds of marketable fish. São Vicente and Brava each have processing plants.

24 FORESTRY

Forests on the island have been cut down for fuel, and the drought damaged many wooded areas. In 1991 there were about 1,000 hectares (2,470 acres) of forest plantations.

25 MINING

Pozzolana (a volcanic rock used in pulverized form in the manufacture of hydraulic cement) and salt are the only minerals exploited commercially. In 1991, about 4,000 tons of salt and 53,000 tons of pozzolana were quarried.

26 FOREIGN TRADE

Cape Verde has been increasingly dependent upon imports, a situation which has led to a severe trade imbalance. The principal exports were fish, bananas, and petroleum and petroleum products.

27 ENERGY AND POWER

In 1991, the islands produced about seven million kilowatt hours of electricity, entirely from thermal sources. Installed capacity totaled about 36,000 kilowatts during the same year.

28 SOCIAL DEVELOPMENT

Social welfare services are being expanded by the government with United Nations assistance. The constitution bans sex discrimination, although social discrimination and violence against women have been reported.

29 HEALTH

Malnutrition (aggravated by the prolonged drought), influenza, and malaria are major health problems in Cape Verde. In 1986, there were 2 hospitals and 60 dispensaries. Average life expectancy in 1992 was 68 years.

30 HOUSING

Housing on the islands varies greatly, from the elegant, Mediterranean-style homes of Europeans and middle-class Cape Verdeans, to the simple timber and mud-block houses of peasants. As of 1980, 95% of all housing units were one-floor dwellings.

31 EDUCATION

Primary education is compulsory and lasts for six years. This is followed by three years of general secondary education. The literacy rate was estimated at 47% in 1993.

32 MEDIA

The government-run newspaper, *Vozde Povo* (1991 circulation 5,000) is published weekly. There are two government radio stations broadcasting to an estimated 61,000 receivers in Portuguese and Crioulo and one television channel. In 1991, Cape Verde had 2,384 telephones.

33 TOURISM AND RECREATION

Tourism is a potentially important source of revenue for the picturesque islands and has increased steadily since the mid-1980s. Between 1986 and 1990, the annual number of tourist arrivals nearly doubled from 13,626 to 22,470. The ruins at Cidade Velha on São Tiago and the beaches at Baia das Gates on Boa Vista hold considerable tourist interest.

34 FAMOUS CAPE VERDEANS

Aristides Maria Pereira (b.1923) was the first president of the independent Republic of Cape Verde.

35 BIBLIOGRAPHY

Foy, Colm. *Cape Verde: Politics, Economics, and Society.* London; New York: Pinter Publishers, 1988.

Meintet, Deirdre. *Race, Culture, and Portuguese Colonialism in Cabo Verde.* Syracuse, N.Y.: Syracuse University Foreign and Comparative Studies Program, 1984.

CENTRAL AFRICAN REPUBLIC

République Centrafricaine

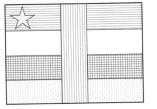

CAPITAL: Bangui.

FLAG: The national flag consists of four horizontal stripes (blue, white, green, and yellow) divided at the center by a vertical red stripe. In the upper left corner is a yellow five-pointed star.

ANTHEM: *La Renaissance (Rebirth)*.

MONETARY UNIT: The Communauté Financière Africaine franc (CFA Fr) is a paper currency. There are coins of 1, 2, 5, 10, 25, 50, 100, and 500 CFA francs, and notes of 50, 100, 500, 1,000, 5,000, and 10,000 CFA francs. CFA Fr1 = $0.0018 (or $1 = CFA Fr571).

WEIGHTS AND MEASURES: The metric system is the legal standard.

HOLIDAYS: New Year's Day, 1 January; Anniversary of President Boganda's Death, 29 March; Labor Day, 1 May; National Day of Prayer, 30 June; Independence Day, 13 August; Assumption, 15 August; All Saints' Day, 1 November; Proclamation of the Republic, 28 November; National Day, 1 December; and Christmas, 25 December. Movable religious holidays include Easter Monday, Ascension, Pentecost Monday.

TIME: 1 PM = noon GMT.

1 LOCATION AND SIZE

Located in Central Africa, entirely within the tropical zone and entirely landlocked, the Central African Republic has an area of 622,980 square kilometers (240,535 square miles). Comparatively, the area occupied by Central African Republic (CAR) is slightly smaller than the state of Texas. The Central African Republic capital city, Bangui, is located in the southwestern part of the country.

2 TOPOGRAPHY

The land consists of an undulating (wave-like) plateau varying in altitude from 610 to 760 meters (2,000–2,500 feet). Two important escarpments (steep slopes) are evident: in the northwest is a high granite plateau, (rising to 1,420 meters/4,659 feet), which is related to the Adamoua Plateau of Cameroon; in the northeast the Bongos Range rises to 1,368 meters (4,488 feet) and extends into Sudan.

3 CLIMATE

The climate is tropical, with abundant rainfall of about 180 centimeters (70 inches) annually in the south, decreasing to about 80 centimeters (31.5 inches) in the extreme northeast. Floods are common. Temperatures at Bangui have an average daily minimum and maximum range from 21°C (70°F) to 32°F (90°F).

4 PLANTS AND ANIMALS

The tropical rain forest in the southwest contains luxuriant plant growth, with some trees reaching a height of 46 meters (150 feet). Toward the north, the forest gradually becomes less dense and eventually gives way to rolling hills, interrupted by taller growths along riverbeds. Almost every animal of the tropics is found, including the elephant.

5 ENVIRONMENT

The most significant environmental problems in the Central African Republic are desertification, water pollution, and the destruction of the nation's wildlife. The Central African Republic reports major losses in its elephant population. As of 1994, it is estimated that 90% of the nation's elephant population has been eliminated over the last 30 years and 85% since 1982. Elephant hunting is now banned. There are 12 national parks and wildlife reserves.

6 POPULATION

A census in 1988 reported the population as 2,539,051, and in 1994, the population was estimated at 3,187,466. A population of 3,862,000 was projected for the year 2000. About half of the population is urban. Bangui, the capital and principal city, had an estimated population of 706,000 in 1990.

7 MIGRATION

Both internal and external migration is mainly seasonal. About 17,700 Sudanese and 1,200 Chadian war refugees were in the country at the end of 1992.

8 ETHNIC GROUPS

The people in the Central African Republic belong to more than 80 ethnic groups, which are classified according to geographic location. The Banda (34%) in the east central region and the Baya (27%) to the west are estimated to be the most numerous groups.

9 LANGUAGES

Many languages and dialects are spoken, but Sango, the language of a group living on the Ubangi River, is spoken by a majority and is the national language. French is the official language of government and is taught in the schools.

10 RELIGIONS

Much of the African population holds traditional religious beliefs. Christianity has spread slowly, and many Christian practices retain traditional overtones. Islam is followed, primarily in the north. About 35% of the population is Protestant; 17.8% is Roman Catholic; 5% is Muslim; and 60% are nonexclusive followers of traditional African beliefs.

11 TRANSPORTATION

Transportation is limited to river, road, and air, with river transportation the most important for movement of freight. The port of Kilongo (at Bangui) is the largest in the country. In 1991, the country had 22,000 kilometers (13,700 miles) of roads, of which only 2% were paved. There are no railroads. There is an international airport at Bangui and 22 secondary airfields and airstrips.

CENTRAL AFRICAN REPUBLIC

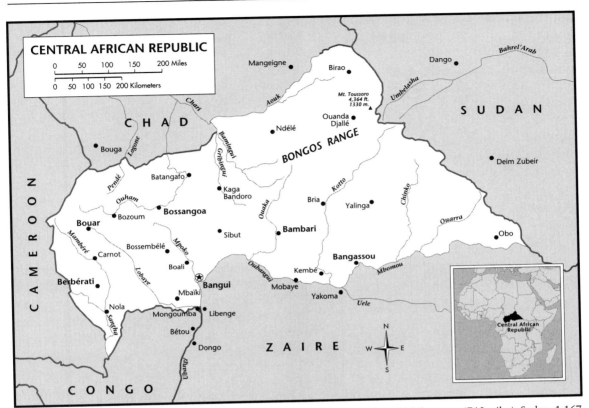

CENTRAL AFRICAN REPUBLIC

0   50   100   150   200 Miles

0   50 100 150 200 Kilometers

Mangeigne
Birao
Dango
Bahrel'Arab
Aouk
Chari
Umbelasha
Mt. Toussoro
4,364 ft.
1330 m.
Ouanda
Djallé
S U D A N
C H A D
Ndélé
BONGOS RANGE
Bouga
Logone
Deim Zubeir
Batangafo
Pendé
Bamingui
Gribingui
Kaga
Bandoro
Kotto
Bria
Ouaka
Yalinga
Chinko
Bossangoa
Ouham
Bozoum
Ouarra
Bouar
Sibut
Bambari
Obo
Bossembélé
Mpoko
C A M E R O O N
Mambéré
Carnot
Boali
Bangassou
Berbérati
Lobaye
Mbaïki
Bangui
Kembé
Mbomou
Mobaye
Ouhangui
Nola
Yakoma
Uele
Mongoumba
Libenge
Sangha
Bétou
Z A I R E
Dongo
Ubangi
N
W   E
S
C O N G O

Central African Republic

LOCATION: 2°13′ to 11°2′N; 14°25′ to 27°26′E. **BOUNDARY LENGTHS:** Chad, 1,199 kilometers (745 miles); Sudan, 1,167 kilometers (725 miles); Zaire, 1,577 kilometers (980 miles); Congo, 467 kilometers (290 miles); Cameroon, 822 kilometers (511 miles).

12 HISTORY

Before its colonial history, the area now known as the Central African Republic was settled by successive waves of peoples, mostly Bantu. Both European and Arab slave traders exploited the area in the 17th, 18th, and 19th centuries, and slave raids and intertribal wars were frequent until the French conquest. In the 19th century, the main population groups, the Baya and the Banda, arrived from the north and east, respectively, to flee the slave trade.

The territory of Ubangi-Shari was formally established in 1894, and its borders fixed by treaties between the European colonial powers. The French explored and conquered the country, chiefly from 1889 to 1900, as part of a plan to link French colonies from the Atlantic to the Nile. In 1910, Gabon, Middle Congo, and Ubangi-Shari (including Chad) were constituted administratively as separate colonies forming parts of a larger French Equatorial Africa. Ubangi-Shari's resources were exploited by French companies, and abuses of the forced labor system were common.

In 1940, the colony quickly rallied to the Free French standard raised at Brazzaville, Congo. In a referendum on 28 September 1958, Ubangi-Shari voted to become an autonomous republic within the French community. The Central African Republic was proclaimed on 1 December 1958, with Barthélémy Boganda as president. In 1961, the constitution was amended to establish a presidential government with a single-party system.

On 1 January 1966, a military coup d'etat (takeover) led by Colonel (later Field Marshal) Jean-Bédel Bokassa abolished the constitution and dissolved the National Assembly. Bokassa, who became president in 1968 and president for life in 1972, proclaimed himself emperor of the newly formed Central African Empire on 4 December 1976. On 20 September 1979, David Dacko, with French support, led a bloodless coup that overthrew Bokassa while he was out of the country. The republic was restored, and Bokassa, who took refuge in Côte d'Ivoire and France, was sentenced to death in absentia for various crimes, including cannibalism.

A new constitution allowing free political activity was approved by referendum in February 1981. A month later, Dacko was elected, but he was overthrown on 1 September 1981 by a military coup. Free elections were not held again until 19 September 1993, when citizens elected Ange-Felix Patasse president.

The transition from military to elected government has gone smoothly, although the economy has faltered. The human rights picture has improved, yet the security forces still exercise arbitrary power and, in 1993, the military engaged in two brief mutinies.

13 GOVERNMENT

After a 1992 election was invalidated by the Supreme Court, new elections were conducted successfully in September 1993. For the 1993 elections, the National Assembly was enlarged to 85 members. President André Kolingba was defeated. A new president, Ange-Felix Patasse, was installed and a graceful transition to multiparty democracy took place. The new coalition government is headed by the MLPC and includes members of three other parties.

14 POLITICAL PARTIES

In 1991, opposition parties were legalized and on 19 September 1993, new elections led to President André Kolingba's defeat. His old rival, Ange-Felix Patasse, became president and the MLPC (Mouvement pour la Libération du Peuple Centrafricain) gained 33 of the 85 seats in the National Assembly. The RDC (Rassemblement Démocratique Centrafricaine) won 14 seats.

15 JUDICIAL SYSTEM

Justices of the peace give cases their first hearing. There are several intermediate level civil courts, including a criminal court and a court of appeal situated in Bangui. At the top is a Supreme Court, also located in Bangui, the members of which are appointed by the President.

There are also provisions for a High Court of Justice, a body of nine judges created to try political cases against the President, members of Congress, and government ministers, which has never convened (assembled officially). Administrative tribunals, several labor tribunals, and a military court also exist.

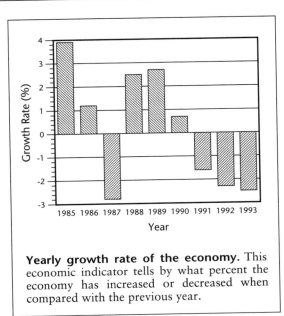

Yearly growth rate of the economy. This economic indicator tells by what percent the economy has increased or decreased when compared with the previous year.

16 ARMED FORCES

The army, numbering about 3,500 in 1993, consisted of seven battalions and helicopters. The 300-man air force had 21 noncombatant aircraft and helicopters.

17 ECONOMY

The Central African Republic has a basically agricultural economy supplemented by the export of diamonds. Coffee, cotton, and timber lead the list of agricultural exports. Economic growth, troubled before, decreased between 1989 and 1991, and was severely affected by declining world prices for its exports. The country has also suffered as a result of its isolation from major markets, a deteriorating transportation infrastructure, and mismanagement of state funds and enterprises.

18 INCOME

In 1992 Central African Republic's gross national product (GNP) was $1,307 million at current prices, or $400 per capita. For the period 1985–92 the average inflation rate was 1.3%, resulting in a real growth rate in GNP of –2.4% per person.

19 INDUSTRY

Textile and leather manufacturing are the leading industries. All cotton produced in the country is ginned locally, with cotton-ginning plants scattered throughout the cotton-producing regions. Refined sugar and palm oil are also produced, as are soap and cigarettes.

20 LABOR

As of the 1988 census, the labor force was 1,186,972. About 70% were employed in agriculture. About 13,029 were private sector wage and salary workers in 1990.

21 AGRICULTURE

Agricultural output is dominated by food crops and the sector employs about 70% of the labor force. The country is nearly self-sufficient in food production and has the potential to be an exporter.

Manioc, the basic food crop, is raised on about 200,000 hectares (494,200 acres); output was about 606,000 tons in 1992. Bananas are the second major food crop. Another important cash crop is high-quality coffee; coffee production was 14,000 tons in 1992.

22 DOMESTICATED ANIMALS

Although most of the Republic is in the tsetse fly belt, some animal husbandry is carried on. In 1992 there were an estimated 2,700,000 head of cattle, 1,300,000 goats, 460,000 pigs, and 137,000 sheep. About 48,000 tons of beef were produced in 1992. Cow's milk production was around 48,000 tons the same year. There were an estimated 3,000,000 chickens in 1992, when some 1,341 tons of eggs were produced.

23 FISHING

Fishing is carried on extensively along the rivers, but most of the catch is sold or bartered (traded) on the Zaire side of the Ubangi. The 1991 fish catch was about 13,500 tons.

24 FORESTRY

There are 35.7 million hectares (88.2 million acres) of forest and woodland (57.3% of the total land area). The CAR's exploitable forests cover 27 million hectares (68 million acres), or 43% of the total land area. A dozen sawmills produced 2,290,000 cubic meters (82 million cubic feet) of sawn logs and veneer logs in 1991.

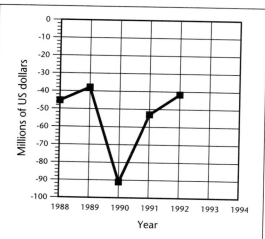

Yearly balance of trade measured in millions of US dollars. The balance of trade is the difference between what a country sells to other countries (its exports) and what it buys (its imports). If a country imports more than it exports, it has a negative balance of trade (a trade deficit). If exports exceed imports there is a positive balance of trade (a trade surplus).

25 MINING

Small amounts of gold are produced, and uranium deposits have been located. In 1991, controlled production of diamonds was only 378,643 carats (78% of gem quality), but diamonds still accounted for 46% of exports. Sizable quantities are smuggled out of the country. Gold production, which began in 1930 and peaked at 521 kilograms in 1980, fell to only 26 kilograms in 1982, but rebounded to 176 kilograms in 1991.

26 FOREIGN TRADE

Coffee, diamonds, timber, and cotton products represent almost all of the Republic's total exports, and machinery and transport equipment are the leading

Selected Social Indicators

These statistics are estimates for the period 1988 to 1993. For comparison purposes, data for the United States and averages for low-income countries and high-income countries are also given.

Indicator	Central African Republic	Low-income countries	High-income countries	United States
Per capita gross national product†	$400	$380	$23,680	$24,740
Population growth rate	2.6%	1.9%	0.6%	1.0%
Population growth rate in urban areas	3.5%	3.9%	0.8%	1.3%
Population per square kilometer of land	5	78	25	26
Life expectancy in years	49	62	77	76
Number of people per physician	25,286	>3,300	453	419
Number of pupils per teacher (primary school)	90	39	<18	20
Illiteracy rate (15 years and older)	62%	41%	<5%	<3%
Energy consumed per capita (kg of oil equivalent)	29	364	5,203	7,918

† The gross national product (GNP) is the total dollar value of all goods and services produced by a country in a year. The per capita GNP is calculated by dividing a country's GNP by its population. The World Bank defines low-income countries as those with a per capita GNP of $695 or less. High-income countries have a per capita GNP of $8,626 or more. Less than 14% of the world's 5.5 billion people live in high-income countries, while almost 60% live in low-income countries.

> = greater than   < = less than

Sources: World Bank, *Social Indicators of Development 1995,* Baltimore: Johns Hopkins University Press, 1995. Central Intelligence Agency, *World Fact Book,* Washington, D.C.: Government Printing Office, 1994.

imports. Imports in 1991 were valued at $4,853,000. Since 1981, imports have exceeded exports.

27 ENERGY AND POWER

Wood supplies 80% of the country's energy needs.

28 SOCIAL DEVELOPMENT

Since 1 July 1956, family allowances have been paid to all salaried workers. Contributions are made by employers at a fixed percentage of the employee's wage.

29 HEALTH

Mobile crews treat local epidemic diseases, conduct vaccination and inoculation campaigns, and enforce local health regulations. The most common diseases are bilharziasis, leprosy, malaria, tuberculosis, and yaws. The Pasteur Institute at Bangui cooperates actively with vaccination campaigns. The average life expectancy is 49 years.

30 HOUSING

The Central African Real Estate Investments Society makes small loans for the repair of existing houses and larger loans (amounting to almost the total cost of the houses) for new construction.

31 EDUCATION

Education is provided free in government-financed schools. Education is compulsory between ages 6 and 14. Primary education lasts for six years; secondary lasts for seven years (four plus three). Adult illiteracy was about 62% in 1990 (males: 48.2% and females: 75.1%).

Specialized institutions include two agricultural colleges, a national college of the performing and plastic arts, and the University of Bangui, founded in 1969.

32 MEDIA

Broadcasting services are government owned and operated by Radio–Télévision Centafrique. Television transmissions are available only in Bangui. In 1991, there were 210,000 radios, 14,000 television sets, and 6,952 telephones. Broadcasting is in Sango and French. The nation's first daily newspaper, the government-controlled *E Le Songo,* began publication in 1986. Its circulation in 1991 was 1,000.

33 TOURISM AND RECREATION

The main tourist attractions are hunting, fishing, the waterfalls, and the many varieties of wild animals. Of special interest are the falls at Boali and Kembé, the megaliths of Bouar, and the Pygmies at Mongoumba.

34 FAMOUS CENTRAL AFRICANS

Barthélémy Boganda (1910–59), a dynamic leader of Central African nationalism, worked toward independence and attained virtually complete political power. The first president of the independent Central African Republic was David Dacko (b.1930), who served from 1960 to 1966, and again from 1979 to 1981.

35 BIBLIOGRAPHY

Kalck, Pierre. *Central African Republic.* Santa Barbara, Calif.: Clio Press, 1993.

O'Toole, Thomas. *The Central African Republic: the Continent's Hidden Heart.* Boulder, Colo.: Westview Press, 1986.

CHAD

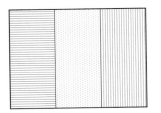

Republic of Chad
République du Tchad

CAPITAL: N'Djamena (formerly Fort-Lamy).

FLAG: The flag is a tricolor of blue, yellow, and red vertical stripes.

ANTHEM: *La Tchadienne* begins "Peuple Tchadien, debout et à l'ouvrage!" ("People of Chad, stand up and set to work!").

MONETARY UNIT: The Communauté Financière Africaine franc (CFA Fr) is a paper currency. There are coins of 1, 2, 5, 10, 25, 50, 100, and 500 CFA francs and notes of 50, 100, 500, 1,000, 5,000, and 10,000 CFA francs. CFA Fr1 = $0.0018 (or $1 = CFA Fr398).

WEIGHTS AND MEASURES: The metric system is the legal standard.

HOLIDAYS: New Year's Day, 1 January; National Holiday, 11 January; Labor Day, 1 May; African Independence Day, 25 May; Independence Day, 11 August; Assumption, 15 August; All Saints' Day, 1 November; Proclamation of the Republic, 28 November; Christmas, 25 December. Movable religious holidays include 'Id al-Fitr, 'Id al-'Adha', Milad an-Nabi, Easter Monday, Ascension, and Pentecost Monday.

TIME: 1 PM = noon GMT.

1 LOCATION AND SIZE

A landlocked country situated in northern Central Africa, the Republic of Chad has an area of 1,284,000 square kilometers (495,755 square miles), extending 1,765 kilometers (1,097 miles) north–south and 1,030 kilometers (640 miles) east–west. Comparatively, the area occupied by Chad is slightly more than three times the size of the state of California. Chad's capital city, N'Djamena, is located in the southwestern part of the country.

2 TOPOGRAPHY

The country's most marked feature is Lake Chad, which is situated at the foot of a gently sloping plain and is surrounded by vast marshes. It has an average depth of 0.9 to 1.2 meters (3–4 feet). From this low point of 230 meters (750 feet) above sea level, the land rises to a maximum of 3,415 meters (11,204 feet) at Emi Koussi, an extinct volcanic peak in the Tibesti Mountains of northern Chad.

3 CLIMATE

The three chief climatic zones are the Saharan, with a wide range of temperatures between day and night; the Sahelian, a semidesert; and the Sudanic, with relatively moderate temperatures. At N'Djamena the average daily maximums and minimums are 42°C (108°F) and 28°C (73°F) in April and 33°C (91°F) and 14°C (57°F) in December. The rains last from April (in the south) or July (farther north) through October.

4 PLANTS AND ANIMALS

Animal and plant life correspond to the three climatic zones. In the Saharan region, the only flora is in the date-palm groves of the oases. Palms and acacia trees grow in the Sahelian region. The southern, or Sudanic, zone consists of broad grasslands or prairies suitable for grazing. Elephants, lions, buffalo, hippopotamuses, rhinoceroses, giraffes, antelopes, leopards, cheetahs, hyenas, snakes, and a variety of birds are found in the savanna country.

5 ENVIRONMENT

There are two national parks and five game reserves. The chief environmental problem is increasing desertification after a decade marked by below-normal rainfall. Warring factions in Chad have damaged the environment and hampered the efforts of the government to address environmental problems for 25 years. The availability of fresh water is also a major problem.

6 POPULATION

According to a 1993 census, the population was 6,288,261. The average annual growth rate was estimated in 1993 at about 2.5%. A population of 7,307,000 was projected for the year 2000. Almost half the population lives in the southwestern 10% of Chad.

7 MIGRATION

At the end of 1992 there were about 16,000 Chadian refugees in Sudan; 1,200 in the Central African Republic; 41,700 in Cameroon; 3,400 in Niger; 2,200 in the Congo; 1,400 in Nigeria; and 200 in Benin. About 150,000 Chadians migrated from rural areas to towns in the early 1990s.

8 ETHNIC GROUPS

The basic population of Chad derives from indigenous African groups, whose composition has been altered over the course of years through successive invasions from the Arabic north. The population can be broadly divided between those who follow the Islamic faith and the peoples of the south, by which is meant the five southernmost administrative areas.

9 LANGUAGES

More than 100 languages are spoken by the different ethnic groups, but Arabic is commonly spoken in the north and Sara languages in the south. French and Arabic are the official languages.

10 RELIGIONS

In 1985, an estimated 44% of the people were Muslims; 33% were Christians; and 23% were followers of African traditional religions. Most of the people of northern Chad are Muslims. Islam, brought both from Sudan and from northern Nigeria, spread through the area around Lake Chad long before the coming of Europeans. The people of the south, particularly those living in the valleys of the Chari and Logone rivers, follow African traditional religions. Protestant and Catholic missionaries have been in the territory only in this century.

CHAD

| 0 | 150 | 300 Miles |

| 0 | 150 | 300 Kilometers |

ALGERIA

LIBYA

Aouzou
Bardaï
Aozou Strip

TIBESTI

Zouar

SAHARA DESERT

▲ Emi Koussi
11,204 ft.
3415 m.

Aozou Strip
The World Court, in
February of 1994, granted
administration of
the Aozou Strip to Chad.

Grand Erg de Bilma

BORKOU
Faya-Largeau

NIGER

Fada

Bodélé
Depression

ENNEDI

Howar

MASSIF DU
KERKOUR NOURENE
Berdoba

Miski

Biltine

SUDAN

Mao

Abéché

Bol

Ghazal

Ati

Batha

Lake
Chad

Farcha
N'Djamena

Mongo

NIGERIA

Massenya

Abou Deïa

Azoum

Am Timan

Melfi

Chari

Bousso

Zakouma
National
Park

Bongor

Logone

Salamat

Aouk

Léré

Lai

Sarh

Pala

Doba

Ouham

Moundou

CAMEROON

CENTRAL AFRICAN REPUBLIC

Chad

N
W   E
S

LOCATION: 7°26′ to 23°N; 13°28′ to 2°E. **BOUNDARY LENGTHS:** Libya, 1,054 kilometers (655 miles); Sudan, 1,360 kilometers (845 miles): Central African Republic, 1,199 kilometers (745 miles); Cameroon, 1,047 kilometers (651 miles); Nigeria, 88 kilometers (55 miles); Niger, 1,175 kilometers (730 miles).

11 TRANSPORTATION

Chad suffers from poor transportation both within the country and to outside markets; its economic development depends on the expansion of transport facilities. During the rainy season, the roads become impassable and the economy slows down almost to a standstill. There are no railways.

In 1991 there were an estimated 31,322 kilometers (19,463 miles) of roads. In 1992 there were about 9,000 passenger cars and 7,000 commercial vehicles in use, including trucks, buses, and tractors. Total waterways cover 4,800 kilometers (3,000 miles), of which 2,000 kilometers (1,250 miles) are navigable all year. Chad has more than 55 airports and landing strips.

12 HISTORY

As early as the 8th century AD, Arabs entered from the north. Their records tell of the existence of great African empires— Kanem, Bornu, Baguirmi, and Ouaddai— between the 9th and 16th centuries. By the end of the 19th century, many small states south of Lake Chad became vassals of the northern kingdoms, which conducted a flourishing slave trade.

The borders of Chad, as they presently stand, were secured by agreements between France and Germany (1894) and France and the United Kingdom (1898). Chad was separated from Ubangi-Shari (today's Central African Republic) in 1916 and became a colony in 1920.

On 26 August 1940, during World War II, French officials in Chad rallied to the Free French standard, making Chad the first colony to do so. After 1945, Chad became one of the territories of French Equatorial Africa in the French Union, and in the referendum of 28 September 1958, the territory of Chad voted to become an autonomous republic within the French Community. On 11 August 1960, Chad achieved full independence, with François (later Ngarta) Tombalbaye as head of state and prime minister. On 4 April 1962, a new constitution was proclaimed and a new government formed, with Tombalbaye as president.

After 1965 there was full-scale rebellion in the Muslim north country. In 1973, Libya, a major source of covert aid for the rebels, occupied and annexed (incorporate territory into an existing country or state) the Aozou Strip in northern Chad. However, in 1994 the World Court granted administration of the Aozou Strip to Chad.

On April 1975, Tombalbaye's 15-year rule ended with his assassination in an army coup. General Félix Malloum became the new president. Four years later, after sustained opposition from the Muslim north, Malloum resigned and fled the country. Hissène Habré, leader of the Armed Forces of the North (Forces Armées du Nord—FAN) became defense minister and Goukouni Oueddei interior minister in a coalition government.

Fighting between FAN and government forces broke out in March 1980, and Habré was dismissed from the cabinet in April. Following Libyan military intervention on Oueddi's behalf, Habré's forces fled to eastern Chad and the Sudan. When Habré reoccupied the capital in June 1982, Oueddei fled to Algeria, and Habré declared himself president of Chad on 19 October 1982.

By early 1983, the Habré regime, with the help of French forces, had extended its control to southern Chad. However, they were meeting increasing difficulties in the north from ousted president Oueddei, who had formed a rival government there. As of early 1984, Chad was effectively divided, and there were growing fears that Libya was moving to annex northern Chad. A November 1984 agreement between France and Libya called for both countries to withdraw their forces from Chad, but although France complied, Libya failed to carry out the agreement. French troops returned in 1985 to help drive back an enemy offensive, and Libya agreed to a cease-fire, effective 11 September. During 1987 fighting, Chad captured $500 million to $1 billion worth of Libyan military equipment, most of it intact.

The Habré regime fell after a three-week campaign in late 1990 by guerrillas loyal to an ex-army commander, Indriss Déby. A Sovereign National Conference that lasted from January to April 1993 confirmed Déby as Chief of State, established a new transitional government, elected 57 counselors to a Higher Transitional Council (a quasi-legislative body), and adopted the Transitional Charter, an interim constitution.

13 GOVERNMENT

The three-month-long National Conference in early 1993 established a new transitional government with a 57-member Higher Transitional Council (elected by the 254 Conference delegates) and a Transitional Charter.

Photo credit: AP/Wide World Photos

Chadians in tribal robes use local drums while singing patriotic songs during ceremonies celebrating Chad's victory over Libyan troops.

14 POLITICAL PARTIES

After the Déby coup, his Patriotic Salvation Movement (MPS) took over from the National Union for Independence and Revolution (Union Nationale pour l'Indépendence et la Révolution—UNIR). Parties were legalized in 1992, and eventually 28 registered with the authorities.

15 JUDICIAL SYSTEM

In most rural areas where there is no access to formal judicial institutions, sultans and chiefs preside over customary

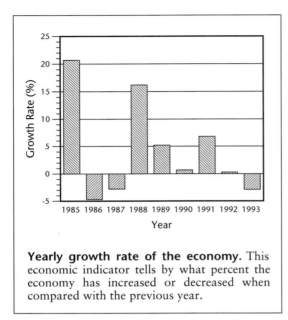

Yearly growth rate of the economy. This economic indicator tells by what percent the economy has increased or decreased when compared with the previous year.

courts. Their decisions may be appealed to ordinary courts.

Under the Transitional Charter the Appellate Court of N'Djamena is charged with responsibility for constitutional review as well as review of decisions of lower courts and criminal convictions involving potential sentences of over 20 years.

16 ARMED FORCES

In 1993, Chad's armed forces totaled about 25,200 men, all but 200 (air force) in the army, which is armed with French armored vehicles and weapons.

17 ECONOMY

Water-resource limitations are the critical factor influencing the Chadian economy. Much of the country is desert—suitable only for very limited agriculture and livestock production—while the remainder is threatened by periodic drought.

Agriculture is Chad's primary sector. Sorghum, millet, and groundnuts are the principal food crops, while cassava, rice, dates, maize, and wheat augment domestic consumption. Cotton is a principal export commodity, but the sector has suffered considerably from a variety of ills.

18 INCOME

In 1992 Chad's gross national product (GNP) was $1,261 million at current prices, or $210 per person. For the period 1985–92 the average inflation rate was a negative –0.2%, resulting in a real growth rate in GNP of 1.3% per person.

19 INDUSTRY

Because it lacks power and adequate transportation, Chad is industrially one of the least developed countries in Africa. Cotton processing is the largest activity, though reduced in scope by the reorganization of the cotton industry in 1986 and competition from Nigeria.

20 LABOR

Over 80% of all Chadian workers are involved in subsistence agriculture, animal husbandry, or fishing. There were some 12,530 wage earners in 1991, with approximately 42% engaged in manufacturing.

21 AGRICULTURE

Only 2.5% of Chad's land is cultivated. Prolonged periodic droughts, civil war,

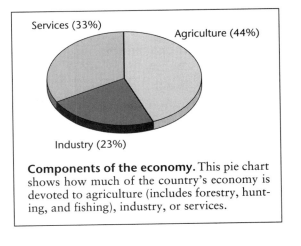

Components of the economy. This pie chart shows how much of the country's economy is devoted to agriculture (includes forestry, hunting, and fishing), industry, or services.

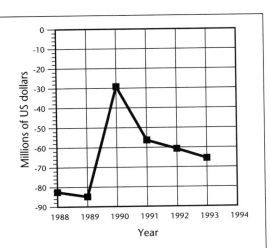

Yearly balance of trade measured in millions of US dollars. The balance of trade is the difference between what a country sells to other countries (its exports) and what it buys (its imports). If a country imports more than it exports, it has a negative balance of trade (a trade deficit). If exports exceed imports, there is a positive balance of trade (a trade surplus).

and political instability have cut agricultural production and necessitated food relief. Cotton production was 70,000 tons in 1992.

Production of peanuts was about 147,000 tons in 1992. Millet is the basic foodstuff. Production of millet and sorghum, another basic food crop, totaled an estimated 674,000 tons in 1992. Rice production was about 52,000 tons in 1992; corn production amounted to 91,000 tons that year.

22 DOMESTICATED ANIMALS

As of 1991, 35% of the total area of Chad was given over to pastureland. In 1992 there were about 5 million sheep and goats and 4.5 million head of cattle; more than 1.5 million cattle died during the 1984–85 drought. Despite the 1990 drought, Chad's livestock herd has increased. In 1992 there were about 570,000 camels and 4 million chickens. Livestock is Chad's second most important export, after cotton.

23 FISHING

Fish, either fresh or dried, forms an important element in the diet of the people living in the major valleys. The catch from the Chari and Logone rivers and the Chad Basin was approximately 60,000 tons in 1991.

24 FORESTRY

Chad has wooded areas covering more than 10% of its land area but no real forests. The only exportable forest product is gum arabic, the yield of which has averaged 300 to 400 tons a year.

Selected Social Indicators

These statistics are estimates for the period 1988 to 1993. For comparison purposes, data for the United States and averages for low-income countries and high-income countries are also given.

Indicator	Chad	Low-income countries	High-income countries	United States
Per capita gross national product†	$210	$380	$23,680	$24,740
Population growth rate	2.5%	1.9%	0.6%	1.0%
Population growth rate in urban areas	3.3%	3.9%	0.8%	1.3%
Population per square kilometer of land	5	78	25	26
Life expectancy in years	48	62	77	76
Number of people per physician	29,412	>3,300	453	419
Number of pupils per teacher (primary school)	64	39	<18	20
Illiteracy rate (15 years and older)	70%	41%	<5%	<3%
Energy consumed per capita (kg of oil equivalent)	16	364	5,203	7,918

† The gross national product (GNP) is the total dollar value of all goods and services produced by a country in a year. The per capita GNP is calculated by dividing a country's GNP by its population. The World Bank defines low-income countries as those with a per capita GNP of $695 or less. High-income countries have a per capita GNP of $8,626 or more. Less than 14% of the world's 5.5 billion people live in high-income countries, while almost 60% live in low-income countries.

> = greater than   < = less than

Sources: World Bank, *Social Indicators of Development 1995,* Baltimore: Johns Hopkins University Press, 1995. Central Intelligence Agency, *World Fact Book,* Washington, D.C.: Government Printing Office, 1994.

25 MINING

Only natron, the natural form of sodium carbonate, is mined. It is used as salt for animal and human consumption, in the preservation of meat and hides, and in soap production.

26 FOREIGN TRADE

Chad's primary export—at 91.1% of the total—is cotton. The other important export is livestock. The Federal Republic of Germany (FRG) is the leading buyer of Chad's exports, taking 8% of the total value. France was the leading source of imports, providing 22% of total value.

27 ENERGY AND POWER

Chad lacks both coal and sources of hydroelectricity. As of 1992, Chad imported 100% of its petroleum requirement from Cameroon and Nigeria. All power plants are thermal. Production of electricity rose from about 31 million kilowatt hours in 1968 to 85 million kilowatt hours in 1991.

28 SOCIAL DEVELOPMENT

Social services were introduced in Chad very slowly and have been largely disrupted by warfare. Legislation calls for

Students studying to be instructors at a new training center and clinic at Koukou Angarana in Bahr Azoum.

family allowances to be paid to all salaried workers.

29 HEALTH

In 1987 Chad had 4 hospitals, 44 smaller health centers, 1 UNICEF clinic, and 239 other clinics—half under religious auspices. Many regional hospitals were damaged or destroyed in fighting, and health services barely existed in 1987.

The most common diseases are schistosomiasis, leprosy, malaria, spinal meningitis, tuberculosis, and yaws, as well as malnutrition. The average life expectancy in 1993 was estimated at 48 years, and the overall death rate was 18 per 1,000.

30 HOUSING

Forty thousand buildings and homes were destroyed during the civil war. According to the latest available figures for 1980–88, the total housing stock numbered 700,000, with 7.2 people per dwelling.

31 EDUCATION

The educational system is patterned on the French system, and the language of instruction is French. Education is compulsory between ages 6 and 14, but it is not enforced. Primary education lasts for six years followed by secondary education which lasts for another seven years.

In 1971, the University of Chad was officially opened in N'Djamena.

32 MEDIA

About 9,856 telephones were in service in N'Djamena in 1991. Radiodiffusion Nationale Tchadienne and Tele–Tchad have broadcasting stations in N'Djamena, which broadcast in French, Arabic, and seven African languages. In 1991 there were 1,385,000 radios and 7,000 television sets. The government press agency publishes the daily news bulletin *Info-Tchad* (circulation about 800 in 1991).

33 TOURISM AND RECREATION

There were 20,501 foreign visitors in 1991; 52% from Africa and 40% from Europe. Most tourists are attracted to the hunting and to Zakouma National Park.

34 FAMOUS CHADIANS

Ngarta Tombalbaye (1918–75) was the first president of the independent Republic of Chad.

35 BIBLIOGRAPHY

Collelo, Thomas, (ed.). *Chad: A Country Study*, 2nd ed. Washington, D.C.: Government Printing Office, 1990.

Decalo, Samuel. *Historical Dictionary of Chad*, 2nd ed. Metuchen, N.J.: Scarecrow Press, 1987.

Lemarchand, Rene. *Chad: Background to Conflict*. Gainesville, Fla.: University of Florida Press, 1979.

Republic of Chile
República de Chile

CAPITAL: Santiago.

FLAG: The flag, adopted in 1817, consists of a lower half of red and an upper section of white, with a blue square in the upper left corner containing a five-pointed white star.

ANTHEM: *Canción Nacional (National Song)* beginning "Dulce Patria, recibe los votos."

MONETARY UNIT: The new peso (P) of 100 centavos replaced the escudo as the nation's monetary unit in October 1975. There are coins of 1, 5, 10, 50, 100, and 500 pesos, and notes of 500, 1,000, 5,000 and 10,000 pesos. P1 = US$0.0023 (or US$1 = P426.89).

WEIGHTS AND MEASURES: The metric system is the legal standard, but local measures also are used.

HOLIDAYS: New Year's Day, 1 January; Labor Day, 1 May; Navy Day (Battle of Iquique), 21 May; Assumption, 15 August; Independence Day, 18 September; Army Day, 19 September; Columbus Day, 12 October; All Saints' Day, 1 November; Immaculate Conception, 8 December; Christmas, 25 December. Movable religious holidays include Good Friday and Holy Saturday.

TIME: 8 AM = noon GMT.

1 LOCATION AND SIZE

Situated along the southwestern coast of South America, Chile has an area of 756,950 square kilometers (292,260 square miles), slightly smaller than the state of Montana. Included in the national territory are the Juan Fernández Islands, Easter Island, and other Pacific islands.

Chile's capital city, Santiago, is located in the center of the country.

2 TOPOGRAPHY

Chile is divided into three general topographic regions: the lofty Andean cordillera (mountain ranges) on the east, occupying from one-third to the entire width of the country; the low coastal mountains of the west; and the fertile central valley between, beginning below the arid Atacama Desert of the north and ending at Puerto Montt in the south. In the extreme north, the coastal mountains join with the Andean spurs to form a series of plateaus separated by deep gorge-like valleys. In the south, the valleys and the coastal range plunge into the sea and form a western archipelago. Some 30 rivers rise in the Andes and descend to the Pacific.

3 CLIMATE

Generally, Chile is divided into three climatic regions. The north, which contains the Atacama Desert, one of the driest regions in the world, has hot, dry weather.

The middle of the country has a Mediterranean climate, with winters averaging 11°C (52°F) and summers, averaging 18°C (64°F). The south, a region of mountains and fjords, has high winds and heavy rains.

Annual rainfall ranges from no recorded precipitation in some parts of the north to 50–100 centimeters (20–40 inches) in south-central Chile, to more than 500 centimeters (200 inches) in some southern regions. The Andean highlands, even in the tropical north, are cold and snowy.

4 PLANTS AND ANIMALS

The northernmost coastal and central region has little vegetation. Grasses and scattered tola desert brush are found on the slopes of the Andes. The central valley is characterized by several species of cactus, the Chilean pine, and the copihue, a red bell-shaped flower that is Chile's national flower. South of the Bío-Bío River, heavy precipitation has produced dense forests of laurels, magnolias, and various species of conifers and beeches.

Only a few of the many distinctive Latin American animals are found in Chile. Among the larger mammals are the puma or cougar, the llama-like guanaco, the Andean wolf, and the foxlike chilla. In the forest region, several types of marsupials and a small deer known as the pudu are found.

There are many species of small birds. Few freshwater fish are native, but North American trout have been successfully introduced into the Andean lakes. Whales are abundant, and six species of seals are found in the area.

5 ENVIRONMENT

Chile's main environmental problems are deforestation, soil erosion, and pollution. The clearing of the nation's forests for commercial purposes contributes to the erosion of the soil. Air and water pollution is especially serious in the urban centers, where the population has doubled in the last 30 years. Industry and transportation are the main sources of air and water pollution. As of 1994, Chile has 112.3 cubic miles of water. While 100% of its urban dwellers have pure water, 79% of its rural population does not.

In 1994, 9 species of mammals, 393 bird species, 1 type of fresh-water fish, and 284 plant species were considered endangered. As of 1987, endangered species in Chile included the tundra peregrine falcon and green sea turtle.

6 POPULATION

Chile's 1992 population was 13,231,803. The population for the year 2000 was projected at 15,272,000. It was estimated that the population density in 1993 was 18 persons per square kilometer (45 per square mile). However, over 80% of the people live in the central region, although this part covers little more than a quarter of the area. Santiago, the largest city, had 233,060 inhabitants in 1992.

7 MIGRATION

Since World War II, permanent immigration has been minimal. In 1990 a National Office of Refugees was established to aid the re-entry of returning exiles who fled the country for political or economic reasons in the 1970s. There is a seasonal pattern of immigration to Argentina by Chilean agricultural workers.

8 ETHNIC GROUPS

Ethnically, the Chilean population is estimated at nearly 75% mestizo (mixed white and Amerindian), almost 20% white, and about 5% Amerindian. Mixtures between the conquering Spaniards, largely Andalusians and Basques, and the Mapuches (Araucanians) produced the principal Chilean racial type. A native population of pure Mapuches numbers as many as 600,000. A small minority of Germans and their descendants live in the Valdivia-Puerto Montt area.

9 LANGUAGES

Spanish is the national language. A sizable segment of Mapuche Amerindians use Spanish in addition to their native tongue. The only other language of any importance is German, spoken mainly in the Valdivia region.

10 RELIGIONS

Roman Catholicism is the principal religion, with about 89% of the population being at least officially Catholic in 1993. The remaining population includes several Protestant denominations, totaling about 11% of the population; an estimated 15,000 Jews (1990); and about 95,000 Amerindians who still practice a native religion.

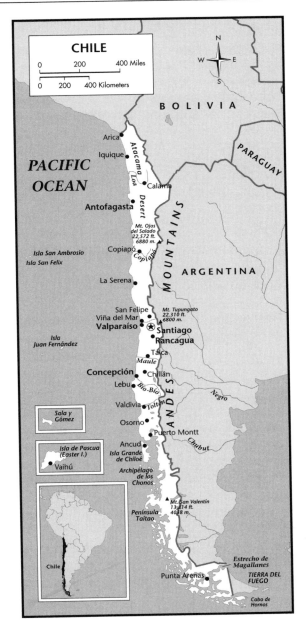

LOCATION: 17°31' to 56°33's; 66°25' to 80°47'w.
BOUNDARY LENGTHS: Peru, 169 kilometers (105 miles); Bolivia, 861 kilometers (535 miles); Argentina, 5,308 kilometers (3,298 miles); coastline, 5,338 kilometers (3,317 miles). **TERRITORIAL SEA LIMIT:** 12 miles.

11 TRANSPORTATION

In 1991, Chile had 8,613 kilometers (5,352 miles) of railways, the fourth largest rail system in Latin America. By 1988, cargo transportation by rail had reached nearly six million tons annually.

There were 79,025 kilometers (49,106 miles) of roads in 1991. In 1992 there were about 1,007,713 passenger cars and 206,790 commercial trucks, buses, and taxis.

Chile has some 20 ports, 10 of which are used principally for coastal shipping. Valparaíso, the principal port for Santiago, is by far the most important. In 1991, the Chilean merchant marine had 38 vessels over 1,000 tons and a gross registered tons of 470,000.

Air transportation has become increasingly important. Chile's largest airline is the state-owned National Airlines of Chile (LAN-Chile), which provides both domestic and international service and flew 922,700 passengers in 1992. Santiago has the principal international airport, which serviced 1,948,000 arriving and departing passengers in 1991.

Photo credit: Susan D. Rock.
Statues of Easter Island.

12 HISTORY

Before the Spanish conquest, central and southern Chile were inhabited by small numbers of Araucanian Amerindians, who came under the influence of the Incas in the early 15th century. The conquistador (conqueror) Pedro de Valdivia founded Santiago in 1541, and brought Chile (north of the Bío-Bío River) under Spanish rule. In the south, however, the Araucanians resisted Spanish rule, killing Valdivia in battle and barring further Spanish settlement. Although subject to the viceroyalty of Peru, Chile was largely governed from Santiago.

Chile had one of Latin America's first independence movements. A *cabildo abierto* ("town meeting") declared independence in 1810 in response to the French usurpation (seizure) of the Spanish crown. However, rival independence leaders fought each other and were overcome by Spanish troops. Eventually, General José de San Martín defeated the Spanish in 1817, and in 1818 Chile formally proclaimed independence.

In the following years, the Conservatives, who wanted a religious, centralized political system, fought bitterly with the Liberals, who favored a parliamentary, secular system. Their struggles plunged Chile into civil war until 1830, when Conservative Diego José Victor Portales assumed control. This began a period of Conservative rule that was to last until 1861. During this time, Chile's territory expanded with new claims to Patagonia (southern Argentina) and the island of Tierra del Fuego, and in 1847, the founding of Punta Arenas on the Strait of Magellan.

Chile defeated Peru and Bolivia in the War of the Pacific (1879–83) over possession of the Atacama Desert and its nitrate deposits. During the war it also won Tarapacá from Peru and Antofagasta from Bolivia. Bolstered by nitrate revenues, Chile's national wealth grew, especially during World War I (1914–18).

The Twentieth Century

After World War I ended, there was a recession, and the country was on the verge of civil war. United States banks loaned large sums to Chilean industry, and efforts were made to salvage the declining nitrate trade and boost copper production. World depression struck, however, bringing an end to foreign loans and a catastrophic drop in world copper prices.

Chile pulled out of the depression by 1938, but popular demand for social reform remained unsatisfied. Juan Antonio Ríos governed moderately amid political conflict aroused by World War II (1939–45). After initially cooperating with Argentina's pro-Axis stand (the Axis powers included Italy, Germany, and Japan), Ríos later led his country into a pro-Allied position, entering the war on the side of the United States in 1944.

After World War II, Chile, an example of stability by Latin American standards for so long, seethed with tensions. Its pursuit of industrialization between the world wars had led to increasing social problems as the cities had many unemployable rural workers. As the cost of living soared, riots and strikes broke out throughout the country.

The 1952 election brought seventy-five-year-old former president Carlos Ibáñez del Campo back to power. Despite his reputation as an authoritarian and his connection with Argentina's Perón, Ibáñez ruled democratically until 1958.

A devastating earthquake and tidal wave in 1960 cut drastically into the programs of newly elected president Jorge Alessandri Rodríguez, and his government was unable to regain momentum. In September 1964, Eduardo Frei Montalva, candidate of the new Christian Democratic Party, was elected by an absolute majority.

The Frei government implemented educational reform, land reform, and a program to give Chile majority ownership of its copper mines. Under Frei, Chile became a cornerstone of the Alliance for Progress, a harsh critic of communism, and a leading exponent of Christian democracy. However, the Frei administration was not able to control the chronic inflation that has plagued Chile for more than 80 years.

Allende in Power

The 1970 presidential election was won by Socialist Senator Salvador Allende. The victory was unique in that for the first time in the Western Hemisphere, a Marxist candidate took office by means of a free election. Doctor Allende, inaugurated on 3 November 1970, called for a socialist economy, a new, leftist constitution, and full diplomatic and trade relations with Cuba, China, and other Communist countries.

After an initial rise in employment and prosperity, the economy began to lag. In June 1973, against a backdrop of strikes and street brawls, a failed coup attempt was staged by a rightist army contingent.

On 11 September 1973, the Allende government was violently overthrown. Allende himself was assassinated—officially reported as a suicide. A four-man junta headed by General Augusto Pinochet Ugarte seized power, dissolved Congress, and banned all political activities. At least 2,500 and possibly as many as 10,000 people were killed during and immediately after the coup. The military declared a state of siege, and assumed dictatorial powers.

During its 16 years in power, the military attempted to return the Chilean economy to private ownership. However, while doing so it tried to maintain dictatorial control of the population, which was continually placed under ever-renewed states of siege.

Although forced to operate in secret, an opposition still emerged. The Church had become increasingly critical of the Pinochet regime, and when Pope John Paul II visited Chile in 1987, he brought accusations of torture and other human rights abuses. Finally, in 1988, Pinochet called for an election to determine whether he should remain president for another eight years. He was soundly defeated.

In 1989, new elections were held. Christian Democrat Patricio Aylwin, running as the candidate of a 17-party Concert of Parties for Democracy was elected and assumed office in 1990. Although Aylwin had some difficult times, he completed his term, as Chilean economic performance improved. In the elections of December 1993 voters gave the Christian Democratic Party candidate, Eduardo Frei Ruiz-Tagle, an impressive 58% of the vote.

13 GOVERNMENT

The 1980 constitution, as amended in 1989, provides for a strong executive with a four-year term. The president has the authority to proclaim a state of emergency for up to 20 days. He can dissolve Congress and call for new elections once per term. The president can also introduce legislation. There is a two-chamber National Congress, consisting of a 120-member Chamber of Deputies and a 46-member Senate. The constitution also provides for an independent judiciary, headed by a 17-member Supreme Court.

Chile is divided into 12 regions and the metropolitan area of Santiago. The regions are subdivided into 40 provinces.

14 POLITICAL PARTIES

The re-emergence of political parties in the aftermath of Pinochet has been dramatic. The ruling Concert of Parties for Democracy includes four major parties: the Christian Democrats (PDC), the Party for Democracy (PPD), the Radical Party (PR), and the Socialist Party (PS). The opposition from the right comes from the Independent Democratic Union (UDI) and the National Renewal (RN), which controlled the Senate until 1993. The Chilean Communist Party (PCCh) and the Allende Leftist Democratic Movement (MIDA) remain active, although they lack any representation in Congress.

15 JUDICIAL SYSTEM

The 1980 constitution, which came into full effect in 1989, provides for an independent judiciary.

The judiciary remains subject to criticism for inefficiency and lack of independence. As of 1993, ten of the seventeen Supreme Court judges are Pinochet appointees. The lower courts are also dominated by appointees of the former military regime. Reforms passed in 1991 (the *cumplido* laws), however, transferred some of the jurisdiction of the military tribunals to the civilian courts.

16 ARMED FORCES

Chilean males between the ages of 14 and 49 are eligible for military service. The period of service for draftees is two years. After their active service, Chilean men serve in the reserve (estimated at 45,000 active in 1993). In addition, there is a national police force, the *carabiñeros,* of

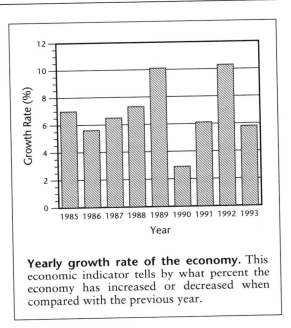

Yearly growth rate of the economy. This economic indicator tells by what percent the economy has increased or decreased when compared with the previous year.

about 27,000. Defense expenditures were $1 billion in 1991.

17 ECONOMY

The Chilean economy is strongly oriented toward commerce and industry, although minerals, chiefly copper and iron ore, provide most of the country's foreign exchange earnings. Chile's leading industries process local raw materials; they include metallurgy, petroleum products, textiles—both wool and synthetics—and paper products. Chilean agriculture, dwarfed in value by mining and manufacturing, supports less than one-sixth of the population. Fertile land is limited, and livestock raising is the main rural enterprise.

The Chilean economy in 1993 completed a decade of strong and sustained expansion. The most active areas were construction, trade, and services, while agriculture and fishing showed the slowest growth. Annual inflation was 12.2%. The unemployment rate kept falling and towards the end of 1993 was approaching 4.4%.

18 INCOME

In 1992, Chile's gross national product (GNP) was $37,064 million at current prices, or $2,730 per person. For the period 1985–92 the average inflation rate was 19.7%, resulting in a real growth rate in GNP of 6.1% per person.

19 INDUSTRY

Chile ranks among the most highly industrialized Latin American countries. Key industries include textiles, automobiles, chemicals, rubber products, steel, cement, and consumer goods.

Output of selected industrial products in 1985 included assembled vehicles, 8,145; iron pellets, 3,604,700 tons; steel ingots, 654,500 tons; cement, 1,429,000 tons; plate glass, 2,977,000 square meters; paper, 369,400 tons; and wheat flour, 1,310,500 tons. Wine production in 1985 was estimated at 450,000,000 liters, nearly all of it consumed domestically.

20 LABOR

In 1991/92, Chile's civilian labor force numbered 4,790,000, or about 36% of the population. Of the employed work force in 1992, 48.6% was engaged in professional and white-collar occupations, 18% in agriculture, 17% in manufacturing, 7.5% in transportation, communications,

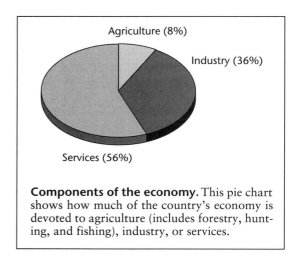

Agriculture (8%)

Industry (36%)

Services (56%)

Components of the economy. This pie chart shows how much of the country's economy is devoted to agriculture (includes forestry, hunting, and fishing), industry, or services.

and utilities, 7.1% in construction, and 1.8% in the mining sector. Unemployment was approaching 4.4% in 1993.

Union membership dropped from about 30% of the labor force in 1975 to about 14.7% in 1991. Recently, the Aylwin government has focused on labor code reforms, professional development and training, freedom of association, and collective bargaining.

21 AGRICULTURE

Of the total land area of 74.8 million hectares (184 million acres), land capable of cultivation was estimated in 1991 at 4.4 million hectares (10.8 million acres) and pastures at 13.5 million hectares (33.4 million acres). Food imports valued at $634.2 million were required to supplement the nation's production in 1992. In 1992, farm output rose 3.6%.

Agricultural production of major crops in the 1991/92 growing season (in thousands of tons) included sugar beets

(2,200); wheat (1,400); potatoes (1,023); corn (790); oats (212); rice (78); beans (91); barley (110); and rapeseed (62).

One of the areas of most rapid growth is in fresh fruit, with grape production rising by 235% between 1981 and 1985. The fruit harvest in 1992 (in tons) included grapes, 1,190,000; apples, 830,000; peaches and nectarines, 223,000; pears, 180,000; oranges, 105,000; and lemons and limes, 92,000.

22 DOMESTICATED ANIMALS

Stock raising is the principal agricultural activity in most rural areas. In 1992 there were an estimated 6.6 million sheep, 3.4 million head of cattle, 1.3 million hogs, 600,000 million goats, and 568,000 horses, mules, llamas, and alpacas. The extreme south of Chile is noted for sheep production, while cattle are raised in the central regions.

Meat products must be imported from Argentina to fulfill domestic demand. In 1992, 195,000 tons of beef and veal, 138,000 tons of pork, and 14,000 tons of mutton and lamb were produced.

The dairy industry is small; milk production totaled 1.5 million tons in 1992. Production of raw wool in 1992 was an estimated 16,400 tons.

23 FISHING

With 1,016 species of fish within its waters, fishing has long been economically important to Chile. The low temperatures and Antarctic current of Chilean waters supply the purest and most oxygenated marine waters in the world.

Photo credit: Embassy of Chile.

Fishermen in Valparaíso, Chile's main seaport.

Anchovies are predominant along the northern coast, whiting and mackerel in the central waters, and shellfish in the south. Leading fish and seafood caught commercially are Spanish sardines and yellow jacks, as well as anchovies, whiting, eels, sea snails, mackerel, and mussels. Tuna fishing has increased, as have catches of clams and lobsters.

Chile is ranked fourth in the world in total landings of fish and is the world's principal exporter of fish meal. The total fish catch soared from 340,000 tons in 1960 to 6,002,967 tons in 1991. In 1992, fisheries' output increased 13.6% over

1991. In 1990, Chile contributed 2% to the world's exports of fresh, chilled, or frozen fish, valued at $266.9 million.

24 FORESTRY

Chile has extensive forests, estimated in the early 1990s at some 8.8 million hectares (21.7 million acres), or 12% of the total land area. Logging operations are concentrated in the areas near the Bío-Bío River. Softwoods include alerce, araucaria, and manio. Chile is a major source of hardwood in the temperate zone, including alamo, laural, lenga, and olivillo.

The establishment of radiata pine and eucalyptus plantations, largely as a result of government assistance, has helped Chile to become an important supplier of paper and wood products to overseas markets. By 1991, forestry exports rose to $836 million. The major markets for Chilean wood are Japan, South Korea, the United States, Taiwan, Belgium, Argentina, and Germany.

25 MINING

During 1987–91, about 18% of the world's copper was produced in Chile, but Chile was estimated to have 22% of the world's copper reserves. In 1991, copper output exceeded 1.8 million tons, the highest in the world. Copper earned an estimated $3.62 billion in 1991.

Chile leads the world in natural nitrate production, although world production of synthetic nitrates has sharply reduced Chile's share of total nitrate output. Exports were 351,230 tons in 1990. The

Salar (salty marsh) de Atacama, which holds significant nitrate reserves, also contains 58% of the world reserves of lithium; in 1991, production of lithium carbonate reached 8,575 tons (second largest after the United States).

Production totals for 1991 included gold, 28,879 kilograms; zinc, 30,998 tons (58% more than in 1987); iron ore, 8.4 million tons; molybdenum, 14,434 tons; and silver, 676,339 kilograms.

Besides copper, Chile's primary export minerals are gold, iodine, iron ore, lithium carbonate, molybdenum, silver, and zinc. Chile is one of the world's ten leading producers of gold, silver, and molybdenum, as well as iodine, rhenium, lithium, and selenium. In 1991, Chile also produced 2.5 million tons of coal.

26 FOREIGN TRADE

In 1992, copper accounted for 38.9% of exports; fresh fruit, 9.4%; and meat, 12%. Other export items include forestry products and processed natural materials, such as fish meal (valued at $540 million in 1992), wood chips (valued at $530 million in 1992), tomato sauce, preserved foods, wine, and furniture. Fuel and energy accounted for 11% of imports in 1992, which grew by 26% from the previous year to total $9.24 billion.

Since 1991, Japan has been Chile's largest export market. In 1992, exports to Japan amounted to about $1.7 billion. Japan, the United States, and the European Community account for about 70% of Chilean exports, and are also the leading suppliers for Chilean imports. Other

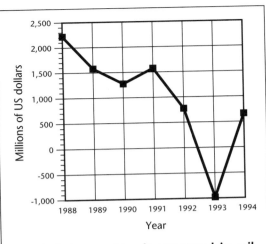

Yearly balance of trade measured in millions of US dollars. The balance of trade is the difference between what a country sells to other countries (its exports) and what it buys (its imports). If a country imports more than it exports, it has a negative balance of trade (a trade deficit). If exports exceed imports, there is a positive balance of trade (a trade surplus).

important trading partners are Taiwan, China, South Korea, Peru, Hong Kong, and Mexico.

27 ENERGY AND POWER

Electric power generation reached 19.9 billion kilowatt hours in 1991, up from 6.9 billion kilowatt hours in 1968; 51% of the power production was hydroelectric. Within South America, Chile is exceeded only by Brazil in its hydroelectric power potential (estimated in 1985 at 18 billion kilowatt hours annually).

In 1991, oil production totaled 6.5 million barrels. The output of natural gas, a by-product of petroleum extraction, grew in the 1970s; 1991 production totaled 4,067 million cubic meters.

28 SOCIAL DEVELOPMENT

Prior to the 1973 coup, Chile had built one of the most comprehensive social welfare systems in the world, with over 50 separate agencies participating in programs. Following the military's takeover of power in 1973, many of the welfare benefits were stopped temporarily, and regulations lapsed. From 1974 to 1981, the junta (military officers holding state powers) remodeled the welfare system along the lines of private enterprise.

Social security covers all members of the work force and their dependents. The system includes pensions, family allowances, medical care, sickness benefits, and unemployment compensation. Pensions are financed exclusively by workers, who must contribute 10% of their taxable income to pension funds monthly, up to a certain limit.

A 1989 law removed many restrictions on women, although some legal distinctions exist, and divorce is illegal.

29 HEALTH

As of 1993, Chile's budget for the public health sector increased for the fourth consecutive year. Chile planned to build and/or expand hospitals in San Felipe, Valdivia, Iquique, and Chillan. In 1991, there were 14,203 physicians. In 1990, there were approximately 32,931 hospital beds (3.3 beds per 1,000 people). From 1985 to 1992, 97% of the population had access to health care services.

Selected Social Indicators

These statistics are estimates for the period 1988 to 1993. For comparison purposes, data for the United States and averages for low-income countries and high-income countries are also given.

Indicator	Chile	Low-income countries	High-income countries	United States
Per capita gross national product†	$2,730	$380	$23,680	$24,740
Population growth rate	1.7%	1.9%	0.6%	1.0%
Population growth rate in urban areas	1.9%	3.9%	0.8%	1.3%
Population per square kilometer of land	18	78	25	26
Life expectancy in years	75	62	77	76
Number of people per physician	2,149	>3,300	453	419
Number of pupils per teacher (primary school)	25	39	<18	20
Illiteracy rate (15 years and older)	7%	41%	<5%	<3%
Energy consumed per capita (kg of oil equivalent)	911	364	5,203	7,918

† The gross national product (GNP) is the total dollar value of all goods and services produced by a country in a year. The per capita GNP is calculated by dividing a country's GNP by its population. The World Bank defines low-income countries as those with a per capita GNP of $695 or less. High-income countries have a per capita GNP of $8,626 or more. Less than 14% of the world's 5.5 billion people live in high-income countries, while almost 60% live in low-income countries.

> = greater than   < = less than

Sources: World Bank, Social Indicators of Development 1995, Baltimore: Johns Hopkins University Press, 1995. Central Intelligence Agency, World Fact Book, Washington, D.C.: Government Printing Office, 1994.

An estimated 15% of Chileans in the early 1980s, including 10% of children under the age of 5, fell below the minimum nutritional requirements established by the Food and Agriculture Organization (FAO) of the United Nations. Protein deficiency among the general population has induced an abnormally high rate of congenital mental handicap. However, Chile has made excellent progress in raising health standards: the infant mortality rate declined from 147 per 1,000 live births in 1948 to 15 in 1992. Average life expectancy in 1993 was 75 years.

30 HOUSING

In 1991, the total housing stock numbered 3,261,000. The number of new dwellings completed jumped from 88,000 in 1991 to 106,000 in 1992.

31 EDUCATION

The adult illiteracy rate, estimated at 50% in 1920, had been reduced to 7% by 1993, per United Nations Educational, Scientific, and Cultural Organization (UNESCO) estimates (males: 6.5% and females: 6.8%).

All state schools provide free education. An eight-year primary and four-year secondary program, with increased emphasis on vocational instruction at the secondary level, was introduced. In 1991, enrollment in secondary and professional schools was 699,455 (general: 436,892 and vocational: 262,563).

The University of Chile (founded as Universidad Real de San Felipe in 1738) and the University of Santiago de Chile are national universities with branches in other cities. There are numerous institutions which provide vocational and technical education. There are also several Roman Catholic universities. Higher educational enrollment was approximately 286,962 in 1991.

32 MEDIA

There were about 150 AM and 153 FM radio stations, and 131 television stations as of 1992. In 1991, Chile had 2.8 million television sets and 4.6 million radios. A total of 866,663 telephones were in use in 1991, the majority located in Santiago.

The largest of some 48 newspapers as of 1991 are in the Santiago-Valparaíso area, where the most important magazines are also published. Among the best-known magazines are *Caras, Analisis,* and *Qué Pasa?* The newspaper *El Mercurio* (founded in 1827) claims to be the oldest newspaper in the Spanish-speaking world. The *El Mercurio* chain includes *La Segunda* and *Las Últimas Noticias* of Santiago, *El Mercurio* of Valparaíso, and *El Mercurio* of Antofagasta.

The names and approximate 1991 circulation figures of the leading daily newspapers are as follows: *La Tercera de la Hora* (200,000); *La Cuarta* (160,000); *Las Últimas Noticias* (140,000); *El Mercurio* (88,500); and *La Nación* (50,000).

33 TOURISM AND RECREATION

Tourist attractions include the Andean lakes of south-central Chile and the famed seaside resort of Viña del Mar, with casinos rivaling those of Monaco. Also popular is Robinson Crusoe Island, in the Pacific. Another Pacific dependency, Easter Island (Isla de Pascua), is a major attraction. The giant Christ of the Andes statue, which commemorates the peaceful settlement of the Chilean-Argentinian border dispute in 1902, is located on the crest of the Andes overlooking the trans-Andean railway tunnel.

Santiago is noted for its colonial architecture, as well as the largest library in South America. Popular national parks include Parque Nacional Lanca in the North, the Nahuelbuta Park near Temuco, and Terres del Paine in the far South. Chilean ski resorts, notably Portillo, near Santiago, have become increasingly popular.

The most popular sport in Chile is soccer. Other pastimes include skiing, horse racing, tennis, fishing in the Pacific for marlin and swordfish, and some of the world's best trout fishing in the Lake District.

In 1991, 1,349,000 tourist visits were reported, 67% from Argentina, 7% from Peru, and 7% from European countries.

Tourism receipts totaled $700 million. There were 25,817 total hotel rooms with 62,340 beds.

34 FAMOUS CHILEANS

Chile's first national hero was the conquistador Pedro de Valdivia (1500?–53), who founded Santiago in 1541. The Indian leader Lautaro (1525–57), another national hero, served Valdivia as a stable boy and then escaped to lead his people to victory against the Spanish. His exploits are celebrated in the great epic poem *La Araucana* by Alonso de Ercilla y Zúñiga (1533?–96), a Spanish soldier. Bernardo O'Higgins (1778–1842), a leader of the fight for independence, was the son of the Irish soldier of fortune Ambrosio O'Higgins (1720?–1801), who had been viceroy of Peru.

Salvador Allende Gossens (1908–73), the Western Hemisphere's first freely elected Marxist head of state, served three years as Chile's president (1970–73), initiating a broad range of socialist reforms and dying in the middle of a violent military coup in September 1973. The coup's leader was General Augusto Pinochet Ugarte (b.1915), a former commander-in-chief of the army.

José Toribio Medina (1852–1930) gained an international reputation with works ranging from history and literary criticism to archaeology and etymology. Important contemporary historians include Arturo Torres Rioseco (b.1897), who is also a literary critic. Benjamín Subercaseaux (1902–73) was a popular historian as well as a novelist.

The novelist and diplomat Alberto Blest Gana (1830–1920) wrote comprehensive novels about Chilean society in the tradition of Balzac. Twentieth-century writers include novelist Eduardo Barrios (1884–1963), an explorer of the abnormal psyche; Joaquín Edwards Bello (1887–1968), an author of realistic novels of urban life; the symbolic novelist, poet, and essayist Pedro Prado (1886–1952); and José Donoso (b.1925), who is perhaps the best-known contemporary novelist.

Poets of note include Gabriela Mistral (Lucila Godoy Alcayaga, 1889–1957), who won the Nobel Prize in 1945; Pablo Neruda (Neftalí Ricardo Reyes, 1904–73), the nation's greatest poet, who was awarded a Stalin Prize as well as the Nobel Prize (1971); and the poet-diplomat Armando Uribe Arce (b.1933).

The nation's first native-born composer was Manuel Robles (1780–1837); Silvia Soublette de Váldes (b.1923) is a leading composer, singer, and conductor. Claudio Arrau (1903-91) is one of the world's leading concert pianists.

35 BIBLIOGRAPHY

Arriaza, Bernardo. "Chinchorro Mummies." *National Geographic,* March 1995, 68–89.

Bizzarro, Salvatore. *Historical Dictionary of Chile,* 2d ed. Metuchen, N.J.: Scarecrow Press, 1987.

Blakemore, Harold. *Chile.* Oxford, England; Santa Barbara, Calif.: Clio Press, 1988.

Chile Since Independence. New York: Cambridge University Press, 1992.

Haverstock, Nathan A. *Chile in Pictures.* Minneapolis: Lerner Publications Co., 1988.

Hintz, M. *Chile.* Chicago. Children's Press, 1985.

Miller, Jack. "Chile's Uncharted Cordillera Sarmiento." *National Geographic,* April 1994, 116–130.

CHINA

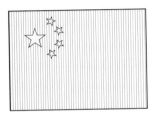

People's Republic of China
Zhonghua Renmin Gongheguo

CAPITAL: Beijing (Peking).

FLAG: The flag is red with five gold stars in the upper left quadrant; one large star is near the hoist and four smaller ones are arranged in an arc to the right.

ANTHEM: *March of the Volunteers.*

MONETARY UNIT: The renminbi, or "people's money," denominated in yuan (Y), is equivalent to 10 jiao or 100 fen. There are coins of 1, 2, and 5 fen, 1, 2, and 5 jiao, and 1 yuan, and notes of 1, 2, and 5 fen, 1, 2, and 5 jiao, and 1, 2, 5, 10, 50, and 100 yuan. Y1 = $0.1148 (or $1 = Y8.7080).

WEIGHTS AND MEASURES: The metric system is the legal standard, but some Chinese units remain in common use.

HOLIDAYS: New Year's Day, 1 January; Spring Festival (Chinese New Year), from the 1st to the 3d day of the first moon of the lunar calendar, usually in February; International Women's Day, 8 March; May Day, 1 May; Army Day, 1 August; Teachers' Day, 9 September; and National Day, 1–2 October.

TIME: 8 pm = noon GMT.

1 LOCATION AND SIZE

The People's Republic of China (PRC), the third-largest country in the world after Russia and Canada and the largest nation in Asia, claims an area of 9,596,960 square kilometers (3,705,406 square miles), including Taiwan, which the PRC claims as a province. Comparatively, the area occupied by China is slightly larger than the United States. The mainland has a coastline of 5,774-kilometers (3,588-miles).

China's territory includes several large islands, the most important of which is Hainan, off the south coast. China's total boundary length is 36,643.6 kilometers (22,769 miles). Its capital city, Beijing, is located in the northeastern part of the country.

2 TOPOGRAPHY

China may be divided roughly into a lowland portion in the east, constituting about 20% of the total territory, and a larger section consisting of mountains and plateaus in the west. The highest mountains are the Kunluns and the Himalayas. The Chinese portion of the Tian mountain range rises above 7,000 meters (23,000 feet).

The main river of north China, and the second largest in the country, is the Yellow River (Huang), whose valley covers an area of 1,554,000 square kilometers

(600,000 miles). Central China is drained mainly by the Yangtze, the country's largest river, and its tributaries.

3 CLIMATE

Although most of China lies within the temperate zone, climate varies greatly with topography. Minimum winter temperatures range from –27°C (–17°F) in northern Manchuria to 16°C (61°F) in the extreme south.

Rain falls mostly in summer. Precipitation is heaviest in the south and southeast, with Guangzhou receiving more than 200 centimeters (80 inches), and diminishes to about 60 centimeters (25 inches) in north and northeast China, and to less than 10 centimeters (4 inches) in the northwest.

4 PLANTS AND ANIMALS

Nearly every major plant found in the tropical and temperate zones of the northern hemisphere can be found in China. In all, more than 7,000 species of woody plants have been recorded, of which 2,800 are timber trees. The rare gingko tree, cathaya tree, and metasequoia, long extinct elsewhere, can still be found growing in China.

China's most celebrated wild animal is the giant panda; as of 1994, just over 500 wild pandas were still in their natural state. Other animals unique to China include the golden-haired monkey, the northeast China tiger, the Chinese river dolphin, the Chinese alligator, the rare David's deer, and the white-lipped deer. The lancelet, an ancient species of fish representing a transitional stage between invertebrate and vertebrate development, is found only in Fujian Province. In addition, more than 1,000 species of birds have been recorded. Among the rarer kinds are the mandarin duck, the white-crowned long-tailed pheasant, golden pheasant, Derby's parakeet, yellow-backed sunbird, red-billed leiothrix, and red-crowned crane.

5 ENVIRONMENT

In 1994, the World Health Organization reported that Chinese cities pollute water supplies more than any other country in the world. One-third of China's population does not have a pure water supply. By 1989, 436 of 532 rivers were polluted. Water supplies are limited—per capita consumption in China's cities is about 34 gallons a day, less than half that in many developing countries.

As of 1994, thirty species of mammals out of 394 were endangered along with 83 species of birds and 350 plant species.

6 POPULATION

The 1990 census of population reported a population of 1,130,510,638. The population as of July 1994 was estimated at 1,206,304,256. China is the most populous country in the world, accounting for 22% of the estimated world population. Government policy calls for an extensive family planning program to limit population growth to no more than 1.7 billion by the year 2000; United Nations estimates for that year predict a population of more than 1.3 billion.

CHINA

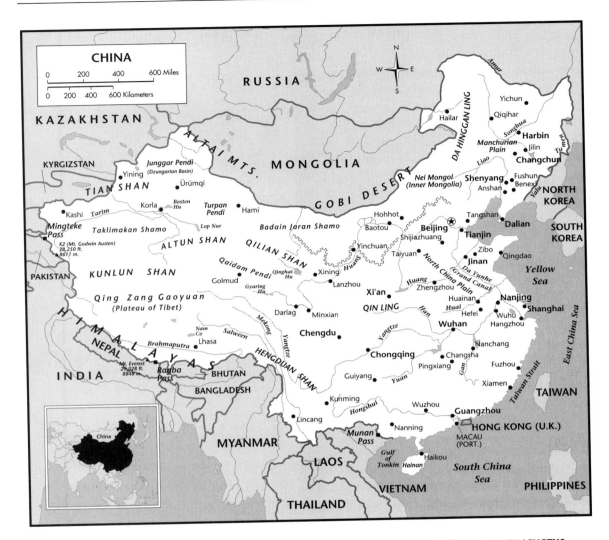

LOCATION: (not including islands south of Hainan): 18°9′ to 53°34′N; 78°38′ to 135°5′E. **BOUNDARY LENGTHS:** Afghanistan, 76 kilometers (47 miles); Bhutan 470 kilometers (292 miles); Myanmar 2,185 kilometers (1,358 miles); Hong Kong, 30 kilometers (19 miles); India 3,380 kilometers (2,100 miles); Kazakhstan 1,533 kilometers (953 miles); North Korea 1,416 kilometers (880 miles); Kyrgyzstan 858 kilometers (533 miles); Laos, 423 kilometers (263 miles); Macau, 0.34 kilometers (0.21 miles); Mongolia 4,673 kilometers (2,904 miles); Nepal, 1,236 kilometers (768 miles); Pakistan, 523 kilometers (325 miles); Russia (NE) 3,605 kilometers (2,240 miles); Russia (NW) 40 kilometers (25 miles); Tajikistan 414 kilometers (257 miles); Vietnam, 1,281 kilometers (796 miles); **TERRITORIAL SEA LIMIT:** 12 miles.

Only 26.2% of the population was urban in 1990. Government policy has sought to limit the growth of the large eastern cities, especially Beijing, Shanghai, and Tianjin, and to promote the growth of smaller cities away from the coast. In 1992, the largest urban centers were Shanghai, 13,450,000; Beijing, 11,020,000; and Tianjin, 9,200,000.

7 MIGRATION

Chinese constitute a majority in Singapore and Hong Kong, are an important ethnic group in Malaysia, and make up a significant minority in the Americas. In 1949, after the Communist victory, some two million civilians and 700,000 military personnel were evacuated to Taiwan.

Emigration from China under the People's Republic of China (PRC) government was once limited to refugees who reached Hong Kong, but is now denied only to a few political dissidents. Immigration, for the most part, is limited to the return of overseas Chinese. At the end of 1992, over 285,500 Vietnamese refugees, all of Chinese ancestry, were in China.

8 ETHNIC GROUPS

In the 1990 census, the largest ethnic group, accounting for 91.9% of the total population, was the Han, who form a majority in most of the settled east and south but remain a minority, despite continuing immigration, in the west. The nation's 55 recognized ethnic minorities had a total population of 91.2 million in 1990. The largest minority, with a population in 1990 of 15,555,820, was the Zhuang, a Buddhist people related to the

Photo credit: Susan D. Rock.
A Chinese man playing a reed flute.

Thai. Other large minorities in 1990 (listed with their populations) were:

Manchu	9,846,776
Hui	8,612,001
Miao	7,383,622
Uygur	7,207,024
Yi	6,578,524
Tujia	5,725,049
Mongolians	4,802,407
Tibetans	4,593,072
Buyi	2,548,294
Dong	2,508,624
Yao	2,137,033
Koreans	1,923,861
Bai	1,598,052
Hani	1,254,800
Li	1,112,498
Kazaks	1,110,758

9 LANGUAGES

Chinese is a branch of the Sino-Tibetan linguistic family, whose words have only one syllable. The meanings of words varies based on the speaker's tone of voice. It is written by means of characters representing complete words.

Spoken Chinese falls into two major groups: the so-called Mandarin dialects known as *putonghua* ("common language") which are spoken in the north and west, and Shanghai, which is spoken in the Yangtze River Delta. Hakka and Hokkien are dialects of the southeastern coastal province. Cantonese, spoken in southern China, is the language of the majority of Chinese emigrants. Mandarin Chinese based on the Beijing dialect was adopted as the official language of China in 1955.

Of the 55 recognized minority peoples in China, only Hui and Manchus use Chinese as an everyday language. More then 20 minority nationalities have their own forms of writing for their own languages.

10 RELIGIONS

Three faiths—Confucianism, Buddhism, and Taoism—have long been established in China. The religious practice of the average Chinese traditionally has been a unique mixture of all three.

Confucianism has no religious organization but consists of a code of ethics and philosophy; honoring one's parents, benevolence, fidelity, and justice are among its principal virtues. Taoism, a native Chinese religion that evolved from a philosophy probably founded in the sixth century BC by Lao-tzu (Laozi), and Buddhism, imported from India during the Han dynasty, both have elaborate rituals.

Suppression of religion and the introduction of programs of antireligious indoctrination began after the Communist revolution of 1949. During the next 15 years, the government closed temples, shrines, mosques, and churches. The Constitution of 1982 provides for freedom of belief and worship, but unofficially religion was still frowned upon.

An estimated 6% of all Chinese were practicing Buddhists, mostly of the Mahayana type; in Tibet, Lamaism (a form of Mahayana Buddhism) has been restored to much of its former importance. Islam claims an estimated 3–6% of the population; most belong to the Sunni branch, but the Tajiks are Shi'ites. In late 1983, the number of Protestants was put at three million and the number of churches at 1,600.

11 TRANSPORTATION

Railways, roads, and inland waterways all play an important role in China's transportation system, which has undergone major growth since the 1940s. China's rail network forms the backbone of the transportation system. Chinese railways increased in length from 21,989 kilometers (13,663 miles) in 1949 to 54,000 kilometers (33,500 miles) in 1991, of which about 6,900 kilometers (4,300 miles) were electrified. However, shortages of freight and tank cars continue to delay deliveries of coal and other industrial raw materials to their destinations.

Road transportation has become increasingly important. Motor roads grew from about 400,000 kilometers (249,000 miles) in 1958 to 1,029,000 kilometers (639,000 miles) by 1991. By 1992, an estimated 1,900,000 passenger automobiles used the highway system, up from 50,000 in 1949. In addition, there were some 4,500,000 commercial vehicles operating in 1992. Bicycles are an important form of transportation throughout China.

The principal inland waterway is the Yangtze River. Major ports on the river include Chongqing, Wuhan, Wuhu, Nanjing, and Shanghai.

China's 1,359 merchant ships can accommodate most of the country's foreign trade; the balance is divided among ships leased from Hong Kong owners and from other foreign sources. The principal ocean ports are Tianjin (the port for Beijing), Lüda, and Huangpu.

The international airports at Beijing, Shanghai, Guangzhou, Tianjin, Ürümqi, Nanning, Kunming, and Hangzhou are equipped to handle large passenger jets. The total scheduled international and domestic service performed in 1992 included 40,605 million passenger-kilometers (25,232 million passenger-miles) and 1,319 million freight ton-kilometers (820 million freight ton-miles).

Photo credit: Susan D. Rock.

A bicycle parking lot.

12 HISTORY

According to tradition, the Xia (Hsia) dynasty (c.2200–c.1766 BC) was the first Chinese state. It was followed, for nearly 1,500 years, by a succession of feudal dynasties. Notable dynasties include the Eastern Zhou dynasty (771–256 BC), which produced the great Chinese philosopher Confucius (K'ung Fu-tzu or Kong Fuzi).

Between 475 and 221 BC, the Qin (Ch'in) dynasty (221–207 BC) gradually emerged from among warring, regional states to unify China into a system of districts and counties under central control. Walls of the feudal states were connected to form what would later become known as the Great Wall of China.

The Han dynasties (206 BC–AD 220) saw the invention of paper and the introduction of Buddhism into China. The

Northern and Southern Song (Sung) dynasties (960–1279) were distinguished for literature, philosophy, the invention of movable type, and the introduction of gunpowder.

In 1279, Kublai Khan (r.1279–94) led the Mongols to bring all of China under their control and became the first ruler of the Mongols' Yuan dynasty (1279–1368). Many European missionaries and merchants, notably Marco Polo, came to the Mongol court.

The Portuguese, Spanish, Dutch, and English explored China in the 15th and 16th centuries. The Manchus, invaders from the northeast, established the last imperial dynasty, the Qing, which was to last from 1644 to 1911. The Qings greatly restricted trade with the outside world and by the close of the eighteenth century, only one port, Guangzhou (Canton), was open to merchants from abroad.

Demands by the British for increased trade, coupled with Chinese prohibition of opium imports from British India, led to the Opium War (1839–42), which China lost. By the Treaty of Nanjing (1842), several ports were opened, and Hong Kong Island was ceded to Britain.

Eventually, the West's interest turned from trade to territory. Between 1884 and 1885 China fought France for control of the territory now known as Vietnam. The war was known as the Sino-French War. China lost the war and France took control of Vietnam. The French joined Vietnam to Cambodia and Laos to form French Indochina. The French ruled this protectorate until after World War II.

In the First Sino-Japanese War (1894–95), Japan obtained the Chinese island of Taiwan. The Boxer Rebellion, an uprising in 1899–1901 by a secret society seeking to expel all foreigners and supported by the Manchu court, was crushed by the intervention of British, French, German, American, Russian, and Japanese troops.

In 1912, a revolution finally overthrew Manchu rule. The new Chinese republic, however, soon passed into the hands of warlords. China joined World War I on the Allied side in 1917. After the war, the Chinese Nationalists in alliance with the Communists built a strong, disciplined political party. The party leader, Chiang Kai-shek (Jiang Jieshi), unified the country under Nationalist rule in 1928 and established a capital in Nanjing.

After gaining control of the government, the Nationalists began a bloody purge of the Communists. The Communists sought refuge in southern Jiangxi Province. They embarked on their difficult and now historic Long March during 1934–35 under the leadership of Mao Zedong (Tse-tung) and set up headquarters at Yan'an (Yenan).

Increasing Japanese pressure against northern China led, in July 1937, to the Second Sino-Japanese War. This war continued into World War II. During World War II, Japanese forces occupied most of China's major economic areas. Nationalist China resisted the Japanese in the south of the country with aid from the United States and United Kingdom. At the same time, the Communists fought the Japanese in the north. After Japan's defeat in 1945, the rift between the two Chinese factions erupted into civil war. Although supported by the United States, the Nationalists were defeated. They were expelled from the mainland by early 1950 and took refuge in Taiwan. Even though they no longer controlled the county, the Nationalists still claimed to be the legitimate government of China. Their claim was recognized by the United States and the United Nations.

The People's Republic

Meanwhile on the mainland, the Communists, under the leadership of Mao as chairman of the Chinese Communist Party (CCP), proclaimed the People's Republic of China (PRC) on 1 October 1949, with the capital at Beijing. A year later, China entered the Korean War (1950–53) on the side of the Democratic People's Republic of Korea (DPRK). This action further angered the United States, which was fighting on the side of democratic South Korea. In the fall of 1950, China entered Tibet, and in 1959, the Tibetan ruler, the Dalai Lama, fled to India. Tibet became an autonomous region within China in 1965.

In domestic affairs, the government pursued rapid programs of industrialization and socialization, including, in 1958–59, the Great Leap Forward. The Great Leap Forward was a crash program designed to quickly improve China's economy. The results were disasterous and resulted in starvation among the population. The Chinese blamed the failure on the Soviets who were acting as advisors to the Chinese government. Tensions between China and the USSR grew and in 1960, the former USSR withdrew its scientific and technical advisers from China.

In 1966, Mao again steered the country onto the revolutionary path with the Great Proletarian Cultural Revolution, one of the most dramatic and turbulent periods in modern Chinese history. It continued until Mao's death in 1976, but the stormiest years were from 1966 to 1969. During those years, cities witnessed fighting between factions, accompanied by attacks on bureaucrats, intellectuals, scientists and technicians, and anyone known to have overseas connections. Amid the rising conflict, the party structure collapsed in major cities, and from January 1967 through mid-1968 the discredited political establishment was replaced by Revolutionary Committees. Estimates place the number of dead as a direct result of the Cultural Revolution at 400,000.

Throughout the late 1960s and early 1970s, China played a major role in supporting communist North Vietnam in the Vietnamese conflict. This once again brought China in conflict with the United States. The United States was fighing on the side of democratic South Vietnam. North Vietnam won the war, causing the United States a painful and humiliating defeat.

In November 1971, the People's Republic of China (PRC) government replaced Taiwan's Nationalist government as China's representative at the United Nations. Following two preliminary visits by United States Secretary of State Henry Kissinger, President Richard M. Nixon

China's first McDonald's fast-food restaurant.

Photo credit: Susan D. Rock.

The 1980s saw a gradual process of economic reforms, beginning in the countryside. The reforms, which included a limited return to a market economy for farm goods, were very effective and the countryside began to prosper. As the rural standard of living rose, reforms of the more complex urban economy began. In the mid-1980s, China began to move away from a socialist system of central planning to a market economy. At the same time, China began to open its economy to the outside world and to encourage foreign investment.

Until 1989, economic reforms were accompanied by relatively greater openness in intellectual spheres. However, student pro-democracy demonstrations began in the mid-1980s, and economic problems, including inflation of up to 35% in major cities, led to major disagreements within the government. This led to a slowdown in reforms.

Student demonstrations began in Beijing in the spring of 1989 and spread to other cities. The urban population, unhappy with high inflation and corruption, largely supported the students. The Beijing demonstrations drew one million people, including journalists, salaried workers, and private entrepreneurs. Martial law was imposed, and the government attempted to send troops to clear Beijing's Tiananmen Square, where demonstrators were camped. Finally, in the early hours of June 4th, armed troops, armored personnel carriers, and tanks, firing on demonstrators and bystanders, managed to reach the Square. Firing continued in the city for several days, and estimates of the total

journeyed to China on 21 February 1972 for an unprecedented state visit, and the two countries took major steps toward normalization of relations. The two nations sought common ground in their mutual distrust of Soviet intentions. In the period following the Nixon visit, United States-China trade accelerated, and cultural exchanges were arranged. Full diplomatic relations were established by 1979.

After Mao

China's long-time leader, Mao Zedong, died on 9 September 1976, and Hua Guofeng was quickly confirmed as party chairman and premier.

number killed range from 200 to 3,000. The events of June 4th sparked protests across the country, and thousands were arrested as the movement was suppressed.

There were also ongoing demonstrations by ethnic minorities. The most visible were those of the Tibetans. Following 4 June 1989, economic reforms were decreased and some private enterprises closed down. In 1993 and 1994, there were peasant protests and riots over local corruption. In addition, there were workers' disputes and strikes in response to low pay and poor working conditions.

Hong Kong

At the end of the Opium War in 1842, the Chinese island of Hong Kong was granted to the United Kingdom. Additional adjacent territories were leased to the British for 99 years in the Anglo-Chinese Convention of Beijing in 1898.

The British developed Hong Kong as a warehousing and distribution center for British trade with southern China. However it declined in size and importance relative to Shanghai. Not until after 1949 did Hong Kong develop into a leading manufacturing, commercial, and tourist center. The people of Hong Kong created a standard of living matched by few developing areas.

In October 1982, talks began between Chinese and British representatives concerning Hong Kong's future after June 30, 1997, the expiration date of the 99 year lease. After two years of negotiations, both sides agreed to a plan that would return Hong Kong to Chinese control on July 1, 1997. In the agreement, China, a Communist state, agreed to allow Hong Kong to maintain its political, economic, and judicial systems. Many people, however, are anxious about the future of the territory.

13 GOVERNMENT

On 4 December 1982, China adopted its fourth constitution since 1949, succeeding those of 1954, 1975, and 1978. In theory, the highest organ of state power is the National People's Congress (NPC), in which legislative power is vested. The constitution stipulates, however, that the Congress is to function under the direction of the Chinese Communist Party.

The PRC consists of 23 provinces, or sheng, of which Taiwan is claimed as the 23rd; 5 autonomous regions (zizhiqu), and 3 centrally administered municipalities (zhixiashi).

14 POLITICAL PARTIES

The Chinese Communist Party (CCP) has been the ruling political organization in China since 1949. Eight other minor parties have existed since 1949 as members of a United Front, but their existence has been purely a formality. The party, with 50 million members (1990 estimate), plays a decisive role in formulating and implementing government policies.

15 JUDICIAL SYSTEM

China's legal system, instituted after the establishment of the PRC in 1949, is largely based on that of the former USSR. The highest judicial body is the Supreme People's Court which supervises the administration of justice in the basic people's courts. Defendants do not enjoy a presumption of innocence and, if convicted, may appeal their case to a higher level only once.

Capital punishment may be administered for more than two dozen offenses, including embezzlement and theft. Criminal defendants have no right to an attorney. Cases are rapidly processed and conviction rates are about 99%. Appeal is possible but with little chance of success.

16 ARMED FORCES

Army personnel in 1993 numbered 2.3 million (1 million draftees). In addition, there are some 5 million men and women in the "basic militia," and up to 7 million in the "ordinary militia" who receive some training but are mostly unarmed.

The Chinese navy in 1993 consisted of 260,000 personnel including 6,000 marines, 25,000 naval air personnel, and 27,000 coastal defense forces. The navy is equipped with 54 major combat ships, 44 attack submarines, and 1 nuclear-powered strategic missile submarine. The naval air force had 880 land-based combat aircraft, including 160 anti-ship bombers. The air force in 1993 was estimated to have 470,000 personnel, with about 4,000 jet fighters and a bomber fleet of about 500.

China has developed a sizable nuclear capacity. China's first nuclear test occurred on 16 October 1964 and consisted of a 20-kiloton bomb exploded at the test site. In 1993 the Strategic Rocket Forces (90,000 personnel) manned eight

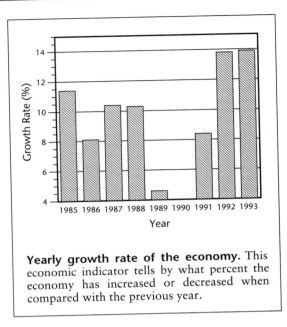

Yearly growth rate of the economy. This economic indicator tells by what percent the economy has increased or decreased when compared with the previous year.

Intercontinental Ballistic Missiles (ICMBs) with single 3–5 megaton warheads.

17 ECONOMY

During the 1980s, the Chinese economy underwent a major restructuring, as the government moved to make the transition from a fully centrally planned (or socialist) economy to a mixed free-market and socialist (or "socialist market") economy. The commune (or communally owned farm) system was disbanded in 1983–84 and replaced by a system of townships, and the household or family became the main unit of rural production. Following the success of these rural reforms, the CCP Central Committee published "A Decision on the Reform of the Economic Structure" in October 1984, with the goal of totally overhauling the national economy and

Photo credit: Susan D. Rock.
Selling eggs at market.

reforming urban industries in ways that were similar to the recent rural reforms.

Under the new program, all urban businesses would be responsible for their own profits and losses, managers would have greater decision-making authority, and national and local government would give up direct control over business and take a regulatory and supervisory position, similar to those of Western governments with a free enterprise system. Pay would be based on productivity, government subsidies would be abolished, wages and prices would find their own level, and private enterprise would be encouraged.

These reforms were remarkably successful, leading to much higher rates of industrial and general economic growth than previously expected. Real gross national product grew by an average of 9.6% annually between 1979–1988, reaching over 10% in 1988. However, inflation increased to 20.7%, and shortages of raw material and energy worsened rapidly. Government measures initiated in late 1988 brought inflation to below 10% by the end of 1989, although gross national product growth declined to just over 4% in that year. While China has thus emerged as the fastest growing economy in the world today, troubling problems of rising inflation (back up to 14.5% in 1993) and inadequate transport and communication networks remain, reminders of the need for further improvements.

18 INCOME

In 1992, China's gross national product (GNP) was $442,346 million at current prices, or about $490 per capita.

19 INDUSTRY

In 1992, the coastal provinces of Jiangsu, Guangdong, Shandong, Shanghai and Zhejiang provinces together accounted for close to 33% of the country's total industrial output and most of its merchandise exports. Approximately 50% of total industrial output still comes from state-owned factories. However, a notable feature of China's recent industrial history has been the dynamic growth of collectively owned rural and village enterprises, as well as private businesses and joint business ventures with foreign investors.

China's cotton textile industry, the largest in the world, produced five million tons of yarn and 19.1 billion meters of cloth in 1992. In that year, 337.9 million meters of woolen piece goods and 350,600 tons of knitting wool were produced. Other products of the textile industry include silk, jute bags, and synthetic fibers.

Light industries employing large amounts of labor have played a particularly large role in the recent industrial boom, presently accounting for 48.9% of total industrial output. In addition to garments and textiles, output from these industries included electric fans, television sets, cameras, sewing machines, household washing machines, radios, telephones, and watches. The electronics industry has also developed the capacity to produce high-speed computers, 600 types of semiconductors, and specialized electronic measuring instruments.

Production of a variety of industrial goods has expanded, including power-generating equipment and machine tools. In addition to fertilizers, the chemicals industry produces calcium carbide, ethylene, and plastics.

By 1992, China was producing 80.9 million tons of steel and 75.9 million tons of pig iron. China now produces varied lines of passenger cars, trucks, buses, and bicycles. In 1992, output included 1.07 million motor vehicles (more than double the 1985 figure), 40.8 million bicycles, 563 diesel and 200 electric locomotives, as well as 21,600 freight cars.

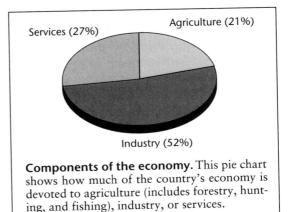

Components of the economy. This pie chart shows how much of the country's economy is devoted to agriculture (includes forestry, hunting, and fishing), industry, or services.

[20] LABOR

In 1992, China's total civilian employment was estimated at 594,320,000. In 1990, the civilian labor force was 647,200,000, or twice as large as the populations of the United States and Canada combined. About 43% of the labor force was female in 1992. About 59% of civilian employment was in agriculture, forestry, and fishing; 22% in industry; and 19% in services. Unemployment in urban areas for those aged 16–25 was 2.3% in 1992.

[21] AGRICULTURE

With some 60% of the population engaged in farming, agriculture forms the foundation of China's economy. Limitations in topography, soil, and climate, however, have restricted cultivation to only about 10.3% of the total land area. Grains are the chief crop, accounting for 70% of the total value of crop output and occupying 80% of all land under cultivation.

The main food crops are rice, wheat, and corn, followed by kaoliang (a type of sorghum), millet, potatoes, and soybeans. China is the world's leading producer of rice, with production at 188 million tons (36% of the world's total) in 1992. The total wheat crop in 1992 (including Taiwan, which China considers a province), amounted to 101 million tons, more than double the 1970 output.

Crops grown for use in industry occupy only 8–9% of the cultivated areas. Among the most important are cotton (the chief raw material for the important textile industry), various oil-bearing crops, sugar, tobacco, silk, tea, and rubber.

22 DOMESTICATED ANIMALS

China leads the world in swine production, the total number of hogs reaching about 379 million in 1992. Pig raising, often pursued as a private sideline by peasants, is the fastest-growing sector of the livestock industry, and hogs and pork products are becoming valuable export earners.

Most sheep are raised by ethnic minorities, in the desert-like lands of Xinjiang, Inner Mongolia, Gansu, and Sichuan (Szechuan). Goats are increasingly promoted throughout China as a profitable household sideline for milk and dairy production.

Chickens and ducks are raised throughout China on private plots and, together with fish and pork, comprise China's chief sources of dietary protein.

China produced nearly 192,000 tons of honey in 1992, more than any other nation. China also led the world in silk production in 1992, approximately 64,000 tons.

23 FISHING

With a coastline of some 6,500 kilometers (4,000 miles), China has excellent coastal fisheries. A vast number of inland lakes and ponds, covering a total area of about 300,000 square kilometers (116,000 square miles), are also used for fish raising. China typically accounts for about 10% of the world's catch.

24 FORESTRY

China's forested area was estimated at 115 million hectares (284 million acres), or about 14% of the total territory. Most of the forests are in remote regions, however, and lack of transportation limits access to them. While China is a major producer of softwood logs and lumber, virtually all of its production is domestically consumed.

25 MINING

China is the world's largest coal producer. Almost all provinces contain coal deposits, and production rose to 1,090 million tons in 1991. The top ten producing coal mines in China had proven reserves in 1990 of 12,996 million tons.

Iron ore reserves were estimated at 55 billion tons in 1991, with production estimated at 176 million tons in that year. China is the world's largest producer of tin and a major producer of tungsten and antimony. Other important minerals are bauxite, copper, and lead.

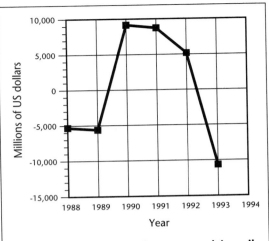

Yearly balance of trade measured in millions of US dollars. The balance of trade is the difference between what a country sells to other countries (its exports) and what it buys (its imports). If a country imports more than it exports, it has a negative balance of trade (a trade deficit). If exports exceed imports there is a positive balance of trade (a trade surplus).

26 FOREIGN TRADE

Though China has only recently become a major trading nation, its enormous trading potential is attracting great attention by both advanced and newly industrializing nations.

Textiles accounted for 11% of all exports in 1992, and clothing for about 17.9%. Besides textiles and clothing, the principal exports in 1992 were food and live animals, chemicals, petroleum and petroleum products, and machinery and transport equipment. Principal imports in 1992 were light manufactured goods, mineral fuels and lubricants, food and live animals, and chemicals.

In recent years, as China has rapidly enlarged its role on the international market, the importance of Hong Kong has increased. In 1992, Hong Kong accounted for close to 35% of China's total trade (up from about 21% in 1986). Japan ranks as the second largest trading partner, importing oil and other raw material and claiming 15% of China's total trade. The most dramatic change in the mid-1980s was the emergence of the United States as China's third-largest trading partner, a rank it still maintains with 11% of total trade.

27 ENERGY AND POWER

Traditionally, coal has been the major primary-energy source, with additional fuels provided by brushwood, rice husks, dung, and other noncommercial materials. Coal still dominates the energy sector, supplying 75% of China's energy needs. China also ranks as the world's fifth-largest producer of crude oil and has proven reserves of natural gas totaling 1.4 trillion cubic meters (49.4 trillion cubic feet).

Total output of electricity increased during the 1988–91 period from 545 billion to 677 billion kilowatt hours. Nuclear generation is to play a secondary but important role, especially in areas that lack both hydropower potential and major coal resources.

28 SOCIAL DEVELOPMENT

Population control and family planning have been given major emphasis at various times by the government, but with limited success. Under a population policy announced in 1978, couples agreeing to have no more than one child enjoy special benefits in the form of cash payments, improved housing, and higher pensions. Penalties are imposed on couples having more than two children, including reduced rations for each child over the limit. Many rural families, however, scorn the new rules. There were reports of infanticide (the killing of an infant) of females, as the traditional Chinese preference for males to continue the family line clashed with the new regulations.

Since 1950, the situation of women has improved due to legislation guaranteeing equal pay for equal work. In 1993, the government continued to condemn and took steps to curb traditional abuse of women, including their abduction and sale for wives or prostitutes, abuse of female children, and female infanticide.

29 HEALTH

At the end of 1990, there were a total of 208,000 health care organizations and 62,000 hospitals (a rise of 3,000 over 1985). From 1985 to 1992, approximately 90% of the population had access to health care services.

During the Cultural Revolution, medical personnel from hospitals were sent in groups to the countryside to provide health care to the people. They worked with locally trained paramedical personnel, called barefoot doctors. Today, barefoot doctors and brigade health stations are still the major deliverers of health care in the countryside.

30 HOUSING

China has an acute shortage of housing, attributable not only to the large annual increases in population (over 10 million a year) that must be accommodated, but also to the long-standing policy of directing investment funds into heavy industry rather than into housing and other social amenities.

In 1992, the total number of housing units in China stood at 276,502,000. In 1990, 400,000 new dwellings were completed. In 1991, 90.6% of all homes had piped water.

31 EDUCATION

The Cultural Revolution affected education more than any other area of society. Schools were shut down in mid-1966 to give the student Red Guards the opportunity to "make revolution" on and off campus; upper- and middle-level bureaucrats throughout the system were removed from office, and virtually entire university faculties and staffs dispersed. Education was reoriented in 1978 under the Four Modernizations policy, and universal primary education by 1990 became a main target.

In 1991, there were 729,158 primary schools with 5,532,300 teachers and 121,641,500 students. At the secondary level, there were 3,557,000 teachers and 52,267,900 students. In 1985 there were 1,016 colleges and universities in China. Among the largest and most prestigious institutions were Beijing University and Qinghua University, both in Beijing.

32 MEDIA

In 1990 there were 6,850,300 telephones and 3,826 fax machines. China had 274 radio broadcasting stations at the end of 1989. The most important station is Beijing's Central People's Broadcasting Station (CPBS), which broadcasts daily on several channels using a variety of languages.

In 1991, China had 213 million radios and 35.8 million television sets. Many of the sets are installed in public meeting places, although increasingly a television set has become a much-prized private acquisition. Since large segments of the rural population are as yet without radios and television sets, the government operates a massive wired broadcast network linked to 100 million loudspeakers.

The press is closely controlled by the government. In 1990 there were 773 national and provincial newspapers and 5,751 magazines and other periodicals.

33 TOURISM AND RECREATION

In 1991, 2,710,103 foreign nationals visited China, of whom about 1,395,000 came from Southeast and Eastern Asia; 789,534 from Europe; and 418,498 from the Americas. In the same year, there were 321,116 hotel rooms.

Tourist Attractions

The most famous tourist attraction in China is the Great Wall, the construction of which began in the third century BC, as a barrier against northern invaders. Other leading tourist attractions include the Forbidden City, or Imperial Palace, in Beijing; the nearby tombs of the Ming emperors; historic Hangzhou, with its famous West Lake and gardens; busy Shanghai, with its well-stocked stores and superb cuisine; Xi'an, the site of monumental Qin dynasty excavations; and Guangzhou, the center of Cantonese cooking, with an extensive Cultural Park.

Sports

Distinctively Chinese pastimes include wushu, a set of ancient exercises known abroad as gonfu (kung fu), or the "martial arts"; taijiquan, or shadow boxing, developed in the seventeenth century; and liangong shibafa, modern therapeutic exercises for easing neck, shoulder, back, and leg ailments. Qigong (literally "breathing exercises") is also widely practiced both as a sport and as physical therapy. A popular traditional spectator sport is Chinese wrestling.

34 FAMOUS CHINESE

Confucius (K'ung Fu-tzu or Kong Fuzi, 551–479 BC) is generally regarded as the most important historical figure, as well as the greatest scholar, of ancient China. His philosophy and social ideas include respect for parents, the sanctity of the family, and social responsibility. Other early philosophers were Lao-tzu (Laozi; Li Erh, c.604–531 BC), the traditional founder of Taoism, and Mencius (Mengtzu or Mengzi, 385–289 BC), who stressed the essential goodness of human nature and the right of subjects to revolt against unjust rulers.

Selected Social Indicators

These statistics are estimates for the period 1988 to 1993. For comparison purposes, data for the United States and averages for low-income countries and high-income countries are also given.

Indicator	China	Low-income countries	High-income countries	United States
Per capita gross national product†	$490	$380	$23,680	$24,740
Population growth rate	1.2%	1.9%	0.6%	1.0%
Population growth rate in urban areas	4.1%	3.9%	0.8%	1.3%
Population per square kilometer of land	121	78	25	26
Life expectancy in years	69	62	77	76
Number of people per physician	1,063	>3,300	453	419
Number of pupils per teacher (primary school)	22	39	<18	20
Illiteracy rate (15 years and older)	22%	41%	<5%	<3%
Energy consumed per capita (kg of oil equivalent)	632	364	5,203	7,918

† The gross national product (GNP) is the total dollar value of all goods and services produced by a country in a year. The per capita GNP is calculated by dividing a country's GNP by its population. The World Bank defines low-income countries as those with a per capita GNP of $695 or less. High-income countries have a per capita GNP of $8,626 or more. Less than 14% of the world's 5.5 billion people live in high-income countries, while almost 60% live in low-income countries.   > = greater than   < = less than

Sources: World Bank, Social Indicators of Development 1995, Baltimore: Johns Hopkins University Press, 1995. Central Intelligence Agency, World Fact Book, Washington, D.C.: Government Printing Office, 1994.

Zhang (Chang) Heng (78–139), an astronomer, is credited with having invented the first seismograph. Zu Zhongzhi (Tsu Chung-chih, 429–500) calculated the figure 3.14159265 as the exact value for π.

Mao Zedong (Tse-tung, 1893–1976), the foremost figure of postrevolutionary China, served as chairman of the Central Committee of the CCP from 1956 to 1976.

35 BIBLIOGRAPHY

Ellis, William S. "Shanghai." National Geographic, March 1994, 2–35.

Feinstein, Steve. China in Pictures. Minneapolis: Lerner Publications Co., 1989.

Hsu, Immanuel Chung-yueh. The Rise of Modern China. New York: Oxford University Press, 1990.

McLenighan, V. People's Republic of China. Chicago: Children's Press, 1984.

Nagel, Rob and Anne Commire. "Chiang Kai-Shek." In World Leaders, People Who Shaped the World. Volume I: Africa and Asia. Detroit: U*X*L, 1994.

———. "Confucius." In World Leaders, People Who Shaped the World. Volume I: Africa and Asia. Detroit: U*X*L, 1994.

———. "Ghenghis Khan." In World Leaders, People Who Shaped the World. Volume I: Africa and Asia. Detroit: U*X*L, 1994.

———. "Mao Zedong." In World Leaders, People Who Shaped the World. Volume I: Africa and Asia. Detroit: U*X*L, 1994.

O'Neill, Thomas. "Mekong River." National Geographic, February 1993, 2–35.

Terrill, Ross. "China's Youth Wait for Tomorrow." National Geographic, July 1991, 110–136.

———. "Hong Kong Countdown to 1997." National Geographic, February 1991, 103–132.

COLOMBIA

Republic of Colombia
República de Colombia

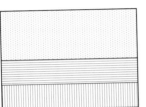

CAPITAL: Bogotá.

FLAG: The national flag consists of three horizontal stripes; the yellow upper stripe is twice as wide as each of the other two, which are blue and red.

ANTHEM: *Himno Nacional,* beginning "O gloria inmarcesible, júbilo inmortal" ("O unwithering glory, immortal joy").

MONETARY UNIT: The Colombian peso (c$) of 100 centavos is a paper currency. There are coins of 10, 20, and 50 centavos and of 1, 2, 5, 10, 20, and 50 pesos, and notes of 100, 200, 500, 1,000, 2,000, 5,000 and 10,000 pesos. Commemorative gold coins of various denominations also have been minted. c$1 = us$0.0038 (or us$1 = c$264.1).

WEIGHTS AND MEASURES: The metric system is the official standard, but Spanish units such as the botella, vara, fonegada, arroba, and quintal are also used.

HOLIDAYS: New Year's Day, 1 January; Epiphany, 6 January; St. Joseph's Day, 19 March; Labor Day, 1 May; Day of St. Peter and St. Paul, 29 June; Independence Day, 20 July; Battle of Boyacá, 7 August; Assumption, 15 August; Columbus Day, 12 October; All Saints' Day, 1 November; Independence of Cartagena, 11 November; Immaculate Conception, 8 December; Christmas, 25 December. Movable religious holidays include Holy Thursday, Good Friday, Holy Saturday, Ascension, Sacred Heart, and Corpus Christi. In addition there are six official commemorative days.

TIME: 7 AM = noon GMT.

1 LOCATION AND SIZE

Colombia is the only South American country with both Caribbean and Pacific coastlines. The fourth-largest country in South America, it has a total area of 1,138,910 square kilometers (439,736 square miles), slightly less than three times the size of the state of Montana. Colombia's total boundary length is 10,616 kilometers (6,596 miles).

Colombia's capital city, Bogotá, is located in the center of the country.

2 TOPOGRAPHY

The Andes Mountains divide just north of Colombia's southern border with Ecuador into three separate chains, or cordilleras, known as the Cordillera Occidental (western), the Cordillera Central, and the Cordillera Oriental (eastern). The western and central cordilleras run roughly parallel with the Pacific coast, extending northward as far as the Caribbean coastal lowlands. The third chain, the Cordillera Oriental, runs northeastward, dividing into two branches. Northward, near the

Caribbean, stands the Sierra Nevada de Santa Marta, whose highest elevation is Cristóbal Colón (5,797 meters/19,020 feet), the tallest peak in Colombia.

Separating the three principal Andean ranges are Colombia's two major rivers, the Cauca and the Magdalena. After emerging from the mountains, the two rivers become one and descend through marshy lowlands to the Caribbean. Open plains immediately adjoin the mountains, but as the distance from the cordillera increases, the plains give way to largely uninhabited and unexplored jungle. Principal rivers on the Pacific coast include the Baudó, San Juan, and Patía.

3 CLIMATE

The country may be divided into four climatic regions by altitude. The hot country, or tierra caliente, is the tropical zone, where the mean annual temperature is 24°C to 27°C (75–81°F). Between 1,100 meters (3,500 feet) and 2,000 meters (6,500 feet) above sea level is the temperate zone, or tierra templada, where the average year-round temperature is about 18°C (64°F).

Between 2,000 meters (6,500 feet) and 3,000 meters (10,000 feet) is the cold country, or tierra fría, with temperatures averaging a little over 13°C (55°F). Above the 3,000-meters (10,000-feet) level the temperature varies from 13°C to –17°C (55°F to 1°F), according to altitude. The annual mean temperature at the capital, Bogotá (altitude 2,598 meters/8,525 feet), is 14°C (57°F). Rainfall is heaviest on the west coast and in the Andean area.

4 PLANTS AND ANIMALS

More than 45,000 species of plants have been identified in Colombia, and it is predicted that when the region has been thoroughly explored the number may be doubled. At the highest and coldest level of mountain meadows, called páramos, the soil supports grasses and dense masses of low bushes.

In the inter-mountain basins some vegetables, European-introduced grains, and corn are found, along with the bushes, trees, and meadow grasses native to the region. The temperate areas support extensive and luxuriant forests, ferns, mosses, trees of the laurel family, Spanish cedars, vegetables, and grain crops.

The tropical zone may be divided into four main groups according to the amount of rainfall received: desertlike areas supporting arid plants, deciduous forests, rainforests, and grass plains. Palm trees of various species abound in the tropics, and there are many edible fruits and vegetables.

Animal life is abundant, especially in the tropical area. Among carnivorous species are the puma (a variety of smaller cat) and raccoons. Herbivorous animals include the tapir, deer, and large tropical rodents. Sloths, anteaters, opossums, and several types of monkeys are also found, as well as some 1,665 species and subspecies of South American and migratory birds.

5 ENVIRONMENT

Columbia's main environmental problems are soil erosion, deforestation, and the

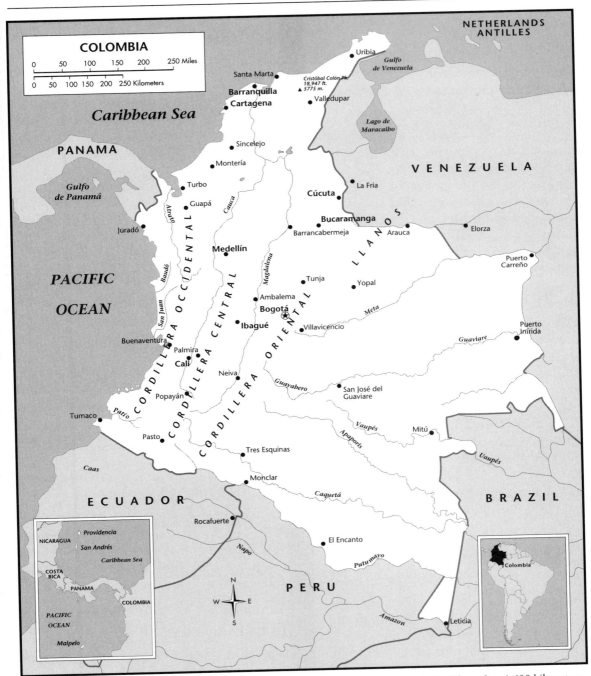

COLOMBIA

Caribbean Sea

PANAMA

PACIFIC OCEAN

Gulfo de Panamá

Gulfo de Venezuela

NETHERLANDS ANTILLES

VENEZUELA

Lago de Maracaibo

Cristóbal Colón Pk. 18,947 ft. 5775 m.

Uribia
Santa Marta
Barranquilla
Cartagena
Valledupar
Sincelejo
Montería
Turbo
Guapá
Juradó
Cúcuta
La Fria
Bucaramanga
Barrancabermeja
Arauca
Elorza
Medellín
Tunja
Yopal
Puerto Carreño
Ambalema
Bogotá
Ibagué
Villavicencio
Buenaventura
Palmira
Cali
Neiva
Popayán
Tumaco
Pasto
Tres Esquinas
Monclar
San José del Guaviare
Mitú
Puerto Inírida

LLANOS

CORDILLERA OCCIDENTAL
CORDILLERA CENTRAL
CORDILLERA ORIENTAL

Atrato
Baudó
San Juan
Cauca
Magdalena
Meta
Guaviare
Guayabero
Vaupés
Apaporis
Vaupés
Patía
Caas
Caquetá
Napo
Putumayo
Amazon

ECUADOR

PERU

BRAZIL

Rocafuerte
El Encanto
Leticia

NICARAGUA
San Andrés
Providencia
COSTA RICA
PANAMA
Caribbean Sea
COLOMBIA
PACIFIC OCEAN
Malpelo

Colombia

N W E S

LOCATION: 12°27′46″N to 4°13′30″s; 66°50′54″E to 79°1′23″W. **BOUNDARY LENGTHS:** Caribbean Sea, 1,600 kilometers (994 miles); Venezuela, 2,219 kilometers (1,379 miles); Brazil, 1,645 kilometers (1,022 miles); Peru, 1,626 kilometers (1,010 miles); Ecuador, 586 kilometers (364 miles); Pacific Ocean, 1,300 kilometers (808 miles); Panama, 266 kilometers (165 miles). **TERRITORIAL SEA LIMIT:** 12 miles.

preservation of its wildlife. Loss of forest land, which also furthers erosion, has been caused by commercial exploitation. Without a major reforestation effort, Colombia's timber resources could be exhausted by the year 2000.

Endangered species in Colombia include the tundra peregrine falcon, gorgeted wood-quail, red siskin, five species of turtle (green sea, hawksbill, olive ridley, leatherback, and arrau), and two species each of alligator and crocodile. By 1994, 25 mammals, 69 bird species, 10 reptile species, and 327 plant species in Colombia were endangered.

6 POPULATION

Colombia is the third most populous country in Latin America, following Brazil and Mexico. The 1985 census set the population total at 27,837,932, and the estimate for 1992 was 33,391,536. The population in the year 2000 was projected at 37,822,000. The population density was an estimated 30 per square kilometer (76 per square mile) in 1992, with about 95% of the population residing in the mountainous western half of the country. In 1992, the estimated population of the capital, Bogotá, was 4,921,264.

7 MIGRATION

Emigration is small but significant, since many of those who leave the country are scientists, technicians, and doctors. Between 1951 and 1985, some 218,724 Colombians settled in the US, at an annual rate that rose to 11,802 in 1985. In 1990 there were more persons in the US of Colombian birth—304,000—than of any other South American nationality. About 300,000 Colombians were internally displaced in 1993 by the country's chronic violence.

8 ETHNIC GROUPS

The predominant racial strain in Colombia is the mestizo (mixed white and Amerindian), constituting about 50% of the total population. An estimated 25% of the inhabitants are of unmixed white ancestry, 20% are mulatto (black–white) or zambo (black–Indian), 4% are black, and 1.5% are pure Amerindian (aboriginals).

Pure Amerindians are rapidly disappearing; the remaining few live mainly in inaccessible and barren regions. The Motilones are one of the few surviving Amerindian groups in South America untouched by civilization; they are famous for their lethal weapon, the black palm bow and arrow. Small, diverse Amerindian groups also inhabit the eastern extremities of the Colombian plains region, the south, and the western coastal jungles.

9 LANGUAGES

The official language, Spanish, is spoken by all but a few Amerindian tribes. Spanish as spoken and written by educated Colombians is generally considered the closest to Castilian Spanish in Latin America.

10 RELIGIONS

The vast majority of the country is Roman Catholic (93.1%). Religious freedom is constitutionally guaranteed to the small Protestant population and the 6,500 Jews.

Photo credit: AP/Wide World Photos

A group of children play in a circle outside a makeshift school set up by Colombia's Paz Indians. The school is at a ranch where 20 of their members were murdered by drug traffickers in 1991.

11 TRANSPORTATION

In 1991 there were about 75,450 kilometers (46,885 miles) of roads. Many roads are plagued by landslides and washouts. Early in 1991, the government proposed a 15-project program, with an estimated cost of $500 million. In 1991 there were 798,606 passenger cars and 670,000 commercial motor vehicles. In the same year, the railroads had a length of 3,563 kilometers (2,214 miles).

Due to Colombia's mountainous terrain and inadequate land transport, air transportation has become the most important means of travel for most passengers. A flight from Bogotá to Medellín takes only half an hour, while a truck requires 24 hours over a winding mountain road. Colombia's airline, Avianca, is the second-oldest commercial airline in the world and one of the largest in Latin America.

Most of the country's air transportation is handled by the six principal airports at Bogotá, Barranquilla, Medellín, Cali, Cartagena, and the island of San Andrés off the coast of Nicaragua. In 1991, these airports serviced about 9,735,000 passengers.

The nation's chief ports on the Caribbean are Barranquilla, Cartagena, and Santa Marta. Buenaventura is the only important Pacific port. Despite the development of roads and railways, river travel has remained the chief mode of transportation for cargo. Navigable inland waterways totaled 14,300 kilometers (8,886 miles) in 1991.

12 HISTORY

Archaeological studies indicate that Colombia was inhabited by various Amerindian groups as early as 11,000 BC. Prominent among the pre-Columbian cultures were the highland Chibchas, an agricultural people located in the eastern chain of the Andes.

The first Spanish settlement, Santa Marta on the Caribbean coast, dates from 1525. In 1536, Gonzalo Jiménez de Quesada and a company of 900 men traveled up the Magdalena River. They entered the heart of Chibcha territory in 1538, conquered the inhabitants, and established Bogotá. Spain consolidated Colombia, then called New Granada, with the areas that are now known as Panama, Venezuela, and Ecuador. The area became Spain's chief source of gold and was exploited for emeralds and tobacco.

In the late 1700s, an independence movement developed, stemming from Spanish taxation and the political and trade restrictions placed on American-born colonists. One of the leaders of this movement was Simón Bolívar. Independence was declared on 20 July 1810. However, independence was not assured until 7 August 1819, when the Battle of Boyacá was won by Simón Bolívar's troops. It was a decisive victory.

In 1819 the Republic of Greater Colombia was formed. It included Colombia, Venezuela, Ecuador, and Panama. Although Venezuela and Ecuador seceded, Panama remained part of Colombia. In 1831 the country became the State of New Granada. Bolívar was elected president of the new republic. However, political and financial order was attained under Francisco de Paula Santander. Santander, who had been Bolívar's vice-president, became president in 1832.

In the decade that followed, there was intense disagreement over the relative amount of power to be granted to the government and the Roman Catholic Church. The supporters of strong central government had organized and became known as the Conservatives. The conservatives favored highly centralized government and the perpetuation of traditional class and church privileges. They also opposed the extension of voting rights to all members of the society. Opposing the Conservatives were the Liberals. The Liberals supported states' rights, universal suffrage, and complete separation of church and state.

The Liberals were in power for most of the years between 1845 and 1880, a period characterized by frequent revolts and civil wars.

During the period 1880–94, the Conservative Rafael Núñez, a poet and intellectual, restored centralized government and the power of the church. During his tenure as president, the State of New Granada formally became the Republic of Colombia.

The differences between the Conservatives and the Liberals eventually led to a civil war known as the War of a Thousand Days (1899–1902). This war resulted in more than 100,000 deaths.

The nation's declining morale was worsened by the loss of Panama in 1903. The United States wanted Colombia to sign a treaty that would lease a zone of land across the Isthmus of Panama to the United States. The United States wanted the land for a canal that would link the Atlantic Ocean with the Pacific. When Columbia refused to ratify the treaty, the United States supported a revolt that created the Republic of Panama. Columbia lost its territory in Panama and the United States went on to build the Panama Canal. Colombia did not recognize Panama's independence until 1914, in exchange for rights in the Canal Zone and a payment from the United States.

During World War II, which Colombia entered on the side of the Allies, social and political divisions within the country intensified. The postwar period was marked by growing social unrest and riots in the capital and in the countryside. An extended and bloody period of rural disorder (La Violencia) claimed 150,000 to 200,000 lives between 1947 and 1958.

The disorder in the country led to a military coup in 1953 that brought General Gustavo Rojas Pinilla to power. Initially, Rojas enjoyed wide popular support, partly for his success in reducing the ongoing violence (La Violencia). When he did not promptly restore democratic government, however, he was overthrown

Photo credit: AP/Wide World Photos

A policeman crosses a street holding the hands of his little girls in the city of Medellín. Policemen are profitable targets since the drug lords will pay thousands of dollars to anyone who kills one.

in 1957 by the military with the backing of both political parties. After his overthrow, a provisional government took office.

In 1957 the Liberals and the Conservatives formed a coalition government that lasted for 16 years. This arrangement, called the National Front, provided for a free election to be held in 1958. The parties would then alternate in power for four-year terms until 1974. In August 1974, with the inauguration of the Liberal Alfonso López Michelsen as president, Colombia returned to a two-party system for presidential and congressional elections.

However, Columbia was plagued by political violence, including numerous kidnappings and political murders by both left- and right-wing organizations. The country also became increasingly plagued by drug traffickers. In 1990, two presidential candidates were assassinated by drug lords intent on intimidating the government from pursuing anti-drug policies. However, the government responded by announcing a new hard-line policy against both the drug traffickers and the anti-government guerrillas.

In 1991 a new constitution was created that included a number of reforms aimed at increasing the democratization of Colombia's elite-controlled political system. In the 1994 elections, Colombians once again chose a Liberal government. The elections were marked by widespread political violence.

13 GOVERNMENT

Colombia is a republic, organized democratically under the current constitution of 1991. The Congress consists of a Chamber of Representatives and a Senate. Members of both are elected directly for four-year terms. In 1990 there were 161 representatives and 102 senators. The chief executive is granted the power to declare a state of emergency during times of economic and social stress. Under such a declaration, the president may rule by decree for a period of not longer than 90 days in any one year.

The president is elected directly for a four-year term and may not succeed himself until one term has passed. There is universal suffrage for those 18 years of age and over.

Colombia is divided into 23 departments (states), 4 intendencies, 5 administrative territories (commissariats), and the Bogotá federal district.

14 POLITICAL PARTIES

For many years, the Colombian constitution allowed only two political parties, the Liberal and the Conservative, to participate in the national government.

The Liberal Party (Partido Liberal—PL) supports religious toleration and a positive response to the social and economic demands of the masses. Liberals have been far more successful in elections than the Conservatives, having won all but one election since 1974, and they continue to enjoy majority support in both houses.

The policy of the Conservative Party (Partido Conservador Social—PCS) has been characterized by close cooperation with the Roman Catholic Church, a lack of tolerance for non-Roman Catholic religious beliefs, maintenance of class privileges, and highly centralized government.

Recent changes allow for more parties, and several have emerged. The Colombian Communist Party (Partido Communista de Colombia—PCC) is a traditional, Moscow-oriented party. After more than two decades as a guerrilla group, it gave up its arms in 1991 and entered candidates in the 1990 elections. Several militant leftist groups remain outside the system.

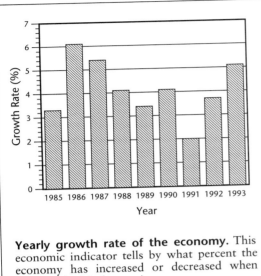

Yearly growth rate of the economy. This economic indicator tells by what percent the economy has increased or decreased when compared with the previous year.

15 JUDICIAL SYSTEM

The Supreme Court in Bogotá is composed of 24 magistrates selected for lifetime terms by justices already in office. The Supreme Court reviews state and municipality laws, frames bills to be submitted to Congress, and proposes reforms. It presides over impeachment trials.

There is a superior court of three or more judges in each of the judicial districts and a number of municipal courts. There are also special labor courts. In criminal cases, the judge chooses a five-member jury; jury duty is obligatory. There is no capital punishment; the maximum penalty for crimes is 20 years in prison.

In practice, the judiciary is overburdened and subject to intimidation in cases involving narcotics or offenses by police.

In 1991, the government set up five regional jurisdictions to handle narcotics, terrorism, and police corruption cases. In these courts, anonymous judges and prosecutors handle the major trials of narcotics terrorists.

16 ARMED FORCES

Colombia's total armed forces in 1993 amounted to 139,000 personnel. All adult males (ages 18–30) are required by the constitution to serve if called, for one or two years.

The army of 120,000 is organized into four divisions of 12 infantry brigades, stationed on a regional basis. Special mobile forces, counterinsurgency forces, rangers, commandoes, and mechanized guard forces number an additional 17 battalions.

Air force personnel numbered 7,000 in 1993; combat aircraft numbered 68; armed helicopters, 51. The navy had 12,000 personnel, including 6,000 marines. Naval ships included 5 frigates, 2 submarines, and 26 patrol craft and gunboats. There is also a 85,000-member national police force.

Colombia's defense forces are frequently occupied in opposing rural violence, often stemming from militant guerrilla groups and drug lords' armies. Defense expenditures in 1991 amounted to around $1 billion.

17 ECONOMY

Despite the gradual expansion of manufacturing, Colombia's economy remains basically agricultural. Coffee is by far the most important crop: its share of total exports ranged from about 40% to 65% of the annual total between 1964 and 1986. Mining has been the area of the most impressive growth in recent years.

Since 1983, the economy has improved significantly, and high growth rates have been recorded. Inflation was kept close to 20% annually through the 1980s. In 1993 it was 23%. By the end of 1993, unemployment had increased to 10.5%.

18 INCOME

In 1992, Colombia's gross national product (GNP) was $44,555 million, or about $1,400 per person. For the period 1985–92 the average inflation rate was 26.1%, resulting in a real growth rate in GNP of 2.4% per person.

19 INDUSTRY

Industrial production figures for 1985 included 33,208 passenger cars and 5,878 other vehicles; 5,314,963 tons of cement; 1,367,352 tons of refined sugar; 274,416 tons of steel; and 64,870 tons of petroleum products.

The country's industrial output grew by 4.1% in 1993. Coffee milling was hurt by the decline in the harvest, which caused a 16.1% fall in the amount produced. Among those areas showing increases were transport and transport materials (42.5%), furniture (16.2%), and glass products (13.7%).

Consumer products represent about one-half of total industrial production.

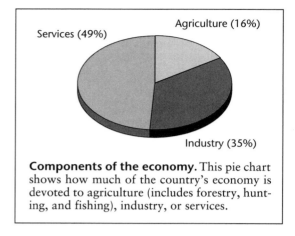

Components of the economy. This pie chart shows how much of the country's economy is devoted to agriculture (includes forestry, hunting, and fishing), industry, or services.

20 LABOR

In 1990, 30% of the labor force of about 10,750,000 held jobs in agriculture and 24% in industry. An average of 350,000 people joined the labor force annually during the 1970s and early 1980s, creating a demand for new positions that could not be met. Urban unemployment is a major problem. The average unemployment rate was 9.6% in 1991, and over 10% by the end of 1993.

The 1991 constitution guarantees the right to strike except against public utilities, equal rights for women workers, workers' participation in management, universal education, and expanded insurance coverage.

21 AGRICULTURE

Agriculture, despite the widespread problem of poor productivity, remains the most important part of the Colombian economy.

Colombia, the world's second-largest coffee grower, contributes 13–16% of the total world production each year. In 1992, coffee exports were valued at $1.26 billion, or 17.1% of the total value of exports.

Sugar, also important, is grown chiefly in the Cauca Valley, with its center at Cali. Many varieties of bananas are grown; bananas for export are produced in the northwest. Corn, yucca, plantains, and, in high altitudes, potatoes have been traditional food staples since before the Spanish conquest. Beans, rice, and wheat, introduced in the nineteenth century, are also important in the diet. Other export crops include fresh-cut flowers, cotton, and tobacco. Cocoa is produced in limited amounts for domestic consumption.

Agricultural production (in thousands of tons) for major crops in 1992 was as follows: sugarcane, 28,930; plantains, 2,745; potatoes, 2,131; rice, 1,735; cassava, 1,836; bananas, 1,900; corn, 1,056; coffee, 1,050; sorghum, 752; cotton, 117; palm oil, 304; and tobacco, 27.

22 DOMESTICATED ANIMALS

Occupying about 40 million hectares (99 million acres) of pasture in 1991, livestock farming, especially cattle breeding, has long been an important Colombian industry. Colombian sheep produce about one-third of the wool used by the country's textile industry. In 1992 there were 24.7 million cattle, 2.5 million sheep, and 2.6 million pigs. The production of beef and veal increased to 678,000 tons in 1995.

23 FISHING

Colombia has an abundance of fish in its Caribbean and Pacific coastal waters and in its innumerable rivers. Lake Tota near Tunja and Lake La Cocha near Pasto abound in trout. About half of the annual catch consists of freshwater fish. Tarpon are caught in the delta waters of the Magdalena, and sailfish, broadbills, and tuna in the Caribbean. The 1991 fish catch was 108,708 tons. In 1991, fish farming production increased, with frozen shrimp exports of $36.7 million and rock lobster exports of $6.5 million.

24 FORESTRY

Colombia's forested area is some 50 million hectares (123.6 million acres), or nearly 50% of the total area. The nation produces enough lumber to meet its own needs. The soft tropical woods that are plentiful are suitable for plywood production, for paper pulp, and for furniture manufacture; the wood pulp, paper, and paperboard output in 1991 was 690,000 tons. Roundwood production was 19,702,000 cubic meters in 1991.

25 MINING

In 1991, the total value of Colombian mineral exports amounted to about $2.9 billion, or 38% of total exports. Colombia is the third largest coal producer in the Western Hemisphere (after the US and Canada). Exports are projected to reach 49 million tons per year by 2001. Colombia is also one of the few countries that is self-sufficient in coking coal for its steel industry.

Colombia is one of the world's largest producers of precious metals and stones; in 1990, production of emeralds surpassed three million carats. Colombia is South America's only producer of platinum, and it ranks second in the region in gold production. Colombia has an estimated 2% of the world's nickel production, which amounted to 20,590 tons in 1991.

The country's substantial copper, iron, nickel, and lead reserves are of major importance to the future development of the economy. Colombia also has a variety of quarried resources, such as limestone, sand, gravel, marble, gypsum, clay, and feldspar. There are also minor deposits of sulfur, asbestos, bauxite, mercury, zinc, and dolomite. Production of marine salt in 1991 was 482,000 tons, and of rock salt, 219,000 tons.

The production of principal minerals (excluding petroleum and natural gas) in 1991 included coal, 20,200,000 tons; iron ore, 685,000 tons; gold, 34,844, kilograms; silver, 8,036 kilograms; and platinum, 1,603 kilograms.

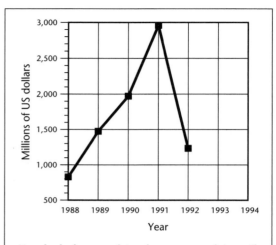

Yearly balance of trade measured in millions of US dollars. The balance of trade is the difference between what a country sells to other countries (its exports) and what it buys (its imports). If a country imports more than it exports, it has a negative balance of trade (a trade deficit). If exports exceed imports, there is a positive balance of trade (a trade surplus).

26 FOREIGN TRADE

Colombia trades in traditional commodities, such as coffee, sugar, and bananas, and in an increasing number of nontraditional products, such as metals, chemicals, and pharmaceuticals. Among the newer export items, fresh-cut flowers have been outstandingly successful.

Exports totaled $7,100 million in 1993, 3.1% more than the comparable figure for 1992. Major export-trading partners include the US, Germany, Venezuela, Japan, UK, and the Netherlands. In the same year, imports jumped 51.1% to total $8,500 million. Major import-trading partners included the US, Japan, Germany, Brazil, Venezuela, and Italy.

The illegal trade in marijuana and cocaine, especially to the US, is known to be substantial.

27 ENERGY AND POWER

Colombia's mountainous terrain and network of rivers offer one of the greatest potentials in the world for the generation of hydroelectric power. These resources remain largely undeveloped, despite intensive government efforts.

Photo credit: AP/Wide World Photos

Six-year-old Nelly Beltran laughs as her cousin, Edwin Riano, 12, unloads freshly baked bricks in the neighborhood of La Paz in southern Bogotá. Nelly's father received a $280 loan to build a small brick factory that has alleviated the family's poverty.

Colombia's recoverable petroleum reserves were estimated at 1.9 billion barrels in 1992. Production of oil had rapidly risen to 22.2 million tons in 1992. Between 1986 and 1991, there were 195 guerrilla attacks on oil facilities, costing $800 million. In 1992, natural gas production totaled 5.3 billion cubic meters.

28 SOCIAL DEVELOPMENT

Social security coverage extends to salaried and self-employed people alike. The government, employers, and employees pay for the program, which includes disability, old age, and death benefits as well as coverage of nonoccupational illnesses, maternity, and job-related accidents.

The Colombian Institute of Social Security administers other programs, including severance pay, pensions, vacation benefits, group life insurance, job training, transportation and clothing subsidies, educational benefits for families, and a scholarship fund. The Family Welfare Institute coordinates an estimated 1,000 public and private charities involved in caring for children and destitute families.

There is still discrimination against women, especially in rural areas. They

Selected Social Indicators

These statistics are estimates for the period 1988 to 1993. For comparison purposes, data for the United States and averages for low-income countries and high-income countries are also given.

Indicator	Colombia	Low-income countries	High-income countries	United States
Per capita gross national product†	$1,400	$380	$23,680	$24,740
Population growth rate	2.3%	1.9%	0.6%	1.0%
Population growth rate in urban areas	3.0%	3.9%	0.8%	1.3%
Population per square kilometer of land	30	78	25	26
Life expectancy in years	69	62	77	76
Number of people per physician	1,236	>3,300	453	419
Number of pupils per teacher (primary school)	28	39	<18	20
Illiteracy rate (15 years and older)	13%	41%	<5%	<3%
Energy consumed per capita (kg of oil equivalent)	661	364	5,203	7,918

† The gross national product (GNP) is the total dollar value of all goods and services produced by a country in a year. The per capita GNP is calculated by dividing a country's GNP by its population. The World Bank defines low-income countries as those with a per capita GNP of $695 or less. High-income countries have a per capita GNP of $8,626 or more. Less than 14% of the world's 5.5 billion people live in high-income countries, while almost 60% live in low-income countries.

> = greater than   < = less than

Sources: World Bank, Social Indicators of Development 1995, Baltimore: Johns Hopkins University Press, 1995. Central Intelligence Agency, World Fact Book, Washington, D.C.: Government Printing Office, 1994.

earn 30–40% less than men for doing similar work and occupy few of the top positions in government.

29 HEALTH

Health standards have improved greatly since the 1950s, but malaria is still prevalent up to 1,100 meters (3,500 feet) in altitude, and many Colombians suffer from intestinal parasites. Malnutrition, formerly a very serious problem, with nutritional goiter, anemia, scurvy, and pellagra frequent, had become less severe by the early 1980s. Average life expectancy in 1993 was 69 years.

According to a study made between 1985 and 1992, 60% of the population had access to health care services. Total health care expenditures in 1990 were US$1,604 million.

30 HOUSING

Colombia's housing shortage is largely a result of the rapid growth of the urban population. With the annual urban population growth rate at over 3%, the housing deficit was estimated to be around 800,000 units and is expanding annually.

Total housing units numbered 6,906,000 in 1992.

31 EDUCATION

Education is free and compulsory for five years in Colombia. Illiteracy is declining, having dropped from an estimated 90% at the end of the nineteenth century to an estimated 13% in 1993 (males: 12% and females: 14%). By law, Colombia must spend at least 10% of its annual budget on education.

There are over 4,000,000 students enrolled in primary schools and 2,000,000 in secondary schools. Although schooling is compulsory for children in the 7–11 age group, dropout rates are high at the primary level, particularly in rural areas, where the students frequently live at considerable distances from their schools.

There are over 475,000 students enrolled in higher education in Colombia. The National University in Bogotá, founded in 1572, is one of the oldest in the Western Hemisphere. Other important universities include the Universidad Javeriana (founded 1622); the Universidad de los Andes; and the Universidad Libre.

32 MEDIA

Most of the nation's 440 radio stations were privately owned in 1991. In 1992 there were 33 television stations in Colombia. In that year there were about 5,800,000 radio receivers and about 3,800,000 television sets. In 1991, over 2,500,000 telephones were in service.

Almost every town publishes at least one daily newspaper. The press varies from the irregular, hand-printed newspapers of the small towns of the interior to such national dailies as *El Tiempo*, one of the most influential newspapers of the Spanish-speaking world.

The country's principal newspapers and their 1991 daily circulations are as follows: *El Tiempo* (220,000); *El Espectador* (160,000); *El Espacio* (92,000); and *El Nuevo Siglo* (70,000).

33 TOURISM AND RECREATION

Colombia has mountains, jungles, modern and colonial cities, and resorts on both the Pacific and the Caribbean. The number of tourists entering Colombia reached 857,000 in 1991, with 798,000 from the Americas and 53,691 from Europe. Earnings from tourism rose to $410 million in 1991. In that year, the country had 43,072 hotel rooms.

Soccer is the most popular sport, followed by basketball, baseball, boxing, and cockfighting; there are also facilities for golf, tennis, and horseback riding, as well as bull rings in the major cities.

34 FAMOUS COLOMBIANS

Outstanding political and military figures in Colombian history include Francisco de Paula Santander (1792–1840), who was the first president of independent Colombia, and José María Córdoba (1800?–1830), a brilliant young soldier of the war of independence, who was made a general at 22 by Simón Bolívar.

Colombia, famous for its literary figures, has produced three outstanding novelists widely read outside the country: Jorge Isaacs (1837–95); José Eustacio Rivera (1880–1929); and Gabriel García

Márquez (b.1928), a Nobel Prize winner in 1982, who is best known for *Cien años de soledad* (*One Hundred Years of Solitude*). Colombia has had a number of noteworthy poets. José Asunción Silva (1865–96) is regarded as the father of Latin American symbolism; his *Nocturnos* are among the finest poems in the Spanish language.

Colombia's most notable painter was Gregorio Vázquez Arce y Ceballos (1638–1711). Francisco José de Caldas (1770–1816) was a brilliant botanist. Guillermo Uribe-Holguín (1880–1971) and José Rozo Contreras (b.1894) are noted composers. The works of the contemporary historian Germán Arciniegas (b.1900) are well known to the English-speaking world in translation.

35 BIBLIOGRAPHY

Bushnell, David. *The Making of Modern Colombia: A Nation in Spite of Itself*. Berkeley: Univ. of California Press, 1993.

Colombia in Pictures. Minneapolis: Lerner, 1987.

Davis, Robert H. *Colombia*. Oxford, England, and Santa Barbara, Calif.: Clio Press, 1990.

McDowell, Bart. "Cartagena Nights." *National Geographic*, April 1989, 494–509.

Morrison, M. *Colombia*. Chicago: Children's Press, 1990.

Pearce, Jenny. *Colombia: The Drug War*. New York: Gloucester Press, 1990.

COMOROS

Federal Islamic Republic of the Comoros
République Fédérale Islamique des Comores
Jumhuriyat al-Qumur al-Ittihadiyah al-Islamiyah

CAPITAL: Moroni.

FLAG: On a green background appears a white crescent set at an angle and encompassing four white stars.

ANTHEM: No information available.

MONETARY UNIT: The Comorian franc (Co Fr) is the equivalent of the Communauté Financière Africaine franc (CFA Fr), which is linked with the French franc at a ratio of 75:1. There are notes of 500, 1,000, and 5,000 Co Fr. Co Fr1 = $0.0023 (or $1 = Co Fr428.25).

WEIGHTS AND MEASURES: The metric system is used.

HOLIDAYS: New Year's Day, 1 January; Second Coup d'État, 13 May; Independence Day, 6 July; Admission to UN, 12 November; Christmas Day, 25 December. The principal Muslim holidays are observed.

TIME: 3 PM = noon GMT.

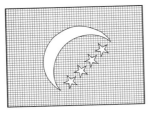

1 LOCATION AND SIZE

Comoros—Grande Comore, Mohéli, and Anjouan islands—is located at the northern entrance of the Mozambique Channel, between the eastern shore of the African continent and the island of Madagascar, which lies about 480 kilometers (300 miles) to the southeast. The area occupied by the Comoros Islands is slightly more than 12 times the size of Washington, D.C. The capital city, Moroni, is located at the western edge of Grande Comore.

2 TOPOGRAPHY

The islands are volcanic in origin, and their highest peak, Mt. Kartala (2,361 meters/7,746 feet), located near the southern tip of the island of Grande Comore, is an active volcano.

3 CLIMATE

The climate in the Comoros is humid and tropical, with coastal temperatures averaging about 28°C (82°F) in March and 23°C (73°F) in August. The monsoon season lasts from November to April.

4 PLANTS AND ANIMALS

The rich volcanic soils on the islands foster the growth of much vegetation. Beyond the coastal zones, where mangroves predominate, there are coconut palms, mangoes, and bananas, and above them is a forest zone, with many varieties of tropical hardwoods.

5 ENVIRONMENT

Although Mohéli has large tracts of fertile land not yet cultivated, parts of Anjouan are so densely populated that farmers have been forced to extend cultivation to the higher slopes, leading to deforestation and soil erosion.

6 POPULATION

The population of the islands in 1994 was estimated at 530,105, excluding Mayotte (which is part of the Comoros chain but is a French territory) which had a population of 94,410 in 1991. Moroni, the capital, had an estimated population of 24,000 in 1990.

7 MIGRATION

About 40,000 Comorians live in France and 25,000 in Madagascar.

8 ETHNIC GROUPS

The islands' indigenous population consists almost entirely of persons of mixed African, Malagasy, Malay, and Arab descent. Small numbers of Indians and Europeans play an important part in the economy.

9 LANGUAGES

French and Arabic are the official languages. The main spoken language, Shaafi Islam (Comorian), is similar to Swahili but has elements of Arabic.

10 RELIGIONS

Islam, the state religion, is followed by more than 99% of Comorians. Almost all Comorians are Sunni Muslims.

11 TRANSPORTATION

Each island has a ringed road, and there were some 750 kilometers (466 miles) of roads in 1991. There is an international airport at Hahaia, on Grande Comore; other islands have smaller airfields.

12 HISTORY

The first settlers were probably Melanesian and Polynesian peoples, who came to the Comoros by the sixth century AD; later immigrants arrived from East Africa, Arab lands, Indonesia, Persia, and Madagascar. The Portuguese discovered the islands about 1503, and Frenchmen first landed in 1517. Malagasy invasions also took place in the sixteenth century.

A French protectorate was placed over Anjouan, Grande Comore, and Mohéli in 1886, and in 1908 the islands were joined administratively with French-ruled Madagascar.

In World War II, the islands were occupied by a British force and turned over to the Free French. The Comoros were granted administrative autonomy within the Republic of France on 9 May 1946, acquiring overseas territorial status, and on 22 December 1961 achieved internal autonomy under special statute.

In a referendum held on 22 December 1974, a large majority on the islands, except Mayotte, voted in favor of independence. On 6 July 1975, the Comoros legislature unilaterally declared independence for all four islands, including Mayotte. The United Nations General Assembly backed the Comorian claim to Mayotte despite French opposition. Nonetheless, Mayotte remained French.

Considerable domestic turmoil accompanied the birth of the new nation. The first Comorian government held power only a month before it was overthrown on 3 August 1975 with the aid of foreign white mercenaries. On 13 May 1978, 'Ali Soilih, who had led the 1975 military coup and had become head of state in January 1976, was overthrown by mercenaries led by Bob Denard, who reinstalled the nation's first president, Ahmad 'Abdallah. 'Abdallah ruled until he was assassinated in November 1989, when Said Mohamed Djohar, head of the Supreme Court, was appointed interim president

A French peacekeeping force enabled the government to lift political restrictions and conduct a presidential election. On 11 March 1990, Djohar won a runoff with 55% of the vote. Subsequently, his coalition government survived three coup attempts.

In the long-delayed and controversial 12 and 20 December 1993 legislative elections, supporters of Djohar won 24 of the 42 seats in the Assembly. Members of the opposition parties contested the validity of both the election results and the choice of Djohar's son-in-law as president of the Assembly on 7 January. On 17 January, the main opposition parties agreed to coordinate their actions in a Forum for National Recovery (FRN).

13 GOVERNMENT

A new constitution was adopted in June 1992. The President and 42-member Federal Assembly are elected by universal suffrage for four- and five-year terms respectively. It also provides for a 15-member Senate to be chosen by an electoral college for a term of six years. The

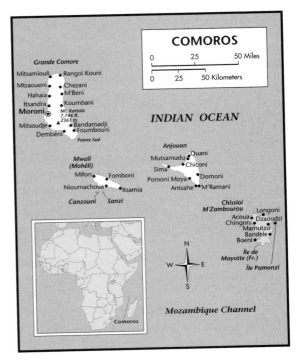

LOCATION: 43°1′N to 44°32′E; 11°21′W to 12°25′S.
TERRITORIAL SEA LIMIT: 12 miles.

post of prime minister is held by a member of the majority party in the Assembly.

14 POLITICAL PARTIES

In February 1982, the Comorian Union for Progress (Union Comorienne pour le Progrés—UCP) was established as the only legal party. Despite earlier assurances of a free ballot, few opposition candidates were allowed to run, and dissidents were subject to intimidation and imprisonment.

On 10 September 1993, the UCP merged with the Union for Democracy and Decentralization (UNDC), the largest party in the Assembly. Djohar hastily created his own party, the RDR, to contest the December 1993 elections.

15 JUDICIAL SYSTEM

The Supreme Court resolves constitutional questions, supervises presidential elections, and arbitrates (judged by an impartial person) any case in which the government is accused of malpractice. The Supreme Court also reviews decisions of the lower courts, including the superior court of appeals at Moroni. Lower courts of the first instance are located in major towns.

16 ARMED FORCES

There is a small French-trained army of almost 1,000 men.

17 ECONOMY

The economy of the Comoros is agriculture based, dependent on trade and foreign assistance. Mineral resources are few; there is little industry. Tourism, however, increased considerably in 1991.

18 INCOME

In 1992 Comoros's gross national product (GNP) was $262 million, or about $430 per person. For the period 1985–92 the average inflation rate was 3.0%, resulting in a real growth rate in GNP of –2.3% per person.

19 INDUSTRY

There are various small-scale industries, mostly for processing the islands' agricultural products.

20 LABOR

The majority of the economically active population is engaged in subsistence agriculture, fishing, or petty commerce. The wage-earning labor force is small, consisting of fewer than 2,000 employees (or 9,500 employees including the public sector).

21 AGRICULTURE

The economy of the Comoros is primarily agricultural, with farmland comprising 44.8% of the total land area as of 1991. Among the chief crops in 1992, in tons, were manioc, 49,000; coconuts, 50,000; bananas, 53,000; sweet potatoes, 10,000; rice, 10,000; corn, 4,000; and copra, 5,000. The chief export crops are vanilla, cloves, ylang-ylang, and copra.

22 DOMESTICATED ANIMALS

Small amounts of livestock are raised. In 1992 there were an estimated 126,000 goats, 47,000 head of cattle, 14,000 sheep, and 5,000 asses. An estimated 1,000 tons of beef and 1,000 tons of other meat were produced in 1992, along with 4,000 tons of milk and 640 tons of eggs.

23 FISHING

The fish catch in the Comoros amounted to about 6,455 tons in 1991, half of which was tuna.

24 FORESTRY

Forest and woodland areas declined from 44,000 hectares (109,000 acres) in 1968 to about 35,000 hectares (86,000 acres) in 1991 (including Mayotte).

25 MINING

There are no commercially exploitable mineral resources. Some sand, gravel, and crushed stone were produced for the domestic construction industry.

26 FOREIGN TRADE

Ylang-ylang essence, vanilla, cloves, copra, and other agricultural commodities make up the bulk of Comorian exports; of these, vanilla is by far the most important export earner. Imports include rice and other foodstuffs, petroleum products, and motor vehicles.

France is the leading trade partner, accounting for 44.5% of exports and 58% of imports in 1989. Other leading trading partners that year were the United States, Botswana, Bahrain, Kenya, Brazil, and South Africa.

27 ENERGY AND POWER

In 1991, 16 million kilowatt hours were generated. Installed capacity was about 5,000 kilowatts, 80% of it thermal. All petroleum products are imported.

28 SOCIAL DEVELOPMENT

Women occupy a subservient position in this extremely traditional society but retain some strength from the matrilineal social structure. Although the government regards the fertility rate as too high, no major population control programs have been launched.

29 HEALTH

In 1987 there were 6 main hospitals, 10 secondary hospitals and medical centers,

Photo credit: Larry Tackett/Tom Stack & Associates

A market scene in Moroni, the capital city of Comoros.

and 4 maternity clinics. Lack of animal protein is a serious problem. In addition, a large percentage of the adult population suffers from malaria, and there is a high incidence of tuberculosis and leprosy.

30 HOUSING

Over 65% of all housing units are straw huts with roofs of cocoa leaves, and 25% are made of durable materials including stone, brick, or concrete.

31 EDUCATION

Primary education lasts for six years followed by seven years of secondary educa-

Selected Social Indicators

These statistics are estimates for the period 1988 to 1993. For comparison purposes, data for the United States and averages for low-income countries and high-income countries are also given.

Indicator	Comoros	Low-income countries	High-income countries	United States
Per capita gross national product†	$430	$380	$23,680	$24,740
Population growth rate	3.8%	1.9%	0.6%	1.0%
Population growth rate in urban areas	5.8%	3.9%	0.8%	1.3%
Population per square kilometer of land	262	78	25	26
Life expectancy in years	56	62	77	76
Number of people per physician	7,551	>3,300	453	419
Number of pupils per teacher (primary school)	45	39	<18	20
Illiteracy rate (15 years and older)	52%	41%	<5%	<3%
Energy consumed per capita (kg of oil equivalent)	30	364	5,203	7,918

† The gross national product (GNP) is the total dollar value of all goods and services produced by a country in a year. The per capita GNP is calculated by dividing a country's GNP by its population. The World Bank defines low-income countries as those with a per capita GNP of $695 or less. High-income countries have a per capita GNP of $8,626 or more. Less than 14% of the world's 5.5 billion people live in high-income countries, while almost 60% live in low-income countries.

> = greater than   < = less than

Sources: World Bank, Social Indicators of Development 1995, Baltimore: Johns Hopkins University Press, 1995. Central Intelligence Agency, World Fact Book, Washington, D.C.: Government Printing Office, 1994.

tion. There is a teacher training college near Moroni, and two technical schools.

32 MEDIA

The weekly newspaper *Al Watwany* (1991 circulation, 1,200) is published by the government. In 1991 there were 4,016 telephones and an estimated 72,000 radios. Radio-Comoros, a government agency, provides services on shortwave and FM, and a television service was begun in 1986.

33 TOURISM AND RECREATION

The tourist industry was undeveloped at independence and has stagnated since 1983. There were 16,942 tourists in 1991.

34 FAMOUS COMORIANS

Heads of state since independence include 'Ali Soilih (1937–78), who came to power as a result of the 1975 coup and who died after the 1978 takeover; and Ahmad 'Abdallah (b.1919), president briefly in 1975 and restored to power in 1978.

35 BIBLIOGRAPHY

Newitt, Malyn. *The Comoro Islands: Struggle Against Dependency in the Indian Ocean.* Boulder, Colo.: Westview, 1984.

CONGO

People's Republic of the Congo
République Populaire du Congo

CAPITAL: Brazzaville.

FLAG: The flag consists of a green triangular section at the hoist and a red triangular section at the fly, separated by a diagonal gold bar.

ANTHEM: *The Congolaise.*

MONETARY UNIT: The Communauté Financière Africaine franc (CFA Fr) is a paper currency, tied to the French franc at the rate of CFA Fr50 = Fr1. There are coins of 1, 2, 5, 10, 25, 50, 100, and 500 CFA francs and notes of 50, 100, 500, 1,000, 5,000, and 10,000 CFA francs. CFA Fr1 = $0.0018 (or $1 = CFA Fr571).

WEIGHTS AND MEASURES: The metric system is the legal standard.

HOLIDAYS: New Year's Day, 1 January; Labor Day, 1 May; Three Glorious Days, 13–15 August (including Independence Day, 15 August); Christmas Day, 25 December. Movable religious holidays include Good Friday and Easter Monday.

TIME: 1 PM = noon GMT.

1 LOCATION AND SIZE

Lying astride the Equator, the People's Republic of the Congo contains an area of about 342,000 square kilometers (132,000 square miles). Comparatively, the area occupied by the Congo is slightly smaller than the state of Montana. The Congo's capital city, Brazzaville, is located in the southeastern part of the country.

2 TOPOGRAPHY

The Congo is roughly divided into four topographical regions: the coastal region, consisting of a low, relatively treeless plain; the escarpment region, made up of a series of forested ridges of moderate height; the plateau region, with savanna, or tropical plains, covering more than 129,000 square kilometers (50,000 square miles); and the northeastern region, a swampy lowland covering some 155,000 square kilometers (60,000 square miles).

3 CLIMATE

The Congo has a tropical climate characterized by high humidity and heat. There are two wet and two dry seasons. Annual rainfall varies from 105 centimeters (41 inches) at Pointe-Noire, in the southwest, to 185 centimeters (73 inches) at Impfondo, in the northeast.

4 PLANTS AND ANIMALS

About half the land area is covered by okoumé, limba, and other trees of the heavy rainforest. On the plateaus, the forest is broken by patches of bushy undergrowth. The plain supports jackals, hyenas, cheetahs, and several varieties of antelope. Elephants, wild boar, giraffes, and monkeys dwell in the forest.

5 ENVIRONMENT

The most significant environmental problems in the Congo are deforestation, increases in urban population, and the protection of its wildlife. The Congo's forests, which cover 50% of the nation's land area, are endangered by fires set to clear the land for agricultural purposes.

The Congo's urban centers are hampered by air pollution from vehicles and water pollution from sewage. The water purity problem is most apparent in rural areas where, as of 1994, 98% of the people did not have safe water.

6 POPULATION

In 1994, the population was estimated at 2,521,923; the projection for the year 2000 was 2,976,000. At least four-fifths of the people live in the southern third of the country. In 1991 Brazzaville, the capital, had 760,300 inhabitants.

7 MIGRATION

There is continuous migration to urban centers, but immigration from other African countries is not significant.

8 ETHNIC GROUPS

The population belongs to four major ethnic groups—the Kongo, Bateke, Mboshi, and Sanga—which comprise more than 40 tribes. In addition, there are small groups of Pygmies, possibly the Congo's original inhabitants, in the high forest region.

9 LANGUAGES

French is the official language. Several related African languages and dialects of the Bantu family are spoken. Monokutuba (Kikongo) and Lingala are the most common.

10 RELIGIONS

Almost half of the population was Christian in the early 1990s; 39.3% of the Christian population was Roman Catholic. About 5% of the people observe African traditional religions exclusively, but traditional beliefs and practices continue to be widespread and coexist with Christianity.

11 TRANSPORTATION

The most important transportation system is the Congo-Ocean Railroad. Dense tropical forests, rugged terrain, and swamps, together with a hot, humid climate and heavy rainfall, make construction and maintenance of roads extremely costly. In 1991 there were about 12,000 kilometers (7,460 miles) of highways.

There are up to 5,000 kilometers (3,100 miles) of navigable rivers. The river port of Brazzaville is an important center for trade with the Central African Republic, Chad, and Zaire.

Because of the great distances and the inadequacy of land transportation, air travel and air freight services are rapidly expanding. Brazzaville and Pointe-Noire airports are the hubs of a network of air routes that connect the four equatorial republics with several European cities.

12 HISTORY

The Congo Empire extended into present-day Angola and reached its height in the

CONGO

0 50 100 150 Miles
0 50 100 150 Kilometers

CENTRAL AFRICAN REPUBLIC

CAMEROON

Lopi · Bétou ·
Bangui ·
Motaba
Lokomo ·
Bomassa ·
Souanké ·
Sembé ·
Ouesso ·
Zalangoye ·
Angouma ·
Djoua
Belinga ·
Liouesso ·
Impfondo ·
Kemboma ·
Zaire (Congo)
Likouala aux
Likouala
Etoumbi ·
Makoua ·
Owando ·
Herbes
Ewo ·
Obili ·
Mossaka ·
Lac Tumba
Moanda ·
Franceville ·
Alima
Mbigou ·
M'Binda ·
Mayoko ·
Djambala ·
N'Gao ·
Lac Mai-Ndombe
Moabi ·
Zanaga ·
Lékéti Mts. 3,412 ft. 1040 m.
Léfini
Mossendjo ·
Bouali ·
Makabana ·
Sibiti ·
Batéké Plateau
Ngabé ·
Madingou ·
Brazzaville
Kayes ·
Nkayi · Mindouli ·
Pool Malebo
Loubomo ·
Mafauati ·
Kinkala ·
Kinshasa
Boko ·
Binza ·
Pointe-Noire ·

EQUATORIAL GUINEA

GABON

Ogooué

ZAIRE

Congo Basin

Lengoué
Sangha
Oubangui
Giri

Nyanga
Kouilou
Niari
Djoué
Congo
MAYOMB MTS.

ATLANTIC OCEAN

CABINDA (ANGOLA)

Congo

N W E S

LOCATION: 3°42′N to 5°1′S; 11°7′ to 18°39′E. **BOUNDARY LENGTHS:** Cameroon, 520 kilometers (323 miles); Central African Republic, 467 kilometers (290 miles); Zaire, 1,625 kilometers (1,010 miles); Angola, 201 kilometers (125 miles); Atlantic coastline, 156 kilometers (97 miles); Gabon, 1,656 kilometers (1,020 miles). **TERRITORIAL SEA LIMIT:** 200 miles.

16th century. By the end of the 17th century, however, this kingdom, as well as those of Loango and Anzico, all had grown weak.

The mouth of the Zaire River was discovered by Diogo Cão in 1484. By 1785, more than 100 French ships annually sailed up the coast trading primarily slaves

Photo credit: International Labour Office

A young child stands at his desk learning his lessons.

and ivory. The Congress of Berlin (1885) gave formal recognition to French claims to the region.

By 1910, Gabon, Middle Congo, and Ubangi-Shari (including Chad) constituted French Equatorial Africa, all under a governor general at Brazzaville. In World War II, French Equatorial Africa joined the Free French movement and the Allied war effort against the Axis powers.

After the war, France promised reforms in French Africa. These reforms eventually led to independence and, on 28 November 1958, the Republic of the Congo was proclaimed. A constitution was adopted the

following year, and Fulbert Youlou was elected prime minister and president. Youlou resigned in 1963, following antigovernment rioting. The military took control of the government, and Alphonse Massamba-Debat was installed as an interim president. He was subsequently elected to a 5-year term. In 1964, relations were established with the former USSR and China, and Massamba-Debat then announced the establishment of a "scientific Socialist state" with one-party control.

However, political stability proved difficult to achieve. Between 1968 and 1979, the Congo had four different presidents, one of whom—Marien Ngouabi—survived seven coup attempts in seven years in office. On 5 February 1979, Denis Sassou-Nguesso became president. He was to hold power for 12 years. During his tenure, a 20-year treaty of friendship and cooperation was signed with the former USSR.

In 1990, a conference of the ruling party agreed to abandon its Marxist ideology and its monopoly of power. Sassou-Nguesso was stripped of his powers the following year, and in 1992 a multiparty government with Pascal Lissouba as president was elected. Strikes, violent civil unrest, and a changing coalition of opposition parties have threatened the new regime. Despite mediation by the Organization of African Unity (OAU) and new elections in 1993, fighting continued into 1994 as armed forces loyal to Lissouba battled independent partisan militias.

13 GOVERNMENT

On 15 March 1992, voters approved a new constitution which provided for a mixed presidential-parliamentary form of government after the French model. Executive authority is vested in a directly elected president, who appoints the prime minister and cabinet. There is also a 60-member Senate.

14 POLITICAL PARTIES

The 1991 National Conference led to an interim government and multiparty elections in 1992. Continual shifts in parties and in coalitions of parties have taken place since. The Pan-African Union for Social Development (UPADS) is currently the largest in the National Assembly and is the party of President Lissouba.

15 JUDICIAL SYSTEM

Judicial bodies include a Supreme Court (appointed by the president), a court of appeals, a criminal court, regional and magistrate's courts, labor courts, and courts of common law, where local chiefs apply traditional laws and customs.

16 ARMED FORCES

In 1993, the Congo had an army of 10,000 personnel, a navy of 350, and an air force of 500.

17 ECONOMY

The Congo's economy is built on its petroleum resources, transport services, and agriculture. After several prosperous years in the early 1980s, the price of oil declined and cast the Congolese economy into the financial turmoil that has yet to

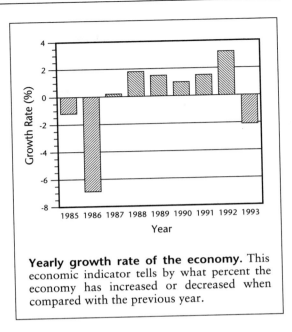

Yearly growth rate of the economy. This economic indicator tells by what percent the economy has increased or decreased when compared with the previous year.

stabilize. The country considered state socialist approaches to its economy before embarking on market-style reforms in 1989.

18 INCOME

In 1992 the Congo's gross national product (GNP) was $2,502 million at current prices, or about $950 per person.

19 INDUSTRY

Until recently, many industries were partially or completely nationalized (converted from private to governmental ownership and control). The largest industries are food processing, including beverages and tobacco, followed by chemicals and petroleum products, woodworking, metalworking and electrical industries,

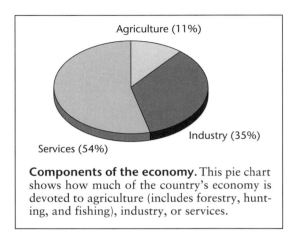

Components of the economy. This pie chart shows how much of the country's economy is devoted to agriculture (includes forestry, hunting, and fishing), industry, or services.

Agriculture (11%)

Industry (35%)

Services (54%)

nonmetallic mineral products, paper and cardboard, and textiles.

20 LABOR

There were about 750,000 economically active people in 1985, the most recent year reported. Almost half of all salaried employees work for the government. The Confederation of Congolese Syndicates is the only trade union organization.

21 AGRICULTURE

In 1991, total arable (fit for cultivation) land was only 169,000 hectares (417,600 acres), or only 0.4% of the total land area. Agricultural activity is concentrated in the south, especially in the Niari River Valley. Main crops for local consumption are manioc, plantains, yams, rice, bananas, sugarcane, tobacco, peanuts, and corn. In 1992, 70% of food requirements were imported.

Export crops are coffee, cocoa, and palm oil; in 1992, 1,000 tons of coffee and 2,000 tons of cocoa were produced. Palm

trees are under the management of a state-owned company. Commercial production of oil from palm kernels fell from 4,935 tons in 1961 to 510 tons in 1992.

22 DOMESTICATED ANIMALS

Animal husbandry has high government priority, and production is steadily increasing. In 1992 there were 385,000 sheep and goats, 55,000 hogs, 69,000 head of cattle, and 2 million chickens.

23 FISHING

Most fishing is carried on along the coast for local consumption. The catch rose from 14,939 tons in 1970 to 45,577 tons in 1991, more than 40% of it from saltwater fishing.

24 FORESTRY

Congolese forests cover some 21.1 million hectares (52.1 million acres), or over three-fifths of the total area of the country. Total production of roundwood was estimated at about 3,760,000 cubic meters in 1991. Okoumé, sapele, sipo, tiama, moaki, and nioré were the main species cut.

25 MINING

Mining, begun in the Congo in 1905, is presently the most important sector of the economy. In addition to petroleum and natural gas, mineral deposits include bauxite, potassium, phosphate, gold, limestone, lead, zinc, copper, and iron. Potash was the main mining product before the rapid growth of oil. Gold, mined in the Mayomb Mountains, reached 158 kilograms in 1967 but fell to 12 kilograms in 1991.

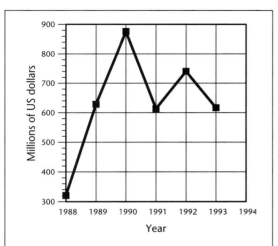

Yearly balance of trade measured in millions of US dollars. The balance of trade is the difference between what a country sells to other countries (its exports) and what it buys (its imports). If a country imports more than it exports, it has a negative balance of trade (a trade deficit). If exports exceed imports, there is a positive balance of trade (a trade surplus).

26 FOREIGN TRADE

The Congo's foreign trade is led by its exports of petroleum products. Imports include food, beverages, and tobacco.

The US takes almost 46% of Congo's exports, followed by France, Spain, Italy, Belgium, Germany, and Portugal. France accounts for 55% of Congo's imports.

27 ENERGY AND POWER

Production of electricity rose from 29 million kilowatt hours in 1960 to 482 million kilowatt hours in 1991, over 98% hydroelectric. Another 65 million kilowatt hours were imported from Zaire. The 1992 petroleum output was 180,000 barrels per day (about 8.8 million tons total), up 17.9% from 1991. Natural gas production was 368 million cubic meters in 1991.

28 SOCIAL DEVELOPMENT

Since 1 July 1956, family allowances have been paid to all salaried workers. Contributions are made by employers at a fixed percentage of the employee's wage. Other payments include a pension scheme, prenatal allowances, a lump sum payable at the birth of each of the first three children, and, if the mother is employed, a recuperation allowance for 14 weeks.

29 HEALTH

In 1992, 83% of the population had access to health care services. A local disease control service conducts vaccination and inoculation campaigns. All medicine, antibiotic, and vaccine imports must be authorized by the Ministry of Health. From 1988 to 1991, only 38% of inhabitants had access to safe water. The average life expectancy is 51 years.

30 HOUSING

As of 1984, 88.3% of all housing units were private houses.

31 EDUCATION

All private schools were taken over by the government in 1965. Education is compulsory between the ages of 6 and 16. Primary schooling lasts for six years and secondary for seven years. The National University, which opened in Brazzaville in 1971, was later renamed Marien Ngouabi University.

Selected Social Indicators

These statistics are estimates for the period 1988 to 1993. For comparison purposes, data for the United States and averages for low-income countries and high-income countries are also given.

Indicator	Congo	Low-income countries	High-income countries	United States
Per capita gross national product†	**$950**	$380	$23,680	$24,740
Population growth rate	**3.1%**	1.9%	0.6%	1.0%
Population growth rate in urban areas	**5.0%**	3.9%	0.8%	1.3%
Population per square kilometer of land	**6.93**	78	25	26
Life expectancy in years	**51**	62	77	76
Number of people per physician	**8,411**	>3,300	453	419
Number of pupils per teacher (primary school)	**67**	39	<18	20
Illiteracy rate (15 years and older)	**43%**	41%	<5%	<3%
Energy consumed per capita (kg of oil equivalent)	**165**	364	5,203	7,918

† The gross national product (GNP) is the total dollar value of all goods and services produced by a country in a year. The per capita GNP is calculated by dividing a country's GNP by its population. The World Bank defines low-income countries as those with a per capita GNP of $695 or less. High-income countries have a per capita GNP of $8,626 or more. Less than 14% of the world's 5.5 billion people live in high-income countries, while almost 60% live in low-income countries.   > = greater than   < = less than

Sources: World Bank, *Social Indicators of Development 1995,* Baltimore: Johns Hopkins University Press, 1995. Central Intelligence Agency, *World Fact Book,* Washington, D.C.: Government Printing Office, 1994.

32 MEDIA

In 1991 there were two daily newspapers: *Journal officiel de la République du Congo* and *Mweti*, both published in Brazzaville. National and international communications are state-owned and state-operated. Radio Brazzaville broadcasts in French and local languages. In 1991 there were 260,000 radios. In 1991 there were 14,000 receiving sets. The Congo had 25,799 telephones in service in 1991.

33 TOURISM AND RECREATION

Reforms and restructuring have enhanced the Congo's potential for tourism (especially ecotourism) depending on attraction of investment capital. In 1990, about 30,786 tourists stayed at hotels and inns, 55% from Europe and 35% from Africa.

34 FAMOUS CONGOLESE

Some well-known Congolese figures are Abbé Fulbert Youlou (1917–72), a former Roman Catholic priest who served as president from 1960 to 1963, as well as mayor of Brazzaville.

35 BIBLIOGRAPHY

Allen, Chris, Michael S. Radu, and Keith Somerville. *Benin, The Congo, and Burkina Faso.* New York: Pinter, 1989.

Chadwick, Douglas. "Ndoki—Last Place on Earth." *National Geographic,* July 1995, 2–45.

Fegley, Randall. *The Congo.* Santa Barbara, Calif.: Clio, 1993.

COSTA RICA

Republic of Costa Rica
República de Costa Rica

CAPITAL: San José.

FLAG: The national flag consists of five horizontal stripes of blue, white, red, white, and blue, the center stripe being wider than the others.

ANTHEM: *Himno Nacional,* beginning "Noble patria, tu hermosa bandera" ("Noble native land, your beautiful flag").

MONETARY UNIT: The colón (c) is a paper currency of 100 céntimos. There are coins of 1, 5, 10, 25, and 50 céntimos and of 1, 2, 5, 10, and 20 colones, and notes of 5, 10, 20, 50, 100, 500, and 1,000 colones. c1 = $0.0065 (or $1 = c153.97).

WEIGHTS AND MEASURES: The metric system is the legal standard, but local measures also are used.

HOLIDAYS: New Year's Day and Solemnity of Mary, 1 January; Day of St. Joseph (Costa Rica's patron saint), 19 March; Anniversary of the Battle of Rivas, 11 April; Labor Day, 1 May; Day of St. Peter and St. Paul, 29 June; Anniversary of the Annexation of Guanacaste, 25 July; Feast of Our Lady of the Angels, 2 August; Assumption (Mother's Day), 15 August; Independence Day, 15 September; Columbus Day, 12 October; Immaculate Conception, 8 December; Abolition of Armed Forces Day, 1 December; Christmas, 25 December. Movable religious holidays include Holy Thursday, Good Friday, Holy Saturday, and Corpus Christi.

TIME: 6 AM = noon GMT.

1 LOCATION AND SIZE

The third-smallest country in Central America, Costa Rica has an area of 51,100 square kilometers (19,730 square miles), including some small islands. The area occupied by Costa Rica is slightly smaller than the state of Virginia. Costa Rica's total boundary length is 1,929 kilometers (1,199 miles). Its capital city, San José, is located in the center of the country.

2 TOPOGRAPHY

The central highlands extend from northwest to southeast, reaching elevations of more than 3,660 meters (12,000 feet) south of San José. Half the population, the centers of culture and government, four of the six main cities, and the bulk of the coffee industry are found in this area. The Atlantic and Pacific coastal lowlands are low, swampy, and heavily forested. Fifteen small rivers drain Costa Rica.

3 CLIMATE

There are three climatic zones. The torrid zone, which includes the coastal and northern plains to an altitude of 900 meters (3,000 feet), is characterized by heavy rains and a temperature range of

Photo credit: Mary A. Dempsey
Isolated beaches at Corcovado Reserve, Costa Rica.

25–38°C (77–100°F). The temperate zone, including the central valleys and plateaus, has a temperature range of 15–25°C (59–77°F). The cold zone, comprising areas higher than 1,800 meters (6,000 feet), has a temperature range of 5–15°C (41–59°F). The average annual rainfall for the country is more than 250 centimeters (100 inches).

4 PLANTS AND ANIMALS

Trees found in the dense tropical forests of the coastal lowlands include ebony, balsa, mahogany, oak, laurel, campana, and cedar. Plant life is abundant; the country has more than 1,000 species of orchids.

Jaguar, deer, puma, and different varieties of monkeys are found in Costa Rica. There are over 790 species of birds and 130 species of snakes and frogs.

5 ENVIRONMENT

Nearly all of Costa Rica was once covered by forests, but over half the country's virgin rainforest has been lost to agriculture. The result has been soil erosion and loss of fertility. In addition, the soil has been contaminated by fertilizers and pesticides. Costa Rica's use of pesticides is greater than that of all other Central American nations combined. Costa Rica contributes 0.1% of the world's total gas emissions and has the highest per person emissions rate in North America.

Costa Rica's national park system is among the most extensive and well developed in Latin America. As of 1986, the system included 12 parks, six nature reserves, four recreation areas, and the International Peace Park, established jointly by Costa Rica and Panama on their common border. As of 1994, ten mammal species, 14 species of birds, two types of reptiles, and 418 plant species are considered endangered.

6 POPULATION

Costa Rica's population according to the 1984 census was 2,416,809. The 1994 estimate was 3,099,000. The United Nations projected population for the year 2000 was 3,798,000. Population density was estimated at 62 persons per square kilometer (158 per square mile) in 1992. The principal city is San José, the capital,

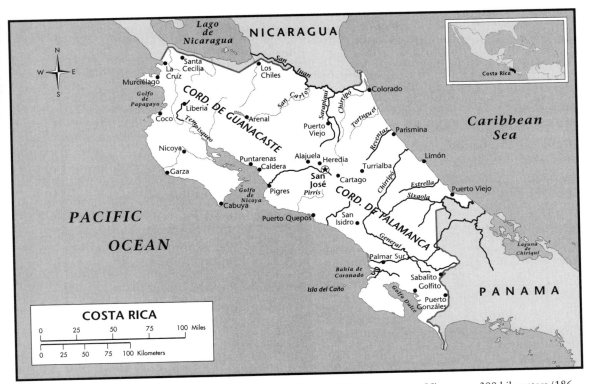

LOCATION: 8°2′26″ to 11°13′12″N; 82°33′48″ to 85°57′57″W. **BOUNDARY LENGTHS:** Nicaragua, 300 kilometers (186 miles); Caribbean coastline, 212 kilometers (132 miles); Panama, 363 kilometers (226 miles); Pacific coastline, 1,016 kilometers (631 miles). **TERRITORIAL SEA LIMIT:** 12 miles.

which had an estimated population of 296,625 in 1991.

7 MIGRATION

Large numbers of Nicaraguans migrate seasonally to Costa Rica seeking employment opportunities. By 1986, approximately 200,000 refugees from Guatemala, El Salvador, and Nicaragua were in Costa Rica. This number had fallen to 113,500 by the end of 1992.

8 ETHNIC GROUPS

The population is fairly homogeneous, primarily of European (mainly Spanish) descent, with a small mestizo (mixed white and Amerindian) minority (about 7%). The remainder are blacks (3%), East Asians (2%), and Amerindians (1%). The blacks for the most part are of Jamaican origin or descent. Some mulattoes (mixed black and white) live mainly in the Limón port area.

9 LANGUAGES

Spanish is the national language, but English is also spoken among the middle class. Descendants of Jamaican blacks speak an English dialect.

10 RELIGIONS

Roman Catholicism is the official religion of the state, but the constitution guarantees religious freedom. Some 91.6% of the population in 1993 was Roman Catholic. Approximately 40,000 Protestants and 2,000 Jews lived in Costa Rica in 1990. Small numbers of Baha'is and Buddhists are also present.

11 TRANSPORTATION

San José is linked to both coasts by railroad and by highway. As of 1991 there were 7,030 kilometers (4,368 miles) of paved roads. Motor vehicle registrations in 1991 included 168,814 passenger automobiles and 95,066 commercial vehicles. Of the three railroad lines, the Atlantic Railway between Limón and San José, and the government-owned Pacific Electric Railway between San José and Puntarenas are interconnected.

Principal ports are Limón on the Caribbean Sea and Puntarenas, Caldera, and Golfito on the Pacific. As of 1991, Costa Rica had only one merchant vessel of more than 1,000 gross registered tons. River traffic is not significant.

Líneas Aéreas Costarricenses, S.A. (LACSA), the national airline, provides domestic and international services centered at Juan Santamaria International Airport near San José. In 1992, LACSA carried 534,500 passengers.

12 HISTORY

There were about 25,000 Amerindians in the region when Columbus landed in 1502. He named the area Costa Rica

Photo credit: Mary A. Dempsey

Pre-Hispanic "balls" used by Costa Rican Indians.

("rich coast"), probably because he saw gold ornaments on some of the Indians. Costa Rica was organized as a province by the Spanish in 1540 and was eventually placed under the provincial administration in Guatemala. Cartago, the colonial capital, was founded in 1563.

When independence came to Central America in 1821, Costa Rica had fewer than 70,000 inhabitants. In the following year, it was absorbed into the short-lived Mexican Empire proclaimed by Agustín de Iturbide. Following the collapse of Iturbide's rule, Costa Rica became a member of the United Provinces of Central America in 1823, and the provincial capital of Costa Rica became San José.

The United Provinces fell apart in 1838, and in 1848, the Republic of Costa Rica was established. The new state was threatened by William Walker, a United States military adventurer who invaded Central America in 1855, but his troops were repelled in 1857, and in 1860 Walker was captured and executed. In 1871, General Tomás Guardia, a dictator, introduced the constitution that, though frequently modified, remained Costa Rica's basic law until 1949.

In the late 19th and early 20th centuries, there were a series of boundary disputes with Panama and Nicaragua, and Costa Rica annexed Guanacaste Province from Nicaragua. In World Wars I and II, Costa Rica was a United States ally, but did not take up arms.

Meanwhile, the success of coffee cultivation had encouraged rapid population growth and the beginnings of modern economic development. The completion of a coast-to-coast railroad played an important role in the nation's progress.

Costa Rica enjoyed political stability from the turn of the century until just after World War II. Between 1948 and 1949, there was a brief period of upheaval, when a dictatorship was imposed on the country by its outgoing president. José Figueres Ferrer, leader of a successful civilian uprising, restored democratic government under the legally elected president, Otilio Ulate Blanco. In 1949, a new constitution restored free elections and banned a standing army.

Figueres was elected president by an overwhelming majority in 1952 (with women voting for the first time), and under his leadership, Costa Rica was one of the most democratic and prosperous countries in Latin America. Costa Rica joined the Central American Common Market (CACM) in 1963. It has benefited from Central American economic cooperation, especially in the area of industrialization.

During the 1980s, Costa Ricans were confronted with a severe economic crisis and increasing political violence, including some terrorist activity in San José. The Monge government introduced a government program to aid economic recovery and avoided being drawn into the war in neighboring Nicaragua between the rebel "contras" and the Sandinista government. Costa Rica resisted pressure from the United States to support the contras and refused to accept United States aid toward the building of a military establishment.

In August 1987, a peace plan for Central America outlined by Costa Rican president Oscar Arias Sánchez was signed in Guatemala by Nicaragua, Guatemala, Costa Rica, El Salvador, and Honduras. Among the provisions were free elections and an eventual reduction in the armed forces in all countries; a guarantee of basic democratic freedoms in Nicaragua; a cease-fire by both Sandinistas and contras; and an end to outside aid to the contras. Arias won the Nobel Prize for peace later that year.

With the pressures of regional warfare and refugees eased, the Costa Rican economy improved. On 6 February 1994, José María Figueres Olsen, son of former president Figueres, was elected president of Costa Rica.

13 GOVERNMENT

Costa Rica is a republic organized under the constitution of 1949. A president, two vice-presidents, and a single-chamber congress (the Legislative Assembly) of 62 members (in 1987) are all directly elected for four-year terms. The cabinet and the president form the Council of Government. Voting is universal and compulsory for all persons of 18 years or more.

Costa Rica is divided into seven provinces, which are further divided into cantons and districts.

14 POLITICAL PARTIES

The largest political grouping is the PLN, a reformist party that has been the nation's leading party since its formation in 1948. The other major party is the more conservative Social Christian Unity Party (Partido Unidad Social Cristiana—PUSC), which, since World War II, has held the presidency only during 1978–82, and from 1990–94. There are also several minor parties.

15 JUDICIAL SYSTEM

The judiciary consists of justices of the peace, lower courts, labor courts, a court of cassation, two civil courts of appeal, two penal courts of appeal, and the Supreme Court, the highest court in the land. The Supreme Court is composed of 17 justices chosen for eight-year terms by the Legislative Assembly. The Supreme

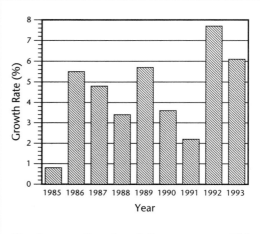

Yearly growth rate of the economy. This economic indicator tells by what percent the economy has increased or decreased when compared with the previous year.

Court, by a two-thirds majority, can declare legislative and executive acts unconstitutional.

16 ARMED FORCES

The 1949 constitution prohibits armed forces. A 4,300-member (in 1993) Civil Guard and a 3,200-member Rural Assistance Guard perform security and police functions. An antiterrorist battalion serves as the presidential guard. Small coast guard and air units (18 planes and helicopters) patrol the coast for revenue purposes. Security expenditures were $60 million in 1992 with no significant arms imports.

17 ECONOMY

As of 1994, Costa Ricans enjoyed the highest per person income in Central

America, although it has been slipping for the past two years. Agriculture continues to be the backbone of the economy. By the end of 1993, it accounted for 26% of total employment and roughly half of exports. The main crops are coffee, bananas and sugar. In recent years, cattle breeding and the production of tropical fruits and vegetables for export have gained in importance. Coffee prices have been rising steadily as of 1994, which will contribute positively to total agricultural earnings.

18 INCOME

From the period 1988–95, Costa Rica's gross national product (GNP) was $6,261 million, or $2,150 per person. For the period 1985–92 the average inflation rate was 18.1%, resulting in a real growth rate in GNP of 2.6% per person.

19 INDUSTRY

Costa Rica is one of the most industrialized countries in Central America, although industries are mostly small-scale and mainly involve assembling or finishing imported semifinished components. Larger-scale manufacturing includes chemical fertilizers, textiles, coffee and cocoa processing, chemicals, and plastics. In 1992, manufacturing advanced by 10.5%.

20 LABOR

In 1992, the labor force amounted to 1,087,000, or 34.1% of the total population. About half the total work force is concentrated in San José and Alajuela provinces. Of all nongovernmental jobs in 1992, industry accounted for 26.9%; agri-

Photo credit: Mary A. Dempsey

A shop at a cheese factory in Costa Rica.

culture, 24.1%; and services, 49%. Government employment grew to 169,371 in 1992. Unemployment was 4.1% in July 1992.

A labor code governs labor-management relations. Minimum wages are set for two-year periods by a mixed labor-management commission. Strikes in the public services are prohibited. About 15% of the total work force is unionized.

21 AGRICULTURE

In 1991, about 10.3% (529,000 hectares/ 1,307,000 acres) of the total land area was used for crop production, with 45.6% in use as permanent pasture. The principal

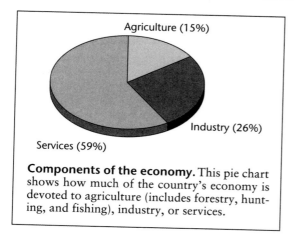

Agriculture (15%)

Industry (26%)

Services (59%)

Components of the economy. This pie chart shows how much of the country's economy is devoted to agriculture (includes forestry, hunting, and fishing), industry, or services.

cash crops are coffee, bananas, cocoa, and sugar. Coffee and bananas together accounted for 40% of exports in 1992, with values of $203 million and $485 million, respectively.

Crops produced mainly for domestic consumption include corn, rice, potatoes, beans, sisal, cotton, citrus fruits, pita (used to make hats, baskets, and mats), yucca, vegetables, pineapples and other fruits, tobacco, abaca (hemp), and vegetable oils (especially African and coconut palms).

Estimated crop production in 1992 (in tons) was sugarcane, 2,840,000; bananas, 1,633,000; rice, 209,000; coffee, 168,000; corn, 40,000; dry beans, 36,000; and cocoa, 2,000. In 1992, the value of agricultural output increased by 3% over that in 1991.

22 DOMESTICATED ANIMALS

About 46% of Costa Rica's total land area was devoted to raising livestock in the early 1990s. Recent improvements in ani-

mal husbandry have allowed the country to meet its own needs in this area, to provide a surplus for export, and to make cattle exports the third most important source of export earnings. Exports of beef were worth $44.2 million in 1992. In that year there were an estimated 1,707,000 head of cattle, 225,000 hogs, 114,000 horses, and 4 million chickens.

23 FISHING

Fish abound in Costa Rican waters, particularly in the Pacific Ocean, where 89% of the annual harvest is caught. Tuna, herring, and shrimp are the most valuable commercial fish. A small native fishing industry contributes to the domestic food supply and exports shark, mollusks, and live lobsters. In 1991, the total volume of fish landed was an estimated 17,905 tons.

24 FORESTRY

Costa Rica's forestland has declined rapidly from about 75% of the total land area in 1940 to 32% in 1991. Varieties of commercial woods include laurel, cedar, oak, quina, espavel, campana, cristobal, pochote, maca wood, cedro macho, cedar, and caoba (mahogany). Forest products include rubber, chicle, ipecac, roots, medicinal plants, seeds, and other plant products. Overall timber output increased to 4,201,000 cubic meters of roundwood cut in 1991, of which about half was used for fuel.

25 MINING

Mineral production in 1991 included iron ore, 65,000 tons; cement, 700,000 tons; common clay, 399,000 tons; limestone,

1,300,000 tons; and marine salt, 50,000 tons. Diatomite, lime, pumice, silver, sandstone, and sand and gravel were also mined in 1991. Gold-mining activity plunged in the early 1980s but recovered in 1985.

26 FOREIGN TRADE

The country's exports have increased moderately in recent years. In 1993, Costa Rica's total exports were estimated at $1,966 million. There is concern about the impact of North American Free Trade Agreement (NAFTA) on the country's exports to the United States. Nevertheless, the United States remained the country's main export destination in the first four months of 1994.

Costa Rica's main exports include bananas, coffee, beef, sugar, ornamental plants, melons, wood products, pineapples, fresh seafood, textiles, and footwear. After the United States, Costa Rica exports mainly to Germany, the Netherlands, the United Kingdom, Guatemala, and Japan.

At year's end 1993, total imports had increased by 11.2% to $2,737 million. Principal import items included petroleum, machinery and transportation equipment, consumer goods, food, paper products (carton), and chemicals. Costa Rica's major suppliers were the United States, Japan, Germany, and Guatemala.

27 ENERGY AND POWER

Costa Rica must import an overwhelming proportion of the petroleum it needs. Because of a scarcity of fuels, the nation

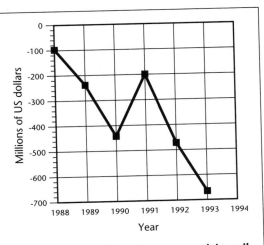

Yearly balance of trade measured in millions of US dollars. The balance of trade is the difference between what a country sells to other countries (its exports) and what it buys (its imports). If a country imports more than it exports, it has a negative balance of trade (a trade deficit). If exports exceed imports there is a positive balance of trade (a trade surplus).

depended on hydroelectric energy for about 85% of its light and power in 1991. Production of hydroelectricity totaled 3,647 million kilowatt hours in 1991.

28 SOCIAL DEVELOPMENT

The national Social Security Fund administers social insurance and pension programs. Most of the population is covered by these social services, which have been extended throughout the country and include workers' compensation and family assistance benefits. The social security program is compulsory for all employees under 65 years of age. The program, however, suffered as a result of the fiscal crisis

Selected Social Indicators

These statistics are estimates for the period 1988 to 1993. For comparison purposes, data for the United States and averages for low-income countries and high-income countries are also given.

Indicator	Costa Rica	Low-income countries	High-income countries	United States
Per capita gross national product†	$2,150	$380	$23,680	$24,740
Population growth rate	2.6%	1.9%	0.6%	1.0%
Population growth rate in urban areas	3.7%	3.9%	0.8%	1.3%
Population per square kilometer of land	62	78	25	26
Life expectancy in years	76	62	77	76
Number of people per physician	1,011	>3,300	453	419
Number of pupils per teacher (primary school)	32	39	<18	20
Illiteracy rate (15 years and older)	7%	41%	<5%	<3%
Energy consumed per capita (kg of oil equivalent)	558	364	5,203	7,918

† The gross national product (GNP) is the total dollar value of all goods and services produced by a country in a year. The per capita GNP is calculated by dividing a country's GNP by its population. The World Bank defines low-income countries as those with a per capita GNP of $695 or less. High-income countries have a per capita GNP of $8,626 or more. Less than 14% of the world's 5.5 billion people live in high-income countries, while almost 60% live in low-income countries.

> = greater than   < = less than

Sources: World Bank, *Social Indicators of Development 1995,* Baltimore: Johns Hopkins University Press, 1995. Central Intelligence Agency, *World Fact Book,* Washington, D.C.: Government Printing Office, 1994.

of the 1980s and was overtaxed by an increase in the number of refugees.

A 1990 law reinforces existing provisions barring sex discrimination and improves women's property rights. Women and men are usually paid equally for equal work.

29 HEALTH

About 95% of the nation's hospital beds are in urban areas. From the period 1988 to 1993, Costa Rica had one physician per 1,011 people. Health services for the rural population are generally inadequate, and the refugee problem has severely taxed urban services. Between 1985 and 1992, it was estimated that 80% of the population had access to health care services.

Health standards have steadily improved in Costa Rica. During the 1980s, the greatest health problem was protein-calorie malnutrition, particularly among infants and children. Diseases of the circulatory system are the leading cause of death. During 1992, life expectancy at birth was an average of 76 years.

30 HOUSING

Sources for housing mortgages include private funds, the Central Bank, the Social

Security Fund, and the national banking system. The National Institute of Housing and Urban Affairs, established in 1954, administers a national low-cost housing program. As of 1980, 30% of all housing had no electricity.

31 EDUCATION

Costa Rica has one of the most literate populations in Latin America; in 1990, adult literacy was 93% according to United Nations Educational, Scientific and Cultural Organization (UNESCO). Nearly one-fifth of the government's expenditure is on education. Primary education lasts for six years followed by three years of secondary education. This again is followed by a two-year highly specialized course. Primary and secondary education is free, and primary-school attendance is compulsory. In 1984, enrollment in primary schools was 353,958, with 12,223 teachers; in secondary schools, enrollment was 148,032 students.

The country has five universities, including an open university. The University of Costa Rica (founded in 1843) is supported by the government and enrolls about 28,000 students. The Open University, in San José, operates 28 regional centers for all students who apply.

32 MEDIA

In 1993 there were over 300,000 telephones in use. There are 71 AM and no FM radio stations and 18 TV stations in Costa Rica. In 1991 there were about 800,000 radios and 435,000 television sets.

Photo credit: Mary A. Dempsey

A schoolboy in Costa Rica whose smile suggests he is on his way home.

Freedom of the press is guaranteed by the constitution and observed in practice. About 120 newspapers, bulletins, and periodicals are issued. There are four daily newspapers, all published in San José. These papers (with 1991 daily circulations) are *La Nación* (97,000); *La Prensa Libre* (63,000 each edition); *La República* (66,000); and *Extra* (95,000).

33 TOURISM AND RECREATION

In 1991, Costa Rica received 504,649 tourists, of whom 425,505 were from the Americas and 69,087 from Europe. Revenues from tourism reached US$331 million. There were 7,196 hotel rooms with a 67.9% occupancy rate.

Popular tourist sights in San José are the National Museum, National Theater, and the Central Bank's gold exhibition. Other attractions include the Irazú and Poás volcanoes, brief jungle excursions, and the Pacific beaches.

Popular recreations are bird-watching, mountain climbing, swimming, water skiing, and deep-sea fishing. Football (soccer) is the national sport, and there are matches every Sunday morning in San José from May through October. Horseback riding is widely available.

34 FAMOUS COSTA RICANS

José María Castro was Costa Rica's first president (1847–49, 1866–68). Juan Rafael Mora Porras, the second president of the republic (1849–59), successfully defended the country against the invasion of United States military adventurer William Walker.

In 1871, General Tomás Guardia (1832–82) introduced the constitution that remained in force until 1949. José Figueres Ferrer (b.1906), president during 1953–58 and 1970–74, is regarded as the father of the present constitution. Oscar Arias Sánchez (b.1940), president since 1986, won the Nobel Prize for peace in 1987 for his plan to bring peace to Central America.

Ricardo Fernández Guardia (1867–1950) is regarded as Costa Rica's greatest historian. Joaquín García Monge (1881–1958) founded the literary review *Repertorio Americano*.

35 BIBLIOGRAPHY

American University. *Area Handbook for Costa Rica.* Washington, D.C.: Government Printing Office, 1970.

Barry, Tom. *Costa Rica: A Country Guide.* Albuquerque, N.Mex.: Inter-Hemisphere Education Resource Center, 1990.

Costa Rica in Pictures. Minneapolis: Lerner, 1987.

Creedman, Theodore S. *Historical Dictionary of Costa Rica, 2nd ed.* Metuchen, N.J.: Scarecrow Press, 1991.

Stansifer, Charles L. *Costa Rica.* Oxford, England; Santa Barbara, Calif.: Clio Press, 1991.

CÔTE D'IVOIRE

Republic of Côte d'Ivoire
République de Côte d'Ivoire

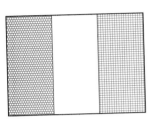

CAPITAL: Yamoussoukro.

FLAG: The flag is a tricolor of orange, white, and green vertical stripes.

ANTHEM: *L'Abidjanaise,* beginning: "Greetings, O land of hope."

MONETARY UNIT: The Communauté Financière Africaine franc (CFA Fr) is the national currency. There are coins of 1, 2, 5, 10, 25, 50, 100, and 500 CFA francs, and notes of 50, 100, 500, 1,000, 5,000, and 10,000 CFA francs. CFA Fr1 = $0.0018 (or $1 = CFA Fr571).

WEIGHTS AND MEASURES: The metric system is the legal standard.

HOLIDAYS: New Year's Day, 1 January; Labor Day, 1 May; Assumption, 15 August; All Saints' Day, 1 November; Independence Day, 7 December; Christmas, 25 December. Movable religious holidays include Good Friday, Easter Monday, Ascension, Pentecost Monday, 'Id al-Fitr, and 'Id al-'Adha'.

TIME: GMT.

1 LOCATION AND SIZE

The Republic of Côte d'Ivoire, on the south coast of the western bulge of Africa, has an area of 322,460 square kilometers (124,502 square miles). Comparatively, the area occupied by Côte d'Ivoire is slightly larger than the state of New Mexico. In 1983, Côte d'Ivoire's capital was moved to Yamoussoukro, about 225 kilometers (140 miles) northwest of the former capital, Abidjan, in the southcentral part of the country. However, the move is not complete, and Abidjan remains the nation's administrative center.

2 TOPOGRAPHY

Except for the Guinea Highlands (in the northwest, from Man to Odienné), which have peaks of over 1,000 meters (3,280 feet), reaching a high point of 1,302 meters (4,272 feet), the greater part of Côte d'Ivoire is a vast plateau, tilted gently toward the Atlantic.

3 CLIMATE

The greatest annual rainfall, 198 centimeters (78 inches), is along the coast and in the southwest. The coastal region has a long dry season from December to mid-May, followed by heavy rains from mid-May to mid-July, a short dry season from mid-July to October, and lighter rains in October and November. Farther north, there is only one wet and one dry season, with rainfall heaviest in summer.

4 PLANTS AND ANIMALS

The southern Côte d'Ivoire forest is a typical rainforest. Farther north, the rainforest gives way to scattered stands of deciduous trees, and mahogany is widespread. Still farther north, oil palm, acacia, breadfruit, and baobab characterize the transition to true savanna, where shea nut and traveler's palm are common. The jackal, hyena, panther, elephant, hippopotamus, numerous monkeys, and many other mammals are widely distributed.

5 ENVIRONMENT

Most of Côte d'Ivoire's forests, once the largest in West Africa, have been cut down by the timber industry, with only slight attempts at reforestation. The land is also affected by climate changes, including decreased rainfall. Water pollution is a significant environmental problem in Côte d'Ivoire due to chemical waste from agricultural, industrial, and mining sources. The country's lack of sanitation facilities also contributes to the pollution problem.

6 POPULATION

The 1988 census counted a population of 10,815,694; an estimate for mid-1994 was 14,566,749. A total of 17,065,000 was forecasted for the year 2000. Movement to the cities has been a problem in recent decades. The population of Abidjan, the former capital, was estimated at 2,751,000 for 1995.

7 MIGRATION

Flourishing economic activity in Côte d'Ivoire has attracted large numbers of workers from neighboring countries. In 1988, they constituted 28% of the national total. The civil war in Liberia created a refugee population in Côte d'Ivoire that numbered 173,700 at the end of 1992.

8 ETHNIC GROUPS

The ethnic composition of Côte d'Ivoire is complex, and accurate statistics are not available. The primary groups are the Baulé, and the Mandingo, or Malinké.

9 LANGUAGES

The official language is French. Of the more than 60 African languages spoken by different ethnic groups, the most important are Agni and Baulé; the Kru languages; the Sénoufo languages; and the Mandé languages.

10 RELIGIONS

The state is secular, and the constitution provides for religious freedom. As of 1993, an estimated 60% of the inhabitants followed traditional animist religions. Animism teaches that spirits inhabit inanimate objects. Muslims accounted for about 20% of the population, and the remaining 20% were Christians, with 1,585,000 belonging to the Roman Catholic Church.

11 TRANSPORTATION

Côte d'Ivoire has one of the best-developed and best-maintained transportation systems in Africa. In 1991, Côte d'Ivoire had 46,600 kilometers of roads, of which 8% were paved. Harbor activity is concentrated at Abidjan (West Africa's largest container port), which has facilities that include a fishing port and equipment for handling containers. San Pedro is a deepwater port that began operations in 1971. In 1991 Abidjan's international airport handled 13,700 commercial planes.

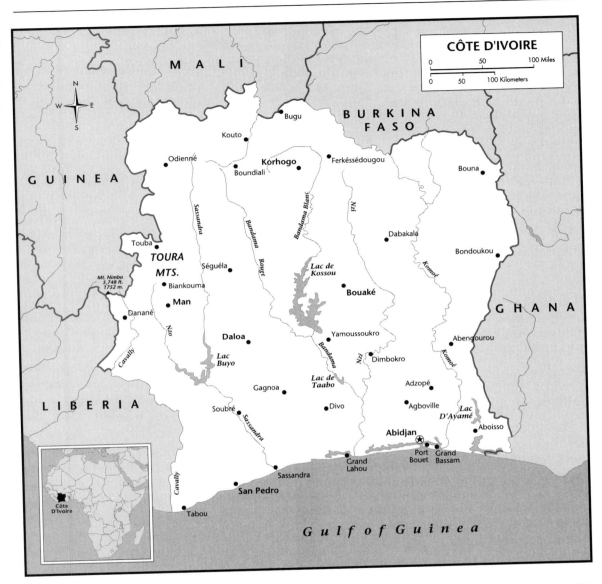

LOCATION: 2°30′ to 7°30′W; 4°20′ to 10°50′N. **BOUNDARY LENGTHS:** Mali, 515 kilometers (320 miles); Burkina Faso, 531 kilometers (330 miles); Ghana, 668 kilometers (415 miles); Gulf of Guinea coastline, 507 kilometers (315 miles); Liberia, 716 kilometers (445 miles); Guinea, 605 kilometers (376 miles); Mali, 515 kilometers (320 miles). **TERRITORIAL SEA LIMIT:** 12 miles.

[12] HISTORY

Little is known of the early history of the area now called Côte d'Ivoire. Most of its peoples entered the country in comparatively recent times, mostly from the northwest and the east.

Modern European acquaintance with the west coast of Africa began with Portuguese discoveries of the 15th century, culminating in the discovery of the route to India around the Cape of Good Hope in 1488, and the establishment of trading posts along the Senegal coast and the Gulf of Guinea. The Portuguese and Spanish were soon followed by the Dutch and English. Gold, ivory, ostrich feathers, gum arabic, and pepper were the first trading commodities. However, slaves became the major trading commodity. French activity in what is now Côte d'Ivoire began in 1687, when missionaries landed at Assinié.

After the Franco-Prussian War of 1870, the French controled not only Côte d'Ivoire but also Upper Volta (modern Burkina Faso), Sudan, and Niger.

French control of Côte d'Ivoire was, however, far from secured. Much of the region remained unexplored, and administrative control had still to be organized with the chiefs who had concluded treaties with the French. In addition, hostile chiefs still had to be subdued. The French prevailed and French rule was finally established in Côte d'Ivoire on the eve of World War I.

During World War I, Côte d'Ivoire became a considerable producer of cocoa, coffee, mahogany, and other tropical products. The railroad, begun in 1904, did not reach the northern part of the colony until 1925. The wharf at Grand Bassam (opened 1901) and that at Port Bouet (opened 1932) remained the principal ports until the cutting of the Ébrié Lagoon in 1950 and the opening of the deepwater port of Abidjan in 1954.

During World War II, Côte d'Ivoire, like the rest of French West Africa, remained under control of France's Vichy government. (The Vichy government was controlled by the Germans, who had invaded France and taken control of the country.) In 1941, the king of Bondoukou and thousands of his people made their way into the Gold Coast to join General Charles de Gaulle's Free French resistance forces. At the end of the war, Côte d'Ivoire was established as an overseas territory under the 1946 French constitution.

Independence

On 7 August 1960, the Republic of Côte d'Ivoire proclaimed its complete independence from France and a new constitution providing for a presidential system was adopted. In elections held on 27 November, Félix Houphouët-Boigny was unanimously elected the country's first president.

Outbreaks of unrest plagued the Houphouët-Boigny government during the late 1960s and early 1970s. However, throughout this period, the government worked to win over new adherents. By the end of the 1970s, Houphouët-Boigny was firmly in control, and Côte d'Ivoire

Soumarhoro Mekinhui, the man in the center, sits in the courtyard of his home with his sister on his right, wearing the white cloth, and 20 of his 24 children. Although polygamy was banned in Côte d'Ivoire more than 20 years ago, it persists among portions of the population. Mekinhui, 64, has had four wives.

became one of black Africa's most prosperous nations. Houphouët-Boigny continued to control the government and won an unopposed sixth term as president in October 1985. He reportedly received 100% of the vote in a turnout of over 99% of the eligible voters. These results were disputed, for in the following month, fewer than 30% turned out for the National Assembly elections.

In 1990, Côte d'Ivoire entered a new political era as months of prodemocracy demonstrations and labor unrest led to the legalization of opposition parties, previously banned. The first multiparty presidential and legislative elections were held, and Houphouët-Boigny was reelected as president with 81% of the vote. Again, outside observers saw the elections as less than free and fair.

Early in 1992, the president rejected the findings of his own investigative commission, which had found army chief of staff General Robert Guei responsible for the shootings of students at Yopougon University in May 1991. Upon doing so, Houphouët-Boigny left for a four-month "private visit" to France. Rioting followed a mass demonstration in February 1992, and the government used this as a pretext to jail opposition leaders. In protest, the FPI withdrew from the National Assembly, leaving it exclusively in the control of the PDCI. Houphouët-Boigny continued to manage affairs from Paris. He returned in June to release the opposition leaders as part of an amnesty that also shielded the soldiers.

After Houphouët-Boigny's death in 1993, power was transferred smoothly to Henri Konan Bédíe.

13 GOVERNMENT

The unicameral (consisting of a single legislative body) National Assembly consists of 175 members, elected by direct voting for a five-year term in the same year as the president. The country had a one-party system until May 1990, when opposition parties were allowed. The post of prime minister was created after the November 1990 elections.

14 POLITICAL PARTIES

From 1959 to 1990, the only political party was the Democratic Party of Côte d'Ivoire, headed by Félix Houphouët-Boigny. In May 1990, opposition parties were legalized and contested the 1990 elections. Among the two dozen parties registered are the Ivoirian Popular Front (FPI), the Ivoirian Workers' Party (PIT), the Ivoirian Socialist Party (PSI), and the Ivoirian Human Rights League. In April 1994, some 19 parties formed a center-left opposition alliance, the Groupement pour la Solidarité (GPS).

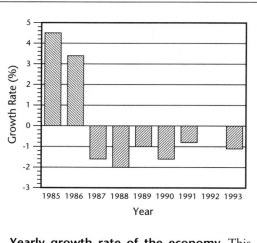

Yearly growth rate of the economy. This economic indicator tells by what percent the economy has increased or decreased when compared with the previous year.

15 JUDICIAL SYSTEM

The Supreme Court has four chambers—constitutional, judicial, administrative, and financial. Appeals courts sit at Abidjan and Bouaké. There are 28 courts of first instance (magistrates' courts). The High Court of Justice, composed of members elected from and by the National Assembly, has the power to impeach any government official, including the president.

16 ARMED FORCES

Côte d'Ivoire's armed forces numbered 7,100 in 1993: 5,500 in the army, including three infantry battalions and one mechanized battalion; 700 in the navy; and 900 in the air force. There is also a paramilitary force of about 7,800. In 1993 the air force had 28 (6 combat) aircraft and helicopters.

17 ECONOMY

Côte d'Ivoire's wealth rests essentially on the production for export of coffee, cocoa, cotton, and tropical woods. The nation is the world's sixth-largest producer of coffee and the world's largest producer of cocoa; bananas, palm oil, and pineapples are other products of importance. Industrial activity, consisting chiefly of processing industries, is well developed. During the mid-1980s, Côte d'Ivoire began experiencing an economic slowdown because of falling export prices, rising import prices, and heavy debt-service costs as a result of borrowing during the boom years.

18 INCOME

In 1992 Côte d'Ivoire's gross national product (GNP) was $8,655 million at current prices, or about $630 per person. For the period 1985–92, the average inflation rate was −2.1%, resulting in a real growth rate in GNP of −5.7% per person.

19 INDUSTRY

Côte d'Ivoire's industrial activity is substantial by African standards. The development of processing industries, especially in the Abidjan region, has been significant. Numerous thriving industries have been built up in the forest zone of the southern coastal region. These include palm oil mills, soap factories, a flour mill, fruit canning factories, a tuna canning factory, breweries, beer and soft drink plants, rubber processing plants, sugar mills, cotton

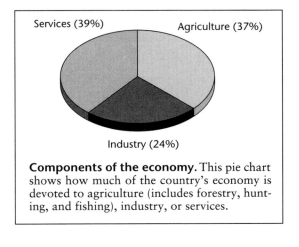

Components of the economy. This pie chart shows how much of the country's economy is devoted to agriculture (includes forestry, hunting, and fishing), industry, or services.

ginning plants, and coffee- and cocoa-bean processing plants.

20 LABOR

Over 80% of the labor force of about 4.2 million is engaged in agriculture, livestock raising, forestry, or fishing, while industry employs only about 8%.

21 AGRICULTURE

Agriculture provides a living for about 75% of Ivoirians and accounts for about one-half of the country's sizable export earnings. Only 11.6% of the land is cultivated, but farming is intensive and efficiently organized.

The main food crops (with their production in tons) are yams, 2,450,000; manioc, 1,350,000; plantains, 1,170,000; rice, 700,000; and corn, 425,000. Sweet potatoes, peanuts, and in the northern districts, millet, sorghum, and hungry rice (fonio) are also grown. During the 1970s the government sought to reduce or eliminate rice imports, but in 1992, about 380,000 tons were imported.

Coffee and cocoa remain the principal cash crops and together provide about 45% of the country's export earnings. Côte d'Ivoire is Africa's leading producer of coffee. Total coffee production in 1992 was 240,000 tons. Cocoa production has increased markedly since the early 1970s; it is now the nation's leading cash crop, and Côte d'Ivoire is the world's leading producer, accounting for 30% of world production in 1992. Output rose to a record 804,000 tons in 1991.

22 DOMESTICATED ANIMALS

Much of the country lies within tsetse-infested areas, and cattle are therefore concentrated in the more northerly districts. In 1992 there were an estimated 1,183,000 head of cattle (compared with 383,000 in 1968), 919,000 goats, 1,200,000 sheep, and 382,000 hogs. There are 26 million chickens; about 15,800 tons of eggs were produced in 1992.

23 FISHING

There are fish hatcheries in Bouaké, and Korhogo. Commercial fishing for tuna is carried on in the Gulf of Guinea; sardines are also caught in quantity. The total catch was 85,182 tons in 1991, almost 75% in Atlantic waters.

24 FORESTRY

At one time, mahogany was the only wood utilized, but now more than 25 different types of wood are used commer-

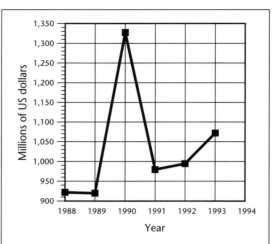

Yearly balance of trade measured in millions of US dollars. The balance of trade is the difference between what a country sells to other countries (its exports) and what it buys (its imports). If a country imports more than it exports, it has a negative balance of trade (a trade deficit). If exports exceed imports there is a positive balance of trade (a trade surplus).

cially. Total 1991 timber production was 13,061,000 cubic meters.

25 MINING

Diamond output declined from 549,000 carats in 1961 to only 15,000 carats in 1991. Gold production went from 20 kilograms in 1990 to 1,100 kilograms in 1991. Copper, titanium, chromite, bauxite, and asphalt are among the known minerals not yet mined commercially.

26 FOREIGN TRADE

Côte d'Ivoire has generally enjoyed a positive trade balance since independence. The major exports are cocoa beans and products, coffee, and fuels; the leading imports

Selected Social Indicators

These statistics are estimates for the period 1988 to 1993. For comparison purposes, data for the United States and averages for low-income countries and high-income countries are also given.

Indicator	Côte d'Ivoire	Low-income countries	High-income countries	United States
Per capita gross national product†	$630	$380	$23,680	$24,740
Population growth rate	3.7%	1.9%	0.6%	1.0%
Population growth rate in urban areas	5.2%	3.9%	0.8%	1.3%
Population per square kilometer of land	40	78	25	26
Life expectancy in years	51	62	77	76
Number of people per physician	14,251	>3,300	453	419
Number of pupils per teacher (primary school)	37	39	<18	20
Illiteracy rate (15 years and older)	46%	41%	<5%	<3%
Energy consumed per capita (kg of oil equivalent)	109	364	5,203	7,918

† The gross national product (GNP) is the total dollar value of all goods and services produced by a country in a year. The per capita GNP is calculated by dividing a country's GNP by its population. The World Bank defines low-income countries as those with a per capita GNP of $695 or less. High-income countries have a per capita GNP of $8,626 or more. Less than 14% of the world's 5.5 billion people live in high-income countries, while almost 60% live in low-income countries.

> = greater than   < = less than

Sources: World Bank, *Social Indicators of Development 1995*, Baltimore: Johns Hopkins University Press, 1995. Central Intelligence Agency, *World Fact Book*, Washington, D.C.: Government Printing Office, 1994.

are miscellaneous manufactured articles, machinery and transportation equipment, and crude oil and petroleum products. In 1991, timber and timber products accounted for $279 million in export value, providing the third most important source of foreign revenue (after coffee and cocoa). Côte d'Ivoire exports primarily to the Netherlands (22.5%) and to France (13.6%), followed by Germany, the United States, and Ghana. The two principal sources of Côte d'Ivoire's imports are France (28.7%) and Nigeria (16.0%).

27 ENERGY AND POWER

Substantial efforts have been undertaken to develop Côte d'Ivoire's hydroelectric potential, and by 1991, hydroelectricity supplied about 40% of electrical demand. Electric power production reached 2,376 million kilowatt hours in 1991. Offshore oil production was 99,000 tons in 1991.

28 SOCIAL DEVELOPMENT

A social welfare service was established in 1950 to coordinate public and private social assistance activities; it occupies itself mainly with casework in the large towns. A system of family allowances for wage earners was instituted in 1956, and workers' compensation has also been introduced. In 1964, the National Assembly abolished polygamy (having more than one wife or husband at a time) and set the legal marriage age at 18 for boys and 16 for girls. There is a cabinet-level Ministry of Women's Affairs.

29 HEALTH

Malaria, yellow fever, sleeping sickness, yaws, leprosy, trachoma, and meningitis are widespread. As of 1990, malnutrition affected 12% of children under 5 years old. Studies show that from 1985 to 1992, only 30% of the population had access to health care services. In 1990 there were 1,020 doctors.

30 HOUSING

Housing remains an issue of major concern in Côte d'Ivoire, particularly in Abidjan, which has been the focus of continued migration from rural areas. Extensive slum clearance has been carried out in the former capital, but shantytowns (poor areas) still persist on the outskirts.

31 EDUCATION

Education is free at all levels. Primary education lasts for six years and secondary for seven years (four years followed by three years). Adult literacy rates in 1990 were estimated at 66.9% for men and 40.2% for women. The National University of Côte d'Ivoire is located in Abidjan.

32 MEDIA

All news media are owned or controlled by the government or the ruling party. The French-language daily *Fraternité Matin* had a circulation of 80,000 in 1991; its Sunday edition, *Ivoire Dimanche,* had a circulation of 60,000. Telephone and telegraph services are government owned; there were 87,700 telephones in use in 1991. The government also controls radio and television broadcasting. Radio broadcasts are in French, English, and indigenous (native) languages; television is in French only. In 1991 there were an estimated 1,765,000 radios and 730,000 television sets in use.

33 TOURISM AND RECREATION

Tourism has developed significantly since the early 1970s. The country has excellent hotels and other tourist facilities, with approximately 6,000 hotel rooms in 1991. There were about 200,000 tourist arrivals in that year. Fine beaches, specially built tourist villages, and photo safaris through the wildlife preserves are principal attractions.

34 FAMOUS IVOIRIANS

Queen Abia Pokou (b. 1720), the legendary heroine of the Baule people, led them to Côte d'Ivoire from the territory that is now Ghana. Félix Houphouët-Boigny (1905–93) was the first African to be a French Cabinet minister; he was also Côte d'Ivoire's first president.

35 BIBLIOGRAPHY

Cote d'Ivoire (Ivory Coast) in Pictures. Minneapolis: Lerner, 1988.

Kakwani, Nanak. *Poverty and Economic Growth.* Washington, D.C.: World Bank, 1990.

Mundt, Robert J. *Historical Dictionary of the Ivory Coast (Côte d'Ivoire).* Metuchen, N.J.: Scarecrow, 1987.

CROATIA

Republic of Croatia

Republika Hrvatska

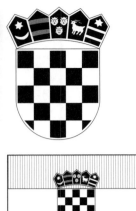

CAPITAL: Zagreb.

FLAG: Red, white, and blue horizontal bands with the Croatian coat of arms (red and white checkered).

ANTHEM: *Lijepa Nasa Domovina.*

MONETARY UNIT: The Croatian kuna was introduced in 1994. us$1 = 5.7 kuna as of fall 1994, but exchange rates are expected to fluctuate.

WEIGHTS AND MEASURES: The metric system is the legal standard.

HOLIDAYS: New Year's Day, 1 January; Epiphany, 6 January; Labor Day, 1 May; Republic Day, 30 May; National Holiday, 22 June; Assumption, 15 August; Christmas, 25–26 December.

TIME: 7 PM = noon GMT.

1 LOCATION AND SIZE

Croatia is located in southeastern Europe. Comparatively, the area occupied by Croatia is slightly smaller than the state of West Virginia with a total area of 56,538 square kilometers (21,829 square miles). Croatia has a total boundary length of 7,633 kilometers (4,743 miles). Its capital city, Zagreb, is located in the northern part of the country.

2 TOPOGRAPHY

Croatia is geographically diverse, with flat plains along the Hungarian border, as well as low mountains and highlands near the Adriatic coast. There are frequent earthquakes.

Croatia's highest point (1,762 meters/ 5,781 feet) is at Mt. Biokovo in the southern part of the country.

3 CLIMATE

Croatia has hot summers and cold winters. Along the coast, the climate is Mediterranean with mild winters and dry summers.

4 PLANTS AND ANIMALS

Ferns, flowers, mosses, and common trees populate the landscape. Along the Adriatic Sea there are subtropical plants. Native animals include deer, brown bears, rabbits, fox, and wild boars.

5 ENVIRONMENT

Air pollution (from metallurgical plant emissions) and loss of forestland are inland environmental problems. Coastal water systems have been damaged by industrial and domestic waste. Environmental management is becoming less centralized, allowing local governments to determine environmental policy.

6 POPULATION

The population of Croatia was 4,784,265 in 1991. It was projected by the World Bank to be 4,800,000 in 2010. The population density in 1991 was 85 persons per square kilometer (219 per square mile). Zagreb, the capital, had a population of 706,770.

7 MIGRATION

At the end of 1992, Croatia was accommodating 648,000 refugees. Some of these were Croats from Bosnia and Herzegovina. Others were from areas of Croatia in Serbian hands. Some 160,000 people had fled to other Yugoslav republics by mid-1991, and about 120,000 had fled abroad.

8 ETHNIC GROUPS

Croats made up 78% of the population in 1991. Serbs were 12% and Muslims 1%. About 2% of the population said they were Yugoslavs. There were smaller numbers of Slovenes, Hungarians, Italians, and other nationalities.

9 LANGUAGES

Serbo-Croatian is the native language. Since 1991, Croats have insisted that their version (now called Croat) is distinctive. The spoken language is basically the same, but Serbs use the Cyrillic (or Russian) alphabet and Croats the Roman alphabet.

10 RELIGIONS

The census of 1991 recorded a Catholic population of 76.5%, with 11.1% Serbian Orthodox, and 1.2% Muslim.

Photo credit: Susan D. Rock

A typical harbor along the coast of the Adriatic Sea.

11 TRANSPORTATION

As of 1991, there were 2,698 kilometers (1,677 miles) of railroads, 34.5% of which used electric power. Highways (paved and unpaved) totaled 32,071 kilometers (19,929 miles) in 1990. Rijeka, Split, and Ploče are the main seaports along the Adriatic. There are 785 kilometers (488 miles) of navigable inland waters; Vukovar, Osijek, Sisak, and Vinkovci are the principal inland ports.

12 HISTORY

Slavic tribes settled in the Balkan area between the fifth and seventh centuries

CROATIA

0	25	50	75 Miles
0	25	50	75 Kilometers

LOCATION: 45°10′N 15°30′E. **BOUNDARY LENGTHS:** Total boundary lengths, 1,843 kilometers (1,145 miles); Bosnia and Herzegovina (east), 751 kilometers (467 miles); Bosnia and Herzegovina (southeast), 91 kilometers (57 miles); Hungary, 292 kilometers (181 miles); Serbia, 239 kilometers (149 miles); Montenegro, 15 kilometers (9.3 miles); Slovenia, 455 kilometers (283 miles); **COASTLINE:** 5,790 kilometers (3,619 miles); mainland coastline, 1,778 kilometers (1,111 miles); islands coastline, 4,012 kilometers (2,506 miles).

AD. The Frankish conqueror Charlemagne won control of Croatia in the ninth century, and the Croatians began converting to Christianity. The land was united as one kingdom for the first time under the reign of Tomislav, beginning around 925, and remained independent until united with Hungary in 1102.

The Hungarian king Koloman and a group of Croatian nobles agreed on a royal union between Hungary and Croatia under which the two would share the same king, but would otherwise be separate nations. Under the agreement, the Croatians retained their own nobility and parliament (the Sabor). This arrangement formed the basis of the Hungarian-Croatian relationship until 1918.

In the 1520s, the Ottoman Turks gained control over most of Croatia just as the Austrian Habsburg king, Ferdinand, claimed both Hungary and Croatia. The Habsburg rulers disregarded the rights of the Croats, and the Croatian peasants were caught between Austrian oppression and repeated Turkish invasions.

King Ferdinand III (r. 1637–57) consolidated Hungary and Croatia under Habsburg rule. This continued until the end of the 18th century, when Leopold II recognized Hungary and Croatia as kingdoms with separate constitutions. Hungarians then began trying to establish the Hungarian language in Croatia, Slavonia, and Dalmatia, thus initiating yet another struggle by the Croats to preserve their own language and culture.

In 1809 Napoleon, having obtained control of Slovenian and Croatian territories, made them part of his Illyrian Provinces. For a few years, these provinces enjoyed an orderly administration—respectful and supportive of the Slovenian and Croatian national individuality and aspirations—and encouraged education and cultural development in national languages. With Napoleon's defeat, Croatia reverted back to direct Austrian administration until the end of World War I in 1918.

Under the Austro-Hungarian dual monarchy agreement, which restructured the Habsburg empire in 1867, Hungary regained control of Croatia. The following year, Croatia-Slavonia-Dalmatia was recognized as a nation with its own territory, and it was granted political autonomy in its internal affairs.

The idea of a separate state uniting the South Slavic nations ("Yugoslavism") grew stronger during World War I. It was fostered by Austro-Hungarian persecution and sympathy for the plight of the Serbian nation. In 1917, an agreement was reached on the Greek island of Corfu on the formation of a "Kingdom of Serbs, Croats, and Slovenes," upon the defeat of Austria-Hungary.

On 1 December 1918, Prince Alexander of Serbia declared the unification of the "Kingdom of Serbs, Croats, and Slovenes," a unitary Kingdom with a strongly centralized government ruled, after 1921, by King Alexander of Serbia. The Slovenes and Croats, while freed from Austro-Hungarian domination, did not win the political and cultural self-rule for which they had hoped. The Croatian "Sabor" was deprived of its authority.

The period between 1921 and 1929 was a confused time, with a sequence of 23 governments and a parliament without the Croatian delegation's 50 votes and the Communist Party's 58 votes. The king dissolved the parliament on 6 January 1929, abolished the 1921 constitution, and

Photo credit: Anne Kalosh

The cemetery at Zagreb.

established his own personal dictatorship as a temporary arrangement. On 3 October 1929, the country was renamed the Kingdom of Yugoslavia. King Alexander was assassinated in Marseille on 9 October 1934 by agents of the extreme Croatian nationalist group, the Ustaša.

Germany's Adolf Hitler unleashed his forces on Yugoslavia on 6 April 1941, bombing Belgrade and other cities without any warning or formal declaration of war. The Yugoslav government fled the country for allied territory, and the Nazis set up a puppet government run by Ustaša. Soon after, Ustaša bands initiated a bloody orgy of mass murders against the Serbs.

In addition, the Ustaša regime organized extermination camps, the most notorious one at Jasenovac where Serbs, Jews, Gypsies, and other opponents were massacred in large numbers. The Serbs reacted by forming their own resistance groups ("Chetniks") or by joining with the Communist-led partisan resistance.

With the entry of Soviet armies into Yugoslav territory in October 1944, the Partisans swept over Yugoslavia in pursuit of the retreating German forces. The Partisans took over Croatia, launching a terrible retaliation in the form of summary executions, people's court sentences, and large scale massacres.

All of the republics of the former Federal Socialist Republic of Yugoslavia share a common history between 1945 and 1991, the year of Yugoslavia's break-up. The World War II Partisan resistance movement, controlled by the Communist Party of Yugoslavia and led by Marshal Josip Tito, won a civil war waged against nationalist groups. They had both recognition and aid from the Western powers and the Soviet Union.

A conflict erupted between Tito and the Russian leader Joseph Stalin in 1948, resulting in Tito's expulsion from the Soviet Bloc. Yugoslavia then developed its own brand of Marxist economy based on workers' councils and self-management of enterprises and institutions, and became the leader of the nonaligned group of nations.

Being more open to Western influences, the Yugoslav Communist regime relaxed its central controls somewhat. This allowed for the development of more liberal wings of Communist parties, especially in Croatia and Slovenia. Also, nationalism reappeared, with tensions especially strong between Serbs and Croats in the Croatian republic, leading to the repression by Tito of the Croatian and Slovenian "Springs" (freedom movements like the one in Czechoslovakia in 1968) in 1970–71.

The 1974 constitution shifted much of the decision-making power from the federal level to the republics, further decentralizing the political process. Following Tito's death in 1980, there was an economic crisis. Severe inflation and the inability to pay the nation's foreign debts led to tensions between the different republics and demands for a reorganization of the Yugoslav federation into a confederation of sovereign states.

Pressure toward individual autonomy for the regions, as well as a market economy grew stronger, leading to the formation of non-Communist political parties. By 1990 they were able to win majorities in multiparty elections in Slovenia and then in Croatia, ending the era of Communist Party monopoly of power.

Slovenia and Croatia declared their independence on 25 June 1991. Within a few weeks, ethnic violence broke out between Croats and the Serbs in the northern region of Croatia, backed by Serbian president Slobodan Milošević. The fighting caused tremendous destruction. Entire cities (for example, Vukovar) were destroyed, and large scale damage was inflicted on medieval Dubrovnik.

Croatia, poorly armed and caught by surprise, fought over a seven-month period and suffered some 10,000 deaths, 30,000 wounded, and over 14,000 missing. Croatia lost about one-third of its territory to the Serbs.

The European community made efforts to stop the killing and destruction in Croatia, as did the United Nations' special envoy, Cyrus Vance. Vance was able to conclude a peace accord on 3 January 1992 that called for a major United Nations peace-keeping force in Croatia. The Serbian side agreed to hand over their heavy weapons to the United Nations' units and to allow thousands of refugees to return home. The second provision had not been honored as of August 1994.

In August 1995, more than 100,000 Croatian troops entered and retook the occupied northern region from rebel Serbs. The Croats also linked up with Bosnian forces to protect the United Nations-designated Muslim "safe area" of Bihać in western Bosnia that had been under Serb attack.

The joint offensive raised fears that hostilities in these neighboring Balkan countries would spread across national borders, especially if the army of the present Yugoslavia (now only Serbia and Montenegro) came directly to the aid of its fellow Serbs in Bosnia and Croatia.

13 GOVERNMENT

Croatia is a united republic with a mix of parliamentary and presidential forms of government. The parliament of Croatia, as formed on 30 May 1990, adopted a constitution for Croatia on 22 December 1990. The executive authority is held by a president, elected for five years, and a government cabinet headed by a prime minister. In 1994, the president was Dr. Franjo Tudjman and the prime minister was Nikica Valentić.

The two-chamber parliament is composed of the House of Representatives (138 seats) and the House of Counties (68 seats) with the chairman of the House of Representatives serving as the Parliament chairman.

The president appoints the prime minister and the cabinet, is the Supreme Commander of the armed forces, declares war, and concludes peace on the basis of the parliament's decisions.

Local government in Croatia consists of municipalities that are grouped into 21 counties.

14 POLITICAL PARTIES

There are some 50 political parties registered in Croatia, but only 9 had elected representatives in the Croatian parliament following the August 1992 elections: the Croatian Democratic Union (HDZ); the Croatian Social Liberal Party (HSLS); the Croatian Peasant Party (HSS); the Croatian People's Party (HNS); the Istrian Democratic Assembly (IDS); Dalmatian Action; the Social Democratic Party (SDP); the Croatian Party of the Right (HSP); and the Serbian People's Party (SNS).

The last presidential elections were held in August 1992 when Dr. Franjo Tudjman, leader of the HDZ, was reelected president.

15 JUDICIAL SYSTEM

The judicial system is comprised of municipal and district courts, a Supreme Court, and a Constitutional Court. A High Judicial Council (made up of the president and 14 other members) appoints judges and public prosecutors.

16 ARMED FORCES

Upon declaring its independence in 1991, Croatia formed an active armed force of 105,000 plus 100,000 reservists (a fighting force used only when strategic need arises). The army of 100,000 is comprised equally of regular and mobilized reservists. The separate air defense service has 4,000 members; the air force, 250 and increasing; and the navy, 5,000 sailors. There are also 40,000 armed police.

Armed with Russian weapons, the army has 9 brigades and 5 separate regiments of combined arms. With only 400 tanks and APCs, the Croatian army is basically a mountain and urban infantry defense force. Croatia is also occupied by 12 United Nations infantry battalions (UNPROFOR), which act as an added barrier to Serbian invasion and other violence. The navy controls one submarine and 12 coastal combat and patrol vessels and craft.

17 ECONOMY

Before the dissolution of the Yugoslav SFR (Federal Socialist Republic of Yugoslavia), Croatia was its second-most prosperous and industrialized area (after Slovenia). As of early 1994, Croatian-Serb nationalists controlled about one-third of Croatia's territory; the resolution of this territorial dispute is necessary for peace and prosperity in Croatia.

Croatia's economic problems are largely inherited from Communist mismanagement and a large foreign debt. More recently, fighting has caused massive damage to bridges, power lines, factories, buildings, and houses.

Croatia's economy also earned the burden of 800,000 refugees and displaced persons from Bosnia and occupied Croat territories in 1993, with some 80% of the refugees finding shelter with families in Croatia.

Photo credit: Susan D. Rock

A boy buys fish in an open air market in Zagreb.

18 INCOME

In 1991, the estimated gross domestic product (GDP) purchasing power equivalent was $26.3 billion, or $5,600 per capita. The national product's real growth rate fell by some 25% in 1991. As of December 1992, consumer prices were rising at a rate of 50% per month.

19 INDUSTRY

Light industry, especially for the production of consumer goods, is more advanced in Croatia than in the other republics of the former Yugoslav SFR (Federal Socialist Republic of Yugoslavia). Croatia's main manufacturing industries include: chemicals and plastics, machine tools, fabricated metal products, electronics, pig iron and rolled steel products, and aluminum processing.

Also important are paper and wood products (including furniture), building materials (including cement), textiles, shipbuilding, petroleum and petroleum refining, and food processing and beverages. Due to the civil war and uncertainty created by the breakup of the Yugoslav SFR (Federal Socialist Republic of Yugoslavia), estimated industrial production declined by nearly one-third in 1991.

20 LABOR

In 1992, about 1,159,000 persons were employed in the following areas: manufacturing, 34%; community, social, and personal services, 23%; transportation and communication, 9%; construction, 7%; agriculture, 5%; public utilities, 2%; mining, 1%; and other services, 19%. In 1992, about 23% of the total labor force was either unemployed or unofficially employed.

All workers, except the military and police, may form and join unions of their own choosing without prior authorization. There are national minimum wage standards, but they are too low to provide a worker and family with a decent living standard.

21 AGRICULTURE

An estimated 1.5 million hectares (3.7 million acres), or 26% of total land, was cultivated in 1991. Permanent pasture land amounted to 1.6 million hectares (3.9 million acres), or 28% of total land area.

Civil war has reduced agricultural output since the breakup of the Yugoslav SFR (Federal Socialist Republic of Yugoslavia). Between 1990 and 1992, crop production dropped by the following amounts (in thousands of tons): wheat, from 1,602 to 658; corn, 1,950 to 1,538; sugar beets, 1,206 to 525; grapes, 398 to 380; and apples, 70 to 62.

22 DOMESTICATED ANIMALS

About 28% of the total land area consists of meadows and pastures. In 1992, there were 1,183,000 pigs, 590,000 cattle, 539,000 sheep, 27,000 horses, and 13,000,000 chickens. In that same year, 246,000 tons of meat were produced, including 135,000 tons of pork, 58,000 tons of poultry, 50,000 tons of beef, and 3,000 tons of mutton. Milk production in 1992 totaled 645,000 tons; eggs, 38,700 tons; and cheese, 11,600 tons.

23 FISHING

With a mainland coastline of 1,778 kilometers (1,105 miles) and island coastlines totaling 4,012 kilometers (2,493 miles) on the Adriatic, Croatia is suited to the development of marine fishing.

24 FORESTRY

About 36% of the total area is forest. Despite the political unrest from the demise of the Yugoslav SFR (Federal Socialist Republic of Yugoslavia), Croatia is still able to supply small but good quality oak and beech. Since 1991, production of lumber and panels has fallen by 50%.

Normally, Croatian exports of hardwood lumber consist of 50% beech, 30% oak, and 6% ash. Panels and veneer are also exported and Croatia is starting to increase the output of value-added products while seeking foreign private joint ventures.

25 MINING

Apart from the petroleum deposits north of the Sava, Croatia contains deposits of bauxite, which are mined at Obrovac, Drniš, and Rovinj. Marine salt is processed at Pag Island.

26 FOREIGN TRADE

In 1990, Croatia's exports amounted to $2.9 billion, of which machinery and transport equipment accounted for 30%; other manufactures, 37%; chemicals, 11%; food and live animals, 9%; raw materials, 6.5%; fuels and lubricants, 5%; and other products, 1.5%. Exports were shipped primarily to the other republics of the former Yugoslav SFR (Federal Socialist Republic of Yugoslavia).

Imports in 1990 totaled $4.4 billion, of which machinery and transport equipment accounted for 21%; fuels and lubricants, 19%; food and live animals, 16%; chemicals, 14%; manufactured goods, 13%; miscellaneous manufactured articles, 9%; raw materials, 7%; and beverages and tobacco products, 1%.

27 ENERGY AND POWER

In 1991, some 8,830 million kilowatt hours were produced and consumption per capita amounted to 1,855 kilowatt hours. Oil fields in Slavonia, natural gas

Photo credit: Susan D. Rock

The rooftops of the Old City in the coastal town of Dubrovnic.

fields in the far north, and coal mines at Labin provide Croatia with energy resources. Much of the energy network has been made inoperable by the civil war, and the oil refining industry has been severely damaged.

28 SOCIAL DEVELOPMENT

The effects of the 1991 war, the great refugee burden, and the absence of significant international aid have strained the country's social fabric and economy. In 1993, the average standard of living stood at less than 50% of its level before 1991. Over 400,000 Croats were displaced by the war and its aftermath.

Selected Social Indicators

These statistics are estimates for the period 1988 to 1993. For comparison purposes, data for the United States and averages for low-income countries and high-income countries are also given.

Indicator	Croatia	Low-income countries	High-income countries	United States
Per capita gross national product†	**$5,600**	$380	$23,680	$24,740
Population growth rate	**0.1%**	1.9%	0.6%	1.0%
Population growth rate in urban areas	**1.5%**	3.9%	0.8%	1.3%
Population per square kilometer of land	**85**	78	25	26
Life expectancy in years	**71**	62	77	76
Number of people per physician	**n.a.**	>3,300	453	419
Number of pupils per teacher (primary school)	**19**	39	<18	20
Illiteracy rate (15 years and older)	**<10%**	41%	<5%	<3%
Energy consumed per capita (kg of oil equivalent)	**1,109**	364	5,203	7,918

† The gross national product (GNP) is the total dollar value of all goods and services produced by a country in a year. The per capita GNP is calculated by dividing a country's GNP by its population. The World Bank defines low-income countries as those with a per capita GNP of $695 or less. High-income countries have a per capita GNP of $8,626 or more. Less than 14% of the world's 5.5 billion people live in high-income countries, while almost 60% live in low-income countries.

n.a. = data not available.   > = greater than   < = less than

Sources: World Bank, *Social Indicators of Development 1995,* Baltimore: Johns Hopkins University Press, 1995. Central Intelligence Agency, *World Fact Book,* Washington, D.C.: Government Printing Office, 1994.

Zagreb and several other major cities have started family crisis associations, such as the Women of Vukovar, for women who have missing relatives, and Tresnjevka, a group working to open a support center for wartime rape victims from Bosnia.

29 HEALTH

Availability of Croatia's health care statistics has been limited by the civil war that has raged since 1991. Between 1991 and 1992, there were 25,000 war-related deaths; deaths for 1993 and 1994 were not yet reported as of late 1994.

30 HOUSING

As of mid-1994, nearly 800,000 displaced persons and refugees from Bosnia and occupied Croat territories were in Croatia, of whom approximately 640,000 have found housing with families in Croatia. The remainder are housed in refugee centers and hotels.

31 EDUCATION

Education at the elementary level is free and compulsory for children between the ages of 6 to 15 years. Secondary education lasts from two to five years.

There are four universities and three polytechnic institutes: the University of Osijek; the University of Rijeka; the University of Split; and the University of Zagreb.

32 MEDIA

In 1990, there were 1,143,376 telephones. Croatian Radio-Television (Hrvatska Radiotelevizija) has charge of all broadcasting. Croatian Radio runs 14 AM and 8 FM stations. Croatian television broadcasts on three channels. In 1991, there were 1,160,000 radios and 1,055,000 television sets.

In 1992, there were 9 daily newspapers with a combined circulation of 342 million, and 603 non-dailies (including 64 weeklies); there were 401 periodicals. In 1990, there were 2,413 book titles published.

33 TOURISM AND RECREATION

Civil unrest since Croatian independence has shattered the profitable tourist business formerly enjoyed by Adriatic coastal resorts, including Dubrovnik and Split, where thousands of European tourists flocked annually to enjoy the climate, scenery, and excellent swimming from April to October.

34 FAMOUS CROATS

Dr. Franjo Tudjman has been president of Croatia since May 1990. Nikica Valentić has been prime minister since April 1993.

Two Nobel prize winners have come from Croatia: Lavoslav Ružička and Vladimir Prelog.

Josip Broz Tito (1892–1980) was the leader of Communist Yugoslavia for many years after World War II. In 1948, he led his country away from the Communist Bloc formed by the Soviet Union. Tito served in the Red Army during the Russian Civil War and led the Yugoslav resistance movement during World War II.

There are several internationally known figures in literature and the arts: Ivan Gundulic (1589–1638) wrote about the Italian influences in Croatia in *Dubravka*. Count Ivo Vojnović (1857–1929) is best known for *A Trilogy of Dubrovnik*.

Double-agent Duško Popov (1912–81), who worked during World War II, was the model for Ian Fleming's James Bond. Religious leader Franjo Seper (1884–1981) was born in Croatia. Musician Artur Rodzinski (1894–1958) became conductor of the Cleveland Orchestra in 1933, the New York Philharmonic in 1943, and the Chicago Symphony in 1947. Zinka Kumc Milanov (1906–) was a dramatic opera soprano with the New York Metropolitan Opera in the 1950s and 1960s.

35 BIBLIOGRAPHY

Gazi, Stephen. *A History of Croatia*. New York: Philosophical Library, 1973.
Glenny, Michael. *The Fall of Yugoslavia: The Third Balkan War*. New York: Penguin, 1992.

CUBA

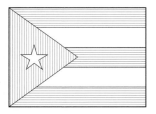

Republic of Cuba
República de Cuba

CAPITAL: Havana (La Habana).

FLAG: The flag consists of five alternating blue and white horizontal stripes penetrated from the hoist side by a red triangle containing a white five-pointed star.

ANTHEM: *Himno de Bayamo (Hymn of Bayamo),* beginning "Al combate corred bayameses" ("March to the battle, people of Bayamo").

MONETARY UNIT: The Cuban peso (c$) of 100 centavos is a paper currency with one exchange rate. There are coins of 1, 2, 3, 5, 20, 40, and 100 centavos and notes of 1, 3, 5, 10, 20, 50, and 100 pesos. The value of the peso was set at exactly US$1 until 1971, when the dollar was devalued against gold but the peso was not. c$1 = US$1.3637 (or US$1 = c$0.7333).

WEIGHTS AND MEASURES: The metric system is the legal standard, but older Spanish units and the imperial system are still employed. The standard unit of land measure is the caballería (13.4 hectares/133.1 acres).

HOLIDAYS: Day of the Revolution, Liberation Day, 1 January; Labor Day, 1 May; Anniversary of the Revolution, 25–27 July; Proclamation of Yara, 10 October. Celebration of religious holidays falling during the workweek was prohibited by a 1972 law.

TIME: 7 AM = noon GMT.

1 LOCATION AND SIZE

The Republic of Cuba consists of one large island and several small ones situated on the northern rim of the Caribbean Sea, about 160 kilometers (100 miles) south of Florida. With an area of 110,860 square kilometers (42,803 square miles), Cuba is the largest country in the Caribbean. The area occupied by Cuba is slightly smaller than the state of Pennsylvania. Cuba's total coastline is 3,764 kilometers (2,339 miles).

Cuba's capital city, Havana, is located on its northeastern coast.

2 TOPOGRAPHY

Cuba's coastline is marked by bays, reefs, keys, and islets. Along the southern coast are long stretches of lowlands and swamps. Slightly more than half the island consists of flat or rolling terrain, and the remainder is hilly or mountainous. Eastern Cuba is dominated by the Sierra Maestra mountains, whose highest peak is Pico Real del Turquino (1,974 meters/6,476 feet). Central Cuba contains the Trinidad (Escambray) Mountains, and the Sierra de los Órganos is located in the west. The largest river is the Cauto.

3 CLIMATE

Except in the mountains, the climate of Cuba is semitropical or temperate. The average minimum temperature is 21°C (70°F), the average maximum 27°C (81°F). The mean temperature at Havana is about 25°C (77°F).

The mountain areas have an average precipitation of more than 180 centimeters (70 inches); most of the lowland area has from 90 to 140 centimeters (35–55 inches) annually; and the area around Guantánamo Bay has less than 65 centimeters (26 inches). Cuba's eastern coast is often hit by hurricanes, causing great economic loss.

4 PLANTS AND ANIMALS

The total number of native flowering species is estimated at nearly 8,000. The mountainous areas are covered by tropical forest, but Cuba is essentially a palm-studded grassland. The royal palm, reaching heights of 15 to 23 meters (50–75 feet), is the national tree. Pines like those in the southeastern United States grow on the slopes of the Sierra de los Órganos. The lower coastal areas have mangrove swamps, and desert plants grow near Guantánamo Bay. Only small animals inhabit Cuba. These include tropical bats, rodents, birds, and many species of reptiles and insects.

5 ENVIRONMENT

As of 1994, Cuba's most pressing environmental problems were deforestation and the preservation of its wildlife. However, the Cuban government has sponsored a successful reforestation program. Another major environmental problem is the pollution of Havana Bay. The nation has 8.3 cubic miles of water with a total of 89% used for agricultural purposes. One hundred percent of Cuba's city dwellers and 91% of its rural people have pure water.

In 1994, 11 mammal species, 15 bird species, 4 types of reptiles, and 860 plant species were considered threatened.

6 POPULATION

According to the 1991 census, the population was 9,723,605. The estimated population in December 1992 was 10,870,000, and the UN projection for the year 2000 was 11,504,000. The estimated population density in 1992 was 98 persons per square kilometer (254 per square mile). Havana, the capital, had an estimated population of 2,096,054 at the end of 1989.

7 MIGRATION

Between April and September 1980, some 125,000 Cubans in small boats (the "freedom flotilla") landed in the US after departing from Mariel harbor. (This exodus was known as the Mariel boatlift.) Cubans have continued to sail to the US in small boats and rafts. A total of 3,656 did so in 1993 as well as 3,864 in the first half of 1994. By the mid-1980s, more than 500,000 Cuban exiles were living in the Miami area. In 1990 there were 751,000 Cuban-born persons in the US. Large numbers have also settled in Puerto Rico, Spain, and Mexico.

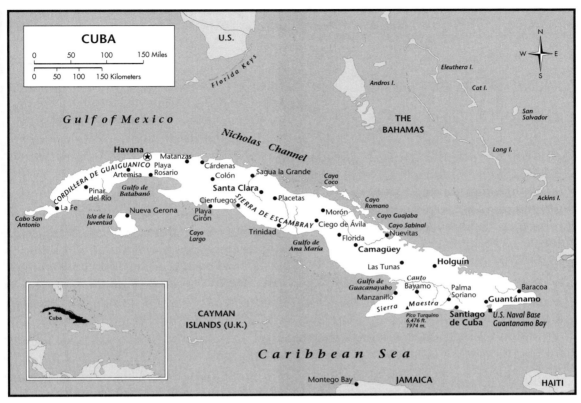

CUBA

| 0 | 50 | 100 | 150 Miles |
| 0 | 50 | 100 | 150 Kilometers |

LOCATION: 74°8′ to 84°57′w; 19°49′ to 23°17′n. **TERRITORIAL SEA LIMIT:** 12 miles.

8 ETHNIC GROUPS

According to the 1981 census, whites (primarily of Spanish descent) made up about 66% of the total; blacks, 12%; and the mixed group (mulattos), 22%. Practically the entire population is native-born Cuban.

9 LANGUAGES

Spanish is the national language of Cuba.

10 RELIGIONS

From the early 1980s to 1993, Roman Catholics represented about 40% of the population. Other religions in Cuba include Santería (a group of cults that combine African beliefs with Christian doctrines), several Protestant churches, including Baptist, Methodist, and Presbyterian, and a very small Jewish population. It is estimated that half of the population belongs to no religion.

11 TRANSPORTATION

In 1991, Cuba had about 21,000 kilometers (13,050 miles) of roads. The first-class Central Highway extends for 1,223 kilometers (760 miles) from Pinar del Río to Guantánamo, connecting all major cities.

Photo credit: Mary A. Dempsey

A memorial at the Bay of Pigs site.

An extensive truck and bus network transports passengers and freight. Railways connect the east and west extremities of the island by 5,295 kilometers (3,290 miles) of standard-gauge track.

By 1991, the Cuban merchant fleet had 83 vessels totaling 585,000 gross registered tons. Cuba's major ports are Havana, Cienfuegos, Mariel, Santiago de Cuba, Nuevitas, and Matanzas.

Cubana Airlines is the national air carrier. The number of air passengers was 672,200 in 1992. In 1991, José Martí airport at Havana serviced 1,199,000 passengers.

12 HISTORY

Cuba was originally inhabited by about 50,000 Ciboney and Taíno Amerindians related to the Arawak peoples, who died from disease and mistreatment soon after the Spanish arrived. Christopher Columbus made the European discovery of Cuba in 1492 on his first voyage to the Americas. The African slave trade began about 1523 and grew with the development of coffee and sugar plantations on the island.

In 1762, the English briefly captured Havana, holding it for almost a year before Spain regained control. Spanish rule was harsh, and periodic rebellions over the next century all ended in failure. The guerrilla revolt of 1868–78, inspired by Carlos Manuel de Céspedes, and the historic rebellion led by national hero José Martí in 1895, failed as well.

In the end, the Cubans won their freedom through the Spanish-American War of 1898. The war was triggered by the mysterious bombing of the battleship *Maine* in Havana harbor. The Treaty of Paris (10 December 1898) established Cuban independence. However, through the Platt Amendment to Cuba's 1901 constitution, the US retained the right to intervene in Cuban affairs and maintain a naval base at Guantánamo Bay.

For the next 30 years, Cuba had a succession of governments, constitutional and otherwise, while American companies controlled about half of Cuba's cultivated land, its utilities and mines, and other natural resources. In 1933, a nationalist uprising drove the brutal dictator Gerardo Machado y Morales from office.

The Batista Regime

After the US attempted to install its own regime, 32-year-old Fulgencio Batista y Zaldívar assumed power and ruled from 1934 until 1940, often through a series of puppet presidents. In 1934, Batista got President Franklin D. Roosevelt to revoke the Platt Amendment, although the United States retained its naval base at Guantánamo Bay (which is currently scheduled to revert to Cuban authority at the end of the century).

Under a new constitution, adopted in 1940, Batista became president. In 1944, he was succeeded by Grau San Martín, whose eight years of rule were ineffective and corrupt. In 1952, with elections scheduled, Batista seized power in a military coup and, for the next seven years, used increasingly harsh measures to keep himself in office. Under the Batista regime, social services suffered, poverty and illiteracy were widespread, and the bureaucracy was glaringly corrupt.

Exiled after a failed 1953 raid on an army barracks, the young revolutionary Fidel Castro gathered supporters in Mexico for a second revolt and in 1956 landed in Cuba. Overcome by Batista's troops, Castro escaped into the Sierra Maestra mountains with only a dozen supporters. His forces never grew to more than a few thousand, but clever use of guerrilla tactics made them a match for Batista's poorly trained army. In addition, there was almost no popular support for Batista, and in 1958, the US ended its military aid to the falling government.

On 1 January 1959, the Batista regime collapsed. Castro seized control of the government and began to rule by decree. Castro instituted a revolutionary government that began large-scale land reforms and other measures aimed at solving Cuba's desperate economic problems.

Castro in Power

After June 1960, Cuban-US relations worsened as Communist influence on the Cuban government grew. Castro's government took control of about $2 billion in US-owned property in Cuba; the US severed diplomatic relations with the Castro government and stopped importing Cuban sugar.

In April 1961, a group of 1,500 Cuban exiles—financed, trained and equipped by the CIA—invaded Cuba at the Bay of Pigs. The invasion turned out to be a politically embarrassing blunder for the newly installed Kennedy administration. The brigade was defeated within 72 hours, and the survivors were captured. They were later released in exchange for a ransom of $50 million in food and medical supplies.

In 1961, Castro declared himself a Marxist-Leninist and part of the Socialist world. All major means of production, distribution, communication, and services were taken over by the government. Cuba's trade and other relations shifted to the Soviet bloc.

In October 1962, US planes photographed Soviet missile bases in Cuba. In what came to be known as the Cuban Missile Crisis, the US blockaded Cuba until the USSR agreed to withdraw the

Photo credit: Mary A. Dempsey

A gasoline shortage has left freeways to bicyclists and horseback riders. Since the breakup of the USSR, Cuba's traditional trading partner, the Cuban economy has begun to falter.

missiles in exchange for a US government pledge to launch no more offensive operations against the island.

However, the US did continue its attempt to isolate Cuba politically and economically from Latin America and the rest of the non-Communist world. Castro responded by trying to weaken certain Central and South American governments. Guerrilla movements became active throughout the region, often with Cuban support.

During the Carter administration, there were moves to normalize relations with Cuba. However, the advent of the Reagan administration brought increased tensions between the two countries. Citing Cuban involvement in Angola, Ethiopia, Nicaragua, and Grenada, the US took a more hostile stance toward Cuba.

Domestically, Castro's administration has had mixed success. Cuba has a strong social welfare system, including free health care and subsidized housing. However, economic mismanagement has led to economic decline. Cubans live frugally under a highly controlled system of rationing.

Cuba was dealt a serious blow in the late 1980s with the collapse of the Soviet Union. This meant a cutoff in economic and military aid, on which Cuba had come to rely. However, Castro remains committed to the original goals of his revolution. He continues to blame Cuba's economic woes on the continuing US trade embargo.

13 GOVERNMENT

A new constitution, adopted in 1975 and ratified in 1976, establishes the National Assembly of People's Power as the supreme state organ. The National Assembly elects the Council of State, which includes the president, who is both head of state and head of government. There are 6 vice-presidents in the Council of State, and 23 other members.

In December 1986, the third National Assembly, with 510 delegates, reelected Castro as president of the state council. He remains the key figure in domestic and foreign policy making.

The country is divided into 14 provinces and 169 municipalities.

14 POLITICAL PARTIES

The constitution recognizes the Cuban Communist Party (Partido Comunista Cubano—PCC) as the "highest leading force of the society and of the state," which, in practice, outlaws other political parties. At the third party congress in 1986, Fidel Castro was reelected as first secretary. PCC membership was about 450,000 in 1986.

15 JUDICIAL SYSTEM

The 1976 constitution established the People's Supreme Court, which proposes laws, issues regulations, and makes decisions to be implemented by the people's courts. There are also seven regional courts of appeal, as well as district courts with civil and criminal jurisdiction.

16 ARMED FORCES

The Castro government has maintained a military draft since 1963, and it now requires two years of military service from men between the ages of 16 and 50. Total armed strength in 1993 was estimated at 175,000. The army has 145,000 personnel, organized into 23 divisions.

The navy has 13,500 personnel, and the air force 17,000. Paramilitary forces included 15,000 state security troops. Except for small military training missions, Cuba has withdrawn its troops from Africa and Central America. In 1993, an estimated 4,300 Russian troops remained in Cuba. Cuba's 1991 budget for defense and internal security was $1.2 billion.

17 ECONOMY

The collapse of the Soviet Union and its control of the Eastern bloc countries resulted in a cutoff of important Soviet assistance and the breakdown of traditional markets for Cuban exports. The Cuban economy slowed significantly in the period 1990–91.

In response, the Castro government has restricted public spending, restructured the economy, and begun trading with market economies. The government has put special emphasis on the promotion of foreign investment and the development of sugar and tourism.

year, 606 sugarcane combines (harvesting machines) were produced, and steel production was 412,900 tons.

The sugar industry produces molasses, ethyl alcohol, rum and liquor, bagasse, torula yeast, and dextran. Other food-processing plants produce cheese, butter, yogurt, ice cream, wheat flour, pasta, preserved fruits and vegetables, alcoholic beverages, and soft drinks. Light industry comprises textiles, shoes, soap, toothpaste, and corrugated cardboard boxes.

20 LABOR

In June 1990, the Cuban labor force of 3,600,000 was distributed as follows: industry, 22%; agriculture, forestry, and fishing, 20%; education and culture, 13.3%; trade, 11%; services, and government, 16.7%; construction, 10%; transportation and communications, 7%. Women constituted 38% of the work force. All Cuban workers belong to a trade union, under the central control of the Confederation of Cuban Workers.

21 AGRICULTURE

In 1991, the state owned 3,330,000 hectares (8,228,000 acres) of cultivated land, and 2,970,000 hectares (7,339,000 acres) of pasture. Sugarcane, Cuba's most vital crop and its largest export, is grown throughout the island, but mainly in the eastern half. Sugar output was 5.8 million in 1992. Cuba has pioneered the introduction of mechanical cane harvesters.

Output of tobacco, the second most important crop, was 44,000 tons in 1992. Other crops in 1992 included (in tons)

Photo credit: Mary A. Dempsey

Cubans wait in line outside a store to buy basic consumer goods.

18 INCOME

In 1992, Cuba's gross national product (GNP) was estimated to be $14.9 billion in current US dollars, or $1,370 per person. In 1992, agriculture contributed approximately 11% to the GNP.

19 INDUSTRY

With technical and financial help from the Russia and Eastern Europe, Cuba has made significant progress in heavy industry. The country's cement plants had an output of 3.2 million tons in 1985. Average annual fertilizer production increased to 1,159,700 tons in 1985. In the same oranges, 570,000; lemons and limes, 60,000; grapefruit, 315,000; rice, 308,000; bananas, 200,000; potatoes, 245,000; sweet potatoes, 240,000; and coffee, 25,000.

22 DOMESTICATED ANIMALS

Milk production in 1992 amounted to 856,000 tons and egg production reached 88,000 tons. Livestock in 1992 included an estimated 4.7 million head of cattle, 1.8 million hogs, and 625,000 horses. In 1992, honey production was an estimated 9,500 tons, higher than any other Caribbean nation.

23 FISHING

Cuban waters support more than 500 varieties of edible fish. The catch in 1991 was 165,236 tons. Tuna, lobster, and other shellfish are the main species caught.

24 FORESTRY

Cutting between the end of World War I (1914–18) and the late 1950s reduced Cuba's woodland to about 14% of the total area and led to soil erosion. Between 1959 and 1985, about 1.8 billion seedlings were planted, including eucalyptus, pine, majagua, mahogany, cedar, and casuarina. By 1991, state forests covered 2,765,000 hectares (6,832,000 acres), or about 25% of the total area. Sawn wood production in 1991 was 130,000 cubic meters.

25 MINING

In 1991, Cuba was the world's sixth-largest nickel producer, with 35,000 tons. Nickel deposits and plants are located in eastern Cuba. Copper production in 1991 was 3,000 tons. Chromite production was 50,000 tons. In 1991, Cuba produced 200,000 tons of salt from seawater.

26 FOREIGN TRADE

The sudden disruption of trade with the former Soviet Union and the Eastern bloc nations after 30 years has caused severe trauma to the Cuban economy since 1990. Cuba has diversified its trading partners in recent years. The country now trades more with Spain, Italy, France, the Netherlands, Canada, several Latin American nations, and China.

Total exports totaled $3.6 billion in 1991, primarily composed of sugar, citrus, shellfish, nickel, coffee, tobacco, and medical products. The main destinations of Cuban products were the former USSR (63%), China (6%), Canada (4%), and Japan (4%).

Imports amounted to $3.7 billion, mainly composed of petroleum, capital goods, industrial raw materials, and food. Cuba's major suppliers were the former USSR (47%), Spain (8%), China (6%), Argentina (5%), Italy (4%), and Mexico (3%).

27 ENERGY AND POWER

Cuba has no coal, and its hydroelectric potential is slight. Bagasse (sugarcane waste) has traditionally supplied most of the sugar industry's fuel. In 1991, Cuba's total electricity production was 16,255 million kilowatt hours. Crude oil output as of 1991 totaled less than 700,000 tons. Natural gas production in 1991 amounted to 34 million cubic meters.

Selected Social Indicators

These statistics are estimates for the period 1988 to 1993. For comparison purposes, data for the United States and averages for low-income countries and high-income countries are also given.

Indicator	Cuba	Low-income countries	High-income countries	United States
Per capita gross national product†	$1,370	$380	$23,680	$24,740
Population growth rate	0.8%	1.9%	0.6%	1.0%
Population growth rate in urban areas	1.5%	3.9%	0.8%	1.3%
Population per square kilometer of land	98	78	25	26
Life expectancy in years	75	62	77	76
Number of people per physician	274	>3,300	453	419
Number of pupils per teacher (primary school)	12	39	<18	20
Illiteracy rate (15 years and older)	6%	41%	<5%	<3%
Energy consumed per capita (kg of oil equivalent)	839	364	5,203	7,918

† The gross national product (GNP) is the total dollar value of all goods and services produced by a country in a year. The per capita GNP is calculated by dividing a country's GNP by its population. The World Bank defines low-income countries as those with a per capita GNP of $695 or less. High-income countries have a per capita GNP of $8,626 or more. Less than 14% of the world's 5.5 billion people live in high-income countries, while almost 60% live in low-income countries.

n.a. = data not available   > = greater than   < = less than

Sources: World Bank, Social Indicators of Development 1995, Baltimore: Johns Hopkins University Press, 1995. Central Intelligence Agency, World Fact Book, Washington, D.C.: Government Printing Office, 1994.

28 SOCIAL DEVELOPMENT

A single system of social security covering almost all workers and protecting them against the risks of old age, disability, and death was enacted in 1963. By 1985 there were 844 nurseries and kindergartens, enrolling 100,600 children.

Family-planning services are integrated within the general health care system. However, with the collapse of the Soviet Union, Cuba no longer receives the same support and has fallen behind in many of its social services. Although women made up 37.3% of the labor force in 1985, they were still concentrated in traditional jobs.

29 HEALTH

Health conditions improved greatly after the 1959 revolution. All health services are provided free of charge. From 1985 to 1992, 98% of the country had access to health care services. Life expectancy was an average of 75 years for women and men in 1993.

30 HOUSING

Cuban housing has not kept pace with the population increase. All large cities have slum problems, despite the construction of 200,000 housing units between 1959 and 1975, 83,000 units between 1976 and

Colonial architecture is a hallmark of Havana, Cuba.

1980, and 335,000 units between 1981 and 1985.

31 EDUCATION

An extensive literacy campaign was started in 1961. In 1990, UNESCO reported the illiteracy rate of persons aged 15 years and over as 6% (males: 5% and females: 7%). Education is free and compulsory for five years (6–11 years of age). Secondary education lasts for another five years.

The Castro government added agricultural and technical programs to the secondary-school curriculum; the work-study principle is now central to Cuban secondary education. Cuba has five universities.

32 MEDIA

In 1992 there were 150 AM and 5 FM radio broadcasting stations and 58 television stations. In the same year, 3,695,000 radios and about 1,746,000 television sets were in use. All telephone service is free. In 1993 there were 321,054 telephones.

Like the radio and television stations, the press is controlled and owned by the government. Cuba's major newspapers, published in Havana, include *Granma*, published by the Communist party (with an estimated 1991 circulation of 420,000) and *Juventud Rebelde* (150,000).

33 TOURISM AND RECREATION

The Cuban government actively promotes tourism to offset the financial decline brought on by the collapse of the Soviet bloc. In 1991, an estimated 424,000 tourists visited Cuba, 207,000 from the Americas and 171,000 from Europe. Direct revenue from tourism was US$300 million. In 1992, tourism became the country's main source of income from abroad.

Among Cuba's attractions are fine beaches, magnificent coral reefs, and historic sites in Old Havana, Trinidad, and Santiago de Cuba. In June 1992, Cuba was admitted to the Caribbean Tourism Organization.

34 FAMOUS CUBANS

José Martí (1853–95), poet, journalist, and patriot, was the moving spirit behind Cuban independence. The major heroes of the revolution against Batista are Fidel Castro Ruz (b.1926); his brother, Gen. Raúl Castro Ruz (b.1931); and Argentine-born Ernesto "Che" Guevara (1928–67). Cubans notable in literature include poet Nicolás Guillén (b.1902) and playwright and novelist Alejo Carpentier y Valmont (1904–80). Desi Arnaz (1917–86) was a bandleader and television star.

35 BIBLIOGRAPHY

Cuba: A Short History. New York: Cambridge University Press, 1993.

Haverstock, Nathan A. *Cuba in Pictures.* Minneapolis: Lerner Publications Company, 1987.

Nagel, Rob, and Anne Commire. "Ernesto 'Che' Guevara." In *World Leaders, People Who Shaped the World.* Volume III: North and South America. Detroit: U*X*L, 1994.

———. "José Martí." In *World Leaders, People Who Shaped the World.* Volume III: North and South America. Detroit: U*X*L, 1994.

Vizquez, A. and R. Casas. *Cuba.* Chicago: Children's Press, 1987.

White, Peter T. "Cuba at a Crossroads." Rudolph, James D. ed. *National Geographic,* August 1991, 90–121.

CYPRUS*

Republic of Cyprus
Kypriaki Dimokratia

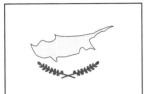

CAPITAL: Nicosia.

FLAG: The national flag consists of the map of Cyprus in gold set above two green olive branches on a white field.

ANTHEM: *Ethnikos Hymnos (National Hymn),* beginning "Se gnorizo apo tin kopsi" ("I recognize you by the keenness of your spade").

MONETARY UNIT: The Cyprus pound (c£) is a paper currency of 100 cents. There are coins of 1, 2, 5, 10, 20, and 50 cents and 1 pound, and notes of 50 cents, and 1, 5, 10, and 20 pounds. c£1 = $1.9833 (or $1 = c£0.5042). The Turkish lira (TL) of 100 kuruş is the currency in the Turkish Cypriot zone.

WEIGHTS AND MEASURES: The metric system is the legal standard. Imperial and local measures are also used.

HOLIDAYS: New Year's Day, 1 January; Epiphany, 6 January; Late President Makarios' Day, 19 January; Greek Independence Day, 25 March; Cyprus National Day, 1 April; Labor Day, 1 May; Cyprus Independence Day, 1 October; Greek Resistance Day, 28 October; Christmas, 25 December; Boxing Day, 26 December. Holidays observed by the Turkish Cypriot community include Founding of the Turkish Federated State of Cyprus, 13 February; Turkish National Sovereignty and Children's Day, 23 April; Turkish Youth and Sports Day, 19 May; Turkish Victory Day, 30 August; Turkish Independence Day, 29 October. Movable Christian religious holidays include Green Monday, Good Friday, Holy Saturday, and Easter Monday. Movable Muslim religious holidays are observed in the Turkish Cypriot zone.

TIME: 2 PM = noon GMT.

1 LOCATION AND SIZE

Cyprus is the third largest Mediterranean island, after Sicily and Sardinia. Its area is 9,250 square kilometers (3,571 square miles), about three-fourths the size of the state of Connecticut. Cyprus has a total coastline of 648 kilometers (403 miles). Since 1975, the northern third of the island, or 3,367 square kilometers (1,300 square miles), has been controlled by the Turkish Cypriot Federated State, which on 15 November 1983 proclaimed its independence as the Turkish Republic of Northern Cyprus; the southern two-thirds (5,884 square kilometers/2,272 square miles) are controlled by the government of the Republic of Cyprus. A narrow zone called the "green line," patrolled by United Nations forces, separates the two regions and divides Nicosia, the national capital.

*Unless otherwise noted, all statistical data refer to that part of the island controlled by the government of the Republic of Cyprus (i.e., the Greek Cypriot zone).

The capital city of Cyprus, Nicosia, is located in the north central part of the country.

2 TOPOGRAPHY

Two diverse mountain systems, the Troodos Mountains in the west and the Kyrenia Mountains in the north, occupy the greater part of the island. Between these principal formations lies a low central plain which contains the bulk of the island's farm and grazing land. There are few lakes.

3 CLIMATE

Cyprus's climate is mostly dry and sunny. The mean annual temperature is about 20°C (68°F). In winter, snow covers the higher peaks of the Troodos; elsewhere the temperature seldom falls below freezing. The annual average precipitation ranges from below 30 centimeters (12 inches) in the west-central lowlands to more than 114 centimeters (45 inches) in the higher parts of the southern massif (mountain mass).

4 PLANTS AND ANIMALS

Forests consist principally of Aleppo pine; other important conifers are the stone pine, cedar, Mediterranean cypress, and juniper. Oriental plane and alder are plentiful in the valleys, while Olympus dwarf oak is found on the hills. Wildflowers grow in great numbers, and herbs are numerous. Cyprus has few wild animals, but bird life is varied and includes partridges, quails, snipes, plovers, woodcocks, and eagles.

5 ENVIRONMENT

The most significant environmental problems in Cyprus are water pollution, erosion, and wildlife preservation. The purity of the water supply is threatened by industrial pollutants, pesticides used in agricultural areas, and the lack of adequate sewage treatment. Cyprus has 0.2 cubic miles of water, of which 91% is used for farming activity. One hundred percent of Cyprus's urban and rural dwellers have access to safe water. The expansion of urban centers threatens the habitat of Cyprus's wildlife. As of 1994, 1 mammal species, 17 types of birds and 43 plant species, in a total of 2,000, are threatened with extinction.

6 POPULATION

At the end of 1992, the population for the whole of Cyprus was estimated at 725,000. The population for the year 2000 was projected at 765,000. The population density in 1992 was estimated at 78 persons per square kilometer (203 per square mile). Nicosia, the capital, had an estimated population (in the Greek-controlled part) of 166,500 in 1992.

7 MIGRATION

Cyprus suffered massive population shifts following the Turkish military occupation of the northern third of the island in July 1974. Some 120,000 Greek Cypriots fled from the occupied area to the south, and about 60,000 Turkish Cypriots fled in the opposite direction. Throughout the 1970s and 1980s, most Greek Cypriot emigrants went to Australia, the United Kingdom, the United States, Canada, South Africa, or Greece. In the late 1980s, about 300,000 were living in seven foreign countries.

8 ETHNIC GROUPS

Following the 16th-century Turkish conquest, Cyprus received a large wave of emigration from Turkey (then known as the Ottoman Empire). There was practically no intermarriage between Turks and Greeks; each community preserved its own religion, language, dress, and other national characteristics.

Greek Cypriots outnumber Turks more than four-to-one. Estimates in 1989 put the proportion of Greek and Turkish Cypriots at 80% and 18.6%, respectively. The rest of the population included about 6,300 Lebanese Maronites and Armenians, and 8,900 others (mainly British).

9 LANGUAGES

After Cyprus's independence in 1960, Greek and Turkish became the official languages. Since 1974, Greek has been the language of the south and Turkish the language of the north. English is also widely used.

10 RELIGIONS

The Church of Cyprus is one of the oldest member bodies of the Holy Orthodox Eastern Church. Nearly all Turkish Cypriots are Sunni Muslims of the Hanafi sect. In 1990, 76.2% of the total population of Cyprus was Greek Orthodox, 18.7% Muslim, 2.7% members of various Christian churches, and 2.4% of other persuasions. Religious minorities include

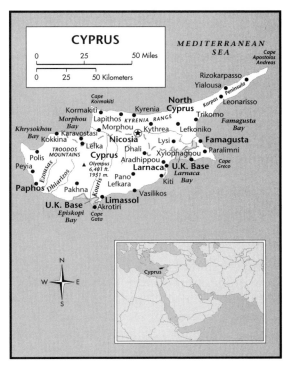

LOCATION: 34°33′ to 35°34′N; 32°16′ to 34°37′E.
TERRITORIAL SEA LIMIT: 12 miles.

Armenian Orthodox, Anglicans, Maronite Christians, and Roman Catholics.

11 TRANSPORTATION

Internal transport is exclusively by road. In 1991, 5,170 kilometers (3,213 miles) of all-weather asphalted highways connected the island's principal towns and larger villages. In 1991 there were 189,701 licensed private motor cars, and 11,180 commercial vehicles.

Although off the main world shipping routes, Cyprus is served by passenger and cargo shipping lines. The Limassol and Larnaca ports have been modernized and are now considered good deep water harbors. In 1991, 1,210 ships totaling 20,036,000 gross registered tons comprised the merchant fleet. There are no inland waterways.

In 1991, Larnaca international airport handled 2.5 million passengers and 26,600 tons of cargo. Cyprus Airways has services to Middle Eastern countries, but there is no regular internal air service.

12 HISTORY

Cyprus was famous in the ancient world for its copper, which, from about 2200 BC, was used in the making of bronze. The island is believed either to have derived its name from or to have given it to this mineral through the Greek word *kypros*— copper. Greek colonizers came to Cyprus in sizable numbers in 1400 BC, and were followed soon afterward by Phoenician settlers. In about 560 BC, Cyprus was conquered by Egypt and then in turn by Persia, Macedonia, Egypt again, Rome, and the Byzantine Empire.

Its Christian history began with the visits of Paul (as described in the Acts of the Apostles). For several centuries after 632 AD, Cyprus underwent a series of Arab invasions. The island was conquered by the English monarch Richard I (the Lion-Hearted) during the Third Crusade. It was later transferred to Guy de Lusignan, under whose dynasty the island thrived for some 300 years before it was conquered in 1489 by Venice and in 1571 by the Turks.

The administration of Cyprus by the United Kingdom began in 1878, under an agreement with Turkey. Upon the entry of Turkey into World War I (1914–18),

Photo credit: Cyprus Tourism Organization.

A lace maker displays her work in the village of Omodhos.

Cyprus was added to the British crown. It was declared a crown colony and placed under a British governor in 1925.

For centuries, under Ottoman and British rule, Greek Cypriots had regarded Greece as their mother country and had sought union (enosis) with it as Greek nationals. In 1931, this desire led to violence, which the British colonial administration put a stop to with severe repressive measures. At the close of World War II (1939–45) demands that the United Kingdom yield the island to Greece were renewed. The National Organization of Cypriot Fighters, led by Colonel George Grivas, a retired Greek army officer, began a campaign of terrorism in 1955 in which upward of 2,000 casualties were recorded.

The prime ministers of Greece and Turkey met in Zürich, Switzerland, early in 1959 in an attempt to reach a settlement. Unexpectedly, the Greek Cypriots set aside their demands for union with Greece and accepted instead proposals for an independent republic. The new republic would have representation from both the Greek and Turkish Cypriot communities. By 1 July 1960, an agreement was reached on all outstanding differences, and independence was officially declared on 16 August.

From the beginning, the two Cypriot communities differed on how the Zürich agreement would be carried out, and how much autonomy the Turkish minority would enjoy. Throughout the 1960s there were outbreaks of violence on the island. The United Nations maintained peace with a peacekeeping force of about 3,500 troops. In addition to the UN forces, both Greek Cypriot National Guard and Turkish Cypriot militia also maintained sizable troops of their own.

Although talks continued between the two communities, no agreement was reached on the two basic points of dispute. Politically, the Turks wanted full freedom, while the Greeks demanded a continued single majority rule. Territorially, the Turks wanted Cyprus divided into Greek- and Turkish-controlled zones, a position that clashed with the Greek Cypriot concept of a unified state.

When peace talks in Geneva broke down, a full-scale Turkish offensive began, and by mid-August, Turkish forces controlled about 38% of the island. On 13 February 1975, the Turkish-held area broke away and proclaimed itself the Turkish Cypriot Federated State.

After the partition, Greek and Turkish Cypriot leaders met several times under United Nations protection to explore a possible solution to the Cyprus problem, but no agreement was reached. On 15 November 1983, the Turkish sector proclaimed itself an independent state. It was named the Turkish Republic of Northern Cyprus (TRNC). However, only Turkey recognizes the TRNC. The United Nations, which condemned the TRNC's declaration of independence, tried repeatedly to end the partition between north and south, but all proposals were rejected by both sides.

Talks between both sides and have taken place at intervals since 1988. In 1991, the United Nations Security Council called on both sides to complete an overall framework agreement. To date no one has been able to find a solution to the problem.

13 GOVERNMENT

The 1960 constitution of the Republic of Cyprus respects the two existing ethnic communities, Greek and Turkish, by providing for representation from each in the government. The president must be Greek and the vice-president Turkish. Legislative authority is vested in the 50-member House of Representatives, elected by the two chief communities in the proportion of 35 Greek and 15 Turkish.

On 13 February 1975, after the Turkish invasion of Cyprus, the Turkish Cypriot Federated State (TCFS) was proclaimed in the northern part of the island, and Rauf Denktash became its president. A draft constitution was ratified by the Turkish Cypriot community in a referendum on 8 June. On 15 November 1983, the TCFS proclaimed itself the Turkish Republic of Northern Cyprus (TRNC), separate and independent from the Republic of Cyprus. In June 1985, TRNC voters approved a new constitution that embodied most of the old constitution's articles.

Cyprus has six administrative districts.

14 POLITICAL PARTIES

The four principal political parties of the Greek community in 1992 were the center-right Democratic Party (Demokratiko Komma—DIKO); the Progressive Party of the Working People (Anorthotikon Komma Ergazomenou Laou—AKEL); the right-wing Democratic Rally (Demokratikos Synagermos—DISY); and the Socialist Party (Eniea Demokratiki Enosi Kyprou—EDEK).

The Turkish Republic of Northern Cyprus held elections for a 50-seat Legislative Assembly in 1985. The right-wing National Unity Party won 24 seats (37% of the vote); the Republican Turkish Party, 12 seats (21%); the Communal Liberation Party, 10 seats (16%); and the New Dawn Party, 4 seats (9%).

15 JUDICIAL SYSTEM

In the Greek Cypriot area, the Supreme Court is the final court of appeal and has final authority in constitutional and administrative cases. The seven Orthodox Church courts have sole jurisdiction in matrimonial cases involving Greek Orthodox Church members. Appeals go from these courts to the appeals tribunal of the Church.

In the Turkish-held area, a Supreme Court acts as a final appeals court, with powers similar to those of the Supreme Court in the Greek Cypriot area. In addition to district courts, there are two Turkish communal courts, as well as a communal appeals court.

16 ARMED FORCES

Under the Zürich agreement, Cyprus was to have an army of 2,000 men, of whom 60% were to be Greek and 40% Turkish. The Cypriot national guard, which is wholly Greek, comprised 8,000 men and 400 women in 1991, backed by 88,000 reservists. About 1,000 troops and advisors from Greece were stationed in the south in 1986.

The Turkish community has its own police force and army of 4,000 regulars and 30,000 reserves. A sizable military force from the country of Turkey (about 30,000 in 1993) has supported these native forces since the 1974 intervention.

British forces, 4,200 ground troops and airmen in 1993, are stationed at two British bases. The United Nations force (UNFICYP) is composed of a 2,300-man brigade from four nations. The Cypriot government spends $284 million for defense.

17 ECONOMY

The 1974 coup and the Turkish armed intervention badly disrupted the economy. Physical destruction and the displacement of about a third of the population reduced the output of the economy's manufacturing, agricultural, and service areas. In general, the Greek Cypriot zone recovered much more quickly and successfully than the Turkish-held region, which was burdened with the weaknesses of Turkey's economy as well as its own. In the south, on the other hand, tourism has exceeded prewar levels, and foreign assistance has been readily available

18 INCOME

In 1992, Cyprus's gross national product (GNP) was $7,070 million at current prices, or $10,380 per person. For the period 1985–92 the average inflation rate was 4.2%, resulting in a real growth rate in GNP of 5.1% per person.

19 INDUSTRY

Industries are numerous and small in scale, most of them employing fewer than 10 workers. Manufacturing, encouraged by income tax breaks and protected by import tariffs, primarily involves the processing of local products for both export and the home market, or the production of consumer items including foods, beverages, apparel, plastic products, and tobacco products.

Major plants include modern flour mills, tire-treading factories, knitting mills, pre-processing facilities, and a petroleum refinery. In 1992, 48,888 persons were employed in manufacturing. In 1992, 1,131,604 tons of cement, 5,117 pairs of footwear, and 55.5 million liters of soft drinks were produced.

20 LABOR

In 1991, according to provisional data, Cyprus's workers totaled 279,900, of whom 8,300 (2.9%) were unemployed. Of those employed, 57.7% worked in services, 27.8% in industry, 13% in agriculture, and 1.5% in other areas. Trade unions represent employees in agriculture, forestry, fishing, mining, quarrying, construction, utilities, governmental services, trade, and general labor.

21 AGRICULTURE

Most farmers raise a variety of staple crops, ranging from grains and vegetables to fruits. Principal crops in 1992 included barley, potatoes, grapes, grapefruit, oranges, lemons, and wheat. Tomatoes, carrots, olives, and other fruits and vegetables are also grown.

The areas that have been Turkish-held since 1974 include much of Cyprus's most fertile land; citrus fruits are a major export.

Favorable weather in 1992 helped grain farmers triple production over the previous year, pushing production of field crops up 90%.

22 DOMESTICATED ANIMALS

Animal husbandry contributes about one-third of total agricultural production.

Photo credit: Cyprus Tourism Organization.

A marketplace in Cyprus where produce is sold.

Output of pork, poultry, and eggs meets domestic demand, but beef and mutton are imported. Sheep and goats provide most of the milk products. In 1992, sheep numbered about 310,000, hogs 285,000, and goats 205,000. Livestock products in 1992 included 32,000 tons of pork, 20,000 tons of poultry meat, 113,000 tons of milk, and 8,000 tons of eggs.

23 FISHING

Year-round fishing is carried on mostly in coastal waters not more than 3.2 kilometers (2 miles) from shore. The 1991 catch was 2,690 tons. Fish exports in 1991 were valued at $4.4 million.

24 FORESTRY

About 175,400 hectares (433,000 acres) are forested; 137,800 hectares (340,500 acres) are reserves managed by the Forest Department. However, most of Cyprus's timber requirements must be met by imports. The timber cut decreased to 56,000 cubic meters in 1991.

25 MINING

In 1991, 700 persons were employed in the mining industry. In the same year, the value of exported minerals was $3.7 million. Production in 1991 included 58,500 tons of bentonite, 5,450,000 tons of sand and gravel, and 37,000 tons of crude gypsum. Other mine and quarry products included marl, umber, and lime.

26 FOREIGN TRADE

With limited natural resources, Cyprus is dependent on other countries for many of its needs. Principal export products are fruits and vegetables, beverages and tobacco, wines, and apparel. More than half of its total output is exported. Imports reflect the heavy demand for fuels and lubricants, machinery, and other manufactured items, as well as for foods, chemicals, and textiles and fabrics.

In 1992, Arab countries took 32% of Cyprus's exports, European Community countries received 41%. The United Kingdom is Cyprus' leading import supplier and export purchaser, accounting for 19.2% of exports and 11.3% of imports in 1992.

27 ENERGY AND POWER

The principal source of power is steam-generated electricity, which is distributed by the Electricity Authority of Cyprus (EAC). Power generation rose to 2,404 million kilowatt hours in 1992. All towns and most villages were supplied. In 1992, the Turkish sector used 380 million kilowatt hours.

28 SOCIAL DEVELOPMENT

Social insurance is required of all employees and self-employed persons in the Greek Cypriot zone. It provides unemployment and sickness benefits; old age, widows', and orphans' pensions; maternity benefits; missing persons' allowances; injury and disablement benefits; and death and marriage grants. A law requiring equal pay for both sexes in private employment was in effect by late 1992.

29 HEALTH

In 1992, there were 1,199 doctors. There are both public and private medical facilities, including about 50 rural health centers. The island has a low incidence of infectious diseases, but hydatid disease (echinococcosis) is widespread. Average life expectancy in 1992 was 77 years. In 1990, 95% of the population had access to health care services, and 100% had access to safe water.

30 HOUSING

Village homes in Cyprus are generally constructed of stone, mud bricks, and other locally available materials; in the more prosperous rural centers, there are houses of burnt brick or concrete. Between 1974 and 1990, 50,227 families were housed in a total of 13,589 low-cost dwellings. The total number of housing units grew from about 75,000 in 1976 to about 125,000 in 1988.

31 EDUCATION

Adult literacy in Cyprus in 1993 was 94%. Education is compulsory for nine years with children attending six years of primary school and six years of secondary. In 1991, there were 390 primary schools with 3,524 teachers and 63,454 students attending them. At the secondary level, there were 3,848 teachers and 47,908 students attending. Of this number, 3,172 were in vocational schools.

32 MEDIA

The Cyprus Telecommunications Authority (CTA) connects Cyprus with 67 other countries. In 1991 there were 303,822 telephones. The Cyprus Broadcasting Corp. transmits radio programs in both AM and FM on three channels in Greek, Turkish, Arabic, and English. In 1991, 207,000 radios and 102,000 television sets were in use.

There were 16 daily newspapers and 8 weeklies published in English, Greek, or Turkish as of 1993. The following are the major daily newspapers (with estimated 1991 circulations): *Phileleftheros* (20,000); *Haravghi* (13,000); *Simerini* (13,000); *Apogevmatini* (10,000); and *Agon* (9,000).

Selected Social Indicators

These statistics are estimates for the period 1988 to 1993. For comparison purposes, data for the United States and averages for low-income countries and high-income countries are also given.

Indicator	Cyprus	Low-income countries	High-income countries	United States
Per capita gross national product†	$10,380	$380	$23,680	$24,740
Population growth rate	1.1%	1.9%	0.6%	1.0%
Population growth rate in urban areas	2.1%	3.9%	0.8%	1.3%
Population per square kilometer of land	78	78	25	26
Life expectancy in years	77	62	77	76
Number of people per physician	1,058	>3,300	453	419
Number of pupils per teacher (primary school)	19	39	<18	20
Illiteracy rate (15 years and older)	6%	41%	<5%	<3%
Energy consumed per capita (kg of oil equivalent)	2,517	364	5,203	7,918

† The gross national product (GNP) is the total dollar value of all goods and services produced by a country in a year. The per capita GNP is calculated by dividing a country's GNP by its population. The World Bank defines low-income countries as those with a per capita GNP of $695 or less. High-income countries have a per capita GNP of $8,626 or more. Less than 14% of the world's 5.5 billion people live in high-income countries, while almost 60% live in low-income countries.   > = greater than   < = less than

Sources: World Bank, Social Indicators of Development 1995, Baltimore: Johns Hopkins University Press, 1995. Central Intelligence Agency, World Fact Book, Washington, D.C.: Government Printing Office, 1994.

33 TOURISM AND RECREATION

Although Cyprus is located off the main routes of travel and has few luxury hotels, the island's pleasant climate, scenic beauties, extensive roads, and rich historic sites have attracted numerous visitors. Tourism generated $1.02 billion in foreign exchange earnings in 1991. During the 1991 tourist season, Cyprus attracted 1.38 million foreign visitors, of whom an estimated 1.2 million came from Europe.

34 FAMOUS CYPRIOTS

Most widely known Cypriot in the pre-Christian world was the philosopher Zeno (335?–263? BC), who preached a philosophy of Stoicism (a philosophy that believes human beings should be free of passion and accept all things that happen to them as the result of divine will).

Makarios III (1913–77), archbishop from 1950 and a leader in the struggle for independence, was elected the first president of Cyprus in December 1959, and reelected in 1968 and 1973.

35 BIBLIOGRAPHY

Cyprus in Pictures. Minneapolis: Lerner, 1992.
Fox, M. Cyprus. Chicago: Children's Press, 1993.
Szulc, Tad. "Cyprus: A Time of Reckoning." National Geographic, July 1993, 104–130.
Solsten, Eric (ed.). Cyprus, a Country Study. 4th ed. Washington, D.C.: Government Printing Office, 1993.

CZECH REPUBLIC

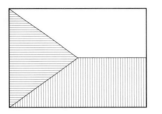

Czech Republic
Ceskaá Republika

CAPITAL: Prague (Praha).

FLAG: The national flag consists of a white stripe over a red stripe, with a blue triangle extending from hoist to midpoint.

ANTHEM: *Kde domov můj (Where Is My Native Land).*

MONETARY UNIT: The koruna (Kc) is a paper currency of 100 haléru, which replaced the Czechoslovak koruna (Kcs) on 8 February 1993. There are coins of 1, 5, 10, 20, and 50 heller and of 1, 2, 5, 10, 20, and 50 koruny, and notes of 10, 20, 50, 100, 200, 500, 1,000, 2,000, and 5,000 koruny. Kc = $0.0340 (or $1 = Kc29.404).

WEIGHTS AND MEASURES: The metric system is the legal standard.

HOLIDAYS: New Year's Day, 1 January; Labor Day, 1 May; Anniversary of Liberation, 9 May; Day of the Apostles, St. Cyril and St. Methodius, 6 July; Christmas, 25 December; St. Stephen's Day, 26 December. Easter Monday is a movable holiday.

TIME: 1 PM = noon GMT.

1 LOCATION AND SIZE

The Czech Republic is a landlocked eastern European country that contains some of the oldest and most significant land routes in Europe. Comparatively, the Czech Republic is slightly smaller than the state of South Carolina with a total area of 78,703 square kilometers (30,387 square miles). It has a total boundary length of 1,880 kilometers (1,168 miles). The capital city of the Czech Republic, Prague, is located in the northcentral part of the country.

2 TOPOGRAPHY

The Czech Republic consists of two main regions. Bohemia in the west is comprised of rolling plains, hills, and plateaus surrounded by low mountains. Moravia in the east is very hilly.

3 CLIMATE

The climate is temperate with cool summers, and cold, cloudy, and humid winters. The average temperature in Prague ranges from about −1°C (30°F) in January to 19°C (66°F) in July. Over three-fifths of the rain falls during the spring and summer. The precipitation range is from 56 centimeters (22 inches) to more than 127 centimeters (50 inches); rainfall is below 58 centimeters (23 inches) in west Bohemia and south Moravia.

4 PLANTS AND ANIMALS

Almost 70% of the forest is mixed or deciduous. Some original steppe grassland areas are still found in Moravia. Mammals commonly found in the Czech Republic include the fox, hare, hart, rabbit, and wild pig. A variety of birds inhabit the lowlands and valleys. Fish such as carp, pike, and trout appear in numerous rivers and ponds.

5 ENVIRONMENT

The Czech and Slovak republics suffer from air, water, and land pollution caused by industry, mining, and agriculture. Acid rain, combined with air pollution from Poland and the former German Democratic Republic (East Germany), has destroyed much of the forest in the northern part of the former Czechoslovakia. Land erosion caused by agricultural and mining practices is also a significant problem.

As of 1994, 2 mammal and 18 bird species in the Czech and Slovak republics were endangered, as well as 2 types of fish and 29 types of plants.

6 POPULATION

According to the 1991 census, the population was 10,302,215. Average density in 1991 was 131 people per square kilometer (338 per square mile).

Prague, the capital and principal city, had a population of 1,215,076 in 1991.

7 MIGRATION

About 100,000 persons left the Czech Republic after the Soviet invasion in August 1968. Emigration slowed during the 1970s to about 5,000 annually, but during the 1980s, some 10,000 people (according to Western estimates) were leaving each year. In 1991 Czechoslovakia received 5,782 immigrants; emigrants totaled 3,896.

8 ETHNIC GROUPS

Between 1945 and 1948 (the period after World War II), the deportation of Germans altered the ethnic structure of the Czech lands. Since the late 1940s, most of the remaining Germans have either assimilated or emigrated to the West.

Slovaks comprised 3% of the population in 1991. There are small numbers of Poles and an uncertain number of Gypsies.

9 LANGUAGES

Czech, which belongs to the Slavic language group, is the major and official language. Many older Czechs speak German; many younger people speak Russian and English.

10 RELIGIONS

In 1990, about 4.7 million Czechs were Roman Catholic. Seventeen other faiths are nationally recognized. Protestants (mainly Lutherans), Greek Catholics, and Russian Orthodox are also present in significant numbers. In 1991, the Jewish population in the Czech Republic was only 4,500.

11 TRANSPORTATION

There are some 9,434 kilometers (5,862 miles) of railroads in the Czech Republic. Highways cover 55,890 kilometers (34,730 miles); the majority are hard surfaced.

As a landlocked nation, the Czech Republic relies on coastal outlets in Poland, Croatia, Slovenia, and Germany for international commerce by sea.

LOCATION: 49°26′ to 51°3′ N; 12°6′ to 18°54′ E. **BOUNDARY LENGTHS:** Poland, 658 kilometers (409 miles); Slovakia, 214 kilometers (133 miles); Austria, 362 kilometers (225 miles); Germany, 646 kilometers (401 miles).

The principal river ports in the Czech Republic are Prague on the Vltava, and Děčín on the Elbe.

Ruzyne airport at Prague is the nation's primary commercial airlink; in 1991 it served 1,342,000 passengers and 17,300 tons of freight. In all, Czech airports in 1992 performed 2,158 million passenger-kilometers and 230 million freight ton-kilometers of service.

12 HISTORY

The first recorded inhabitants of the territory of the present-day Czech Republic settled there about 50 BC. Early ethnic groups included Celts, Slavs, and Franks. The Moravian Empire thrived in the 9th century but was destroyed by invading Magyars (Hungarians), who seized the eastern part, while the Kingdom of Bohemia took control of the west.

Photo credit: Corel Corporation.

A view of St. Vitus' Cathedral in Prague. About 4.7 million Czechs are Roman Catholic.

In the 14th century Charles IV was King of Bohemia, as well as the Holy Roman Emperor, ushering in the Czech "Golden Age." In 1348 he founded Charles University in Prague, beginning the city's tradition as a seat of learning. In the 15th century Bohemia became a center of opposition to the Catholic church, and to German domination. The opposition was led by Jan Hus, who was burned at the stake for heresy in 1415. By 1600 the Czechs were mostly Protestant, while their rulers were Catholic. Although Protestants were able to obtain certain civil freedoms,

peace was fragile. In 1618 two Protestant churches were closed, leading Protestants to throw two royal governors out of the windows of Prague Castle, an act known since as the "Defenestration of Prague." The Thirty Years' War followed, ending in 1648 with the Peace of Westphalia, which led to large-scale immigration of Germans into Bohemia.

Under Empress Maria-Theresa (1740–80) Bohemia became part of Austria. Czech culture and language were suppressed. When rebellions broke out across Europe in 1848, the Czechs demanded greater rights. Austrian authorities responded by imposing a military dictatorship, which struggled to restrain a steadily rising tide of Czech nationalism.

When World War I (1914) began, thousands of Czech soldiers surrendered to the Russians, rather than fight for the Austro-Hungarians. They were reorganized as the Czech Legion, which fought on the Russian side.

Formation of the Czechoslovak Republic

During the war, the Czechs joined with the Slovaks and other suppressed nationalities of the Austro-Hungarian Empire in pushing for their own state. The Czechoslovak Republic, established in October 1918 under President Tomas Masaryk, combined at least five nationalities—Czechs, the so-called Sudeten Germans, Slovaks, Moravians, and Ruthenians. The Czech lands were more developed economically, and Czech politicians dominated the political system. A large number of Slovak nationalists wanted complete independence.

After first occupying the Sudeten-German area in 1938, Hitler took over the remainder of the Czech lands on 15 March 1939, ending the first republic. Eduard Benes, the president, left the country and established a Provisional Government in London in 1940, while Klement Gottwald, the communist leader, went to Moscow. At the end of World War II (1945), negotiations between Benes, Gottwald, and Josef Stalin established the basis for a postwar Czechoslovakian government.

The new National Front government ran Czechoslovakia as a democracy until 1948, when a military coup with Soviet backing forced President Benes to accept a government headed by Gottwald. A wave of purges and arrests rolled over the country from 1949 to 1954. Gottwald died a few days after Stalin died, in March 1953. His successors, presidents Zapotocky and Novotny, both clung to harsh methods of control, holding Czechoslovakia in a tight grip until well into the 1960s.

The Khrushchev-led liberalization in the Union of Soviet Socialist Republics (USSR) encouraged liberals within the Czechoslovak party to try to imitate Moscow. In January 1968, the presidency was separated from the Communist party chairmanship, and Alexander Dubček was named head of the Czechoslovak Communist Party, the first Slovak ever to hold the post.

Novotny resigned in March 1968, and, under Dubček, Czechoslovakia embarked

Photo credit: Corel Corporation.

Socialist art on a doorway in Prague, the capital city of the Czech Republic.

on a radical liberalization, termed "socialism with a human face." The leaders of the USSR and other eastern bloc nations viewed the developments of the "Prague Spring" with alarm and issued warnings to Dubček.

Finally, on the night of 20–21 August 1968, military units from almost all the Warsaw Pact nations invaded Czechoslovakia to "save it from counter-revolution." Dubček and other officials were arrested, and the country was placed under Soviet control. A purge of liberals followed, and Dubček was expelled from the party.

Between 1970 and 1975 nearly one-third of the party was dismissed, as the new communist Party leader Gustav Husak consolidated his power, reuniting the titles of party head and republic president.

Political Change by Popular Demand

Once again it was liberalization in the USSR (under the terms "perestroika" and "glasnost") which set off political change in Czechoslovakia. Husak ignored Soviet leader Mikhail Gorbachev's calls for Party reform. In 1987, Husak announced his retirement and his replacement by Milos Jakes.

In 1989, as the East German government was forced to give in to popular demand for change, Czech citizens were encouraged to make similar demands. On 17 November, a group of about 3,000 youths gathered in Prague's Wenceslas Square, demanding free elections. On Jakes's orders, they were attacked and beaten by security forces; this ignited a swell of public indignation, expressed in ten days of nonstop meetings and demonstrations. This so-called "velvet revolution" ended on 24 November, when Jakes and all his government resigned.

Vaclav Havel, a playwright and founder of the Charter 77 dissident group, was named president on 29 December 1989. The old struggle between the Czechs and Slovaks resulted in the country being renamed the Czech and Slovak Federal Republic. Following the June 1990 elections, economic transformation of the country began.

Meanwhile, pressure for separation by Slovakia continued to build through 1991 and 1992. Legislative attempts to strengthen the central government failed, and the republics increasingly began to behave as though they were already separate. Their prime ministers eventually agreed to separate, in the so-called "velvet divorce," which took effect 1 January 1993. Havel was reconfirmed as president by a vote of the 200-member Czech parliament on 26 January 1993.

13 GOVERNMENT

The constitution of the Czech Republic was adopted in December 1992. It calls for a two-chamber legislative body, consisting of an 81-member senate and a 200-member lower body, or parliament. The former Czech assembly was transformed into the parliament upon the dissolution of Czechoslovakia, but the senate remains unfilled as of late 1994.

The head of the executive branch is the president, who will eventually be elected by popular election. The present president, Vaclav Havel, was elected by the parliament at the time of the republic's formation. The government is headed by the prime minister, who comes from the majority party, or a coalition.

14 POLITICAL PARTIES

At present the strongest political grouping in the republic is the Civic Democratic Party (CDP), headed by Prime Minister Vaclav Klaus.

The CDP has an unbreakable majority in parliament because of its coalition with three other parties, the Civic Democratic Alliance, Christian Democratic Union, and Christian Democratic Party. There are two more left-leaning parties, the Czech Social Democrats, and the Czech People's Party, and a number of small nationalist parties.

15 JUDICIAL SYSTEM

Under the 1992 constitution, the judiciary has been completely reorganized to provide for a system of courts which includes a Supreme Court, a Supreme Administrative Court, high, regional, and district courts, and a Constitutional Court. The 15-member Constitutional Court created in 1993 rules on the constitutionality of legislation.

16 ARMED FORCES

The Czech and Slovak republics' armed forces in 1993 totaled 145,000. The army had 72,000 regular troops and 450,000 reserves. The air force had 44,800 regulars and 45,000 reserves. Defense expenditures in 1990 were equivalent to $1.6 billion.

17 ECONOMY

In 1993, the Czech Republic emerged from 40 years of centralized economic planning in the communist era with a more prosperous and less debt-ridden economy than most other post-communist countries. It has significant industrial production and is strong in both heavy and precision engineering. The annual rate of inflation almost doubled from 11% in 1992 to 20% in 1993.

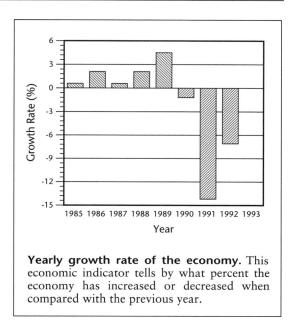

Yearly growth rate of the economy. This economic indicator tells by what percent the economy has increased or decreased when compared with the previous year.

18 INCOME

In 1992, the Czech Republic's gross national product (GNP) was $25,313 million at current prices, or $2,440 per person. For the period 1985–92 the average inflation rate was 8.5%, resulting in a real growth rate in GNP of –5.3% per person.

19 INDUSTRY

Light industry, including consumer goods—such as the world-famous pilsner beer, ham, and sugar—were important in the pre-World War II export trade, but machinery was predominant under the communist regime. Major industries in the Czech Republic include textiles, glass, china, wood and paper, iron, steel, coal, machine tools, and chemicals.

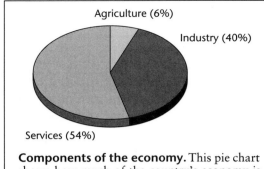

Agriculture (6%)

Industry (40%)

Services (54%)

Components of the economy. This pie chart shows how much of the country's economy is devoted to agriculture (includes forestry, hunting, and fishing), industry, or services.

20 LABOR

As of April 1993 the labor force was estimated at over 5.2 million, with some 2.7% of that total unemployed. Wages are expected to be comparable to European Communities wages within ten years. A severe housing shortage keeps workers in areas with high unemployment from moving to locations, such as Prague, where their chances of finding employment are better.

21 AGRICULTURE

Agriculture is a small but important part of the economy which has steadily declined since the "velvet revolution" of 1989. In 1992, agricultural production fell nearly 12% from the previous year, with a further decline of 10–15% estimated in 1993.

The principal crops are grains (wheat, rye, barley, oats, and corn), which support the Czech Republic's 70 breweries. At 166 liters (44 gallons) per person, the Czech Republic is the world's highest per capita beer-consuming nation. There is a long tradition of brewing in the Czech Republic; some of the world's oldest brands were created there.

22 DOMESTICATED ANIMALS

Hogs, cattle, and poultry are the main income-producers in the livestock sector. In 1990 there were an estimated 3.5 million head of cattle. The number of hogs that year reached an estimated 4.9 million; sheep, 451,000; and horses, 28,000.

23 FISHING

Fishing is a relatively unimportant source of domestic food supply.

24 FORESTRY

Forests cover about one-third of the total area of the Czech Republic. The need for wood products has far outstripped domestic supply, especially for furniture and construction materials.

25 MINING

The Czech Republic's nonfuel mineral resources include clay, tin, tungsten, lead, zinc, and uranium. In 1992, lime production amounted to 1.2 million tons (down from 2.1 million tons in 1991).

26 FOREIGN TRADE

As of 1993, European Community and EFTA countries accounted for 59% of trade by the Czech and Slovak republics. Their most important trading partners were Germany, the Commonwealth of Independent States (CIS), Austria, and Poland; followed by Italy, Switzerland, and France. In 1992, total exports (for

A view of Prague from above. Prague has a population of over 1.2 million people.

both republics) were valued at US$11,155 million, and total imports at US$12,406 million.

27 ENERGY AND POWER

As of 1992, the Czech Republic had a yearly electrical energy supply totaling 55,370 million kilowatt hours, of which 64.5% was produced by thermal power plants, 20.7% was generated at nuclear facilities, 12% came from industrial power plants, and 2.8% came from hydro-electric sources.

Domestic coal mining supplied the former Czechoslovakia with 55% of its annual energy needs.

28 SOCIAL DEVELOPMENT

After World War II, new social legislation made sickness, accident, disability, and old age insurance compulsory. The trade unions administered health insurance and family allowances.

Women exceed the number of men employed in farming, trade, health and social welfare, and education. However, they hold a larger share of lower-paying positions.

29 HEALTH

Factories and offices have health services, ranging from first-aid stations to hospitals. All school children receive medical

Selected Social Indicators

These statistics are estimates for the period 1988 to 1993. For comparison purposes, data for the United States and averages for low-income countries and high-income countries are also given.

Indicator	Czech Republic	Low-income countries	High-income countries	United States
Per capita gross national product†	**$2,440**	$380	$23,680	$24,740
Population growth rate	**-0.1%**	1.9%	0.6%	1.0%
Population growth rate in urban areas	**0.1%**	3.9%	0.8%	1.3%
Population per square kilometer of land	**131**	78	25	26
Life expectancy in years	**72**	62	77	76
Number of people per physician	**272**	>3,300	453	419
Number of pupils per teacher (primary school)	**18**	39	<18	20
Illiteracy rate (15 years and older)	**<1%**	41%	<5%	<3%
Energy consumed per capita (kg of oil equivalent)	**n.a.**	364	5,203	7,918

† The gross national product (GNP) is the total dollar value of all goods and services produced by a country in a year. The per capita GNP is calculated by dividing a country's GNP by its population. The World Bank defines low-income countries as those with a per capita GNP of $695 or less. High-income countries have a per capita GNP of $8,626 or more. Less than 14% of the world's 5.5 billion people live in high-income countries, while almost 60% live in low-income countries.

n.a. = data not available.   > = greater than   < = less than

Sources: World Bank, *Social Indicators of Development 1995*, Baltimore: Johns Hopkins University Press, 1995. Central Intelligence Agency, *World Fact Book*, Washington, D.C.: Government Printing Office, 1994.

attention, including inoculations, X-rays, and annual examinations. An insurance scheme is already in place to encourage private medical practice.

Special attention has been devoted to preventive medicine, with campaigns waged against tuberculosis, venereal diseases, cancer, poliomyelitis, diphtheria, and mental disturbances. Average life expectancy in 1992 was 72 years for men and women.

30 HOUSING

Currently, the lack of affordable housing, which keeps people from relocating for better job opportunities, is a major factor that is slowing economic growth in the Czech Republic. According to the March 1991 census, there were 5,320,095 apartments in the former Czechoslovakia. Housing starts totaled 10,000 in 1991, down nearly 80% from 1990.

31 EDUCATION

Education in the former Czechoslovakia was free up to, and including, the university level, for all who could obtain admission. There was practically no illiteracy. At the start of the 1991 school year, 1,898,470 students were enrolled in 6,480 primary schools; 848,721 students attended secondary schools; and 8,957 attended teacher training schools

Over 36 universities, colleges, and advanced schools in the former Czechoslovakia had a total of 177,110 students in 1991. Universities in the current Czech Republic include the world-famous Charles University at Prague (founded 1348); Palacky′ University; and J. E. Purkyňe University.

32 MEDIA

New investment is expected to increase the number of telephones from 17 to 34 per 100 inhabitants by 1999. The waiting time for new telephone service currently is from five to ten years. In 1992, about 150 private companies provided cable television to some 5% of the 3.4 million Czech households. Several broadcast radio and television channels also operate in the Republic.

Major newspapers, with their estimated 1991 circulations are *Lidove Noving* (450,000); *Mlada Fronta* (391,000); *Rude Pravo* (370,000); *Svobodne Slovo* (314,000); and *Prace* (235,000).

33 TOURISM AND RECREATION

Tourism has doubled since the overthrow of Communism. Hotel space in the Czech Republic is limited; many visitors are invited to rent a room in a private house or apartment. Several new luxury hotels were opened in 1993.

Prague, which survived World War II relatively intact, has numerous palaces

Photo credit: Corel Corporation.

Musicians perform at the spring music festival in Prague. Famous Czechs include the composers Antonín Dvorák and Leos Janácek.

and churches from the Renaissance and Baroque periods. There are many attractive mountain resorts, especially in northern Bohemia. Football (soccer), ice hockey, skiing, canoeing, swimming, and tennis are among the favorite sports.

34 FAMOUS CZECHS

Perhaps the two most famous Czechs are the religious reformer John Huss (Jan Hus, 1371–1415) and the theologian, educator, and philosopher John Amos Comenius (Jan Amos Komenský, 1592–1670), an early advocate of universal education.

The Good Soldier Schweik by Jaroslav Hašek (1883–1923) is a famous satire on militarism. Karel Capek (1890–1938), brilliant novelist, journalist, and playwright, is well known for his play *R.U.R.* (in which he coined the word *robot*). Bedřich Smetana (1824–84), Antonín Dvořák (1841–1904), and Leoš Janáček (1854–1928) were world-famous composers. The leading modern sculptor, Jan Stursa (1880–1925), is best known for his often-reproduced *The Wounded.*

The founder of modern Czechoslovakia was Tomáš Garrigue Masaryk (1850–1937). Alexander Dubček (b.1921) was the principal leader of the 1968 reform movement that ended with Soviet intervention. Gustáv Husák (b.1913) was general secretary of the Communist Party from 1969 to 1987. Parliamentary elections at the end of 1989 saw the rise of the playwright Vaclav Havel (b. 1936) to power. The Czech and Slovak republics decided to split in 1992. Havel was elected president of the Czech Republic in parliamentary elections.

The best-known political dissidents in the 1970s and 1980s were the playwrights Pavel Kohout (b.1928) and Václav Havel (b.1936). Miloš Forman (b.1932), a leader of the "new wave" of Czech cinema, emigrated after 1968 to the United States, where he has directed films including the award-winning *One Flew Over the Cuckoo's Nest.* The novelist Milan Kundera (b.1929), who has lived in France since 1975, is the best-known contemporary Czech writer. Two Czechs have become top world tennis players: Martina Navrátilová (b.1956), an expatriate since 1975, and Ivan Lendl (b.1960).

There have been only two Czechoslovak Nobel Prize winners: Jaroslav Heyrovský (1890–1967) in chemistry (1959), and the poet Jaroslav Seifert (1901–84) for literature in 1984.

35 BIBLIOGRAPHY

Abercrombie, Thomas J. "Czechoslovakia: the Velvet Divorce." *National Geographic,* September 1993, 2–37.

Gawdiak, Ihor, ed.. *Czechoslovakia, A Country Study.* 3d ed. Washington, D.C.: Library of Congress, 1989.

Kriseova, Eda. *Vaclav Havel: the Authorized Biography.* New York: St. Martin's Press, 1993.

Short, David. *Czechoslovakia.* Santa Barbara, Calif.: ABC-Clio, 1986.

Volgyes, Ivan, and Hans Brisch, eds. *Czechoslovakia: The Heritage of Ages Past.* New York: Columbia University Press, 1986.

GLOSSARY

aboriginal: The first known inhabitants of a country. A species of animals or plants which originated within a given area.

acid rain: Rain (or snow) that has become slightly acid by mixing with industrial air pollution.

adobe: A brick made from sun-dried heavy clay mixed with straw, used in building houses. A house made of adobe bricks.

adult literacy: The ability of adults to read and write.

afforestation: The act of turning arable land into forest or woodland.

agrarian economy: An economy where agriculture is the dominant form of economic activity. A society where agriculture dominates the day-to-day activities of the population is called an agrarian society.

air link: Refers to scheduled air service that allows people and goods to travel between two places on a regular basis.

airborne industrial pollutant: Pollution caused by industry that is supported or carried by the air.

allies: Groups or persons who are united in a common purpose. Typically used to describe nations that have joined together to fight a common enemy in war.

In World War I, the term Allies described the nations that fought against Germany and its allies. In World War II, Allies described the United Kingdom, United States, the USSR and their allies, who fought against the Axis Powers of Germany, Italy, and Japan.

aloe: A plant particularly abundant in the southern part of Africa, where leaves of some species are made into ropes, fishing lines, bow strings, and hammocks. It is also a symbolic plant in the Islamic world; anyone who returns from a pilgrimage to Mecca (Mekkah) hangs aloe over his door as a token that he has performed the journey.

Altaic language family: A family of languages spoken in portions of northern and eastern Europe, and nearly the whole of northern and central Asia, together with some other regions. The family is divided into five branches: the Ugrian or Finno-Hungarian, Smoyed, Turkish, Mongolian, and Tunguse.

althing: A legislative assembly.

amendment: A change or addition to a document.

Amerindian: A contraction of the two words, American Indian. It describes native peoples of North, South, or Central America.

amnesty: An act of forgiveness or pardon, usually taken by a government, toward persons for crimes they may have committed.

Anglican: Pertaining to or connected with the Church of England.

animism: The belief that natural objects and phenomena have souls or innate spiritual powers.

annual growth rate: The rate at which something grows over a period of 12 months.

annual inflation rate: The rate of inflation in prices over the course of a year.

anthracite coal: Also called hard coal, it is usually 90 to 95 percent carbon, and burns cleanly, almost without a flame.

anti-Semitism: Agitation, persecution, or discrimination (physical, emotional, economic, political, or otherwise) directed against the Jews.

apartheid: The past governmental policy in the Republic of South Africa of separating the races in society.

appeasement: To bring to a state of peace.

appellate: Refers to an appeal of a court decision to a high authority.

applied science: Scientific techniques employed to achieve results that solve practical problems.

aquaculture: The culture or "farming" of aquatic plants or other natural produce, as in the raising of catfish in "farms."

aquatic resources: Resources that come from, grow in, or live in water, including fish and plants.

aquifer: An underground layer of porous rock, sand, or gravel that holds water.

arable land: Land that can be cultivated by plowing and used for growing crops.

arbitration: A process whereby disputes are settled by a designated person, called the arbitrator, instead of by a court of law.

archipelago: Any body of water abounding with islands, or the islands themselves collectively.

archives: A place where records or a collection of important documents are kept.

arctic climate: Cold, frigid weather similar to that experienced at or near the north pole.

aristocracy: A small minority that controls the government of a nation, typically on the basis of inherited wealth.

armistice: An agreement or truce which ends military conflict in anticipation of a peace treaty.

artesian well: A type of well where the water rises to the surface and overflows.

ASEAN *see* Association of Southeast Asian Nations

Association of Southeast Asian Nations: ASEAN was established in 1967 to promote political, economic, and social cooperation among its six member countries: Indonesia, Malaysia, the Philippines, Singapore, Thailand, and Brunei. ASEAN headquarters are in Jakarta, Indonesia. In January 1992, ASEAN agreed to create the ASEAN Free Trade Area (AFTA).

atheist: A person who denies the existence of God or of a supreme intelligent being.

atoll: A coral island, consisting of a strip or ring of coral surrounding a central lagoon.

atomic weapons: Weapons whose extremely violent explosive power comes from the splitting of the nuclei of atoms (usually uranium or plutonium) by neutrons in a rapid chain reaction. These weapons may be referred to as atom bombs, hydrogen bombs, or H-bombs.

austerity measures: Steps taken by a government to conserve money or resources during an economically difficult time, such as cutting back on federally funded programs.

Australoid: Pertains to the type of aborigines, or earliest inhabitants, of Australia.

Austronesian language: A family of languages which includes practically all the languages of the Pacific Islands—Indonesian, Melanesian, Polynesian, and Micronesian sub-families. Does not include Australian or Papuan languages.

authoritarianism: A form of government in which a person or group attempts to rule with absolute authority without the representation of the citizens.

autonomous state: A country which is completely self-governing, as opposed to being a dependency or part of another country.

autonomy: The state of existing as a self-governing entity. For instance, when a country gains its independence from another country, it gains autonomy.

average inflation rate: The average rate at which the general prices of goods and services increase over the period of a year.

average life expectancy: In any given society, the average age attained by persons at the time of death.

Axis Powers: The countries aligned against the Allied Nations in World War II, originally applied to Nazi Germany and Fascist Italy (Rome-Berlin Axis), and later extended to include Japan.

bagasse: Plant residue left after a product, such as juice, has been extracted.

Baha'i: The follower of a religious sect founded by Mirza Husayn Ali in Iran in 1863.

Baltic states. The three formerly communist countries of Estonia, Latvia, and Lithuania that border on the Baltic Sea.

Bantu language group: A name applied to the languages spoken in central and south Africa.

banyan tree: An East Indian fig tree. Individual trees develop roots from the branches that descend to the ground and become trunks. These roots support and nourish the crown of the tree.

Baptist: A member of a Protestant denomination that practices adult baptism by complete immersion in water.

barren land: Unproductive land, partly or entirely treeless.

barter: Trade practice where merchandise is exchanged directly for other merchandise or services without use of money.

bedrock: Solid rock lying under loose earth.

bicameral legislature: A legislative body consisting of two chambers, such as the U.S. House of Representatives and the U.S. Senate.

bill of rights: A written statement containing the list of privileges and powers to be granted to a body of people, usually introduced when a government or other organization is forming.

bituminous coal: Soft coal; coal which burns with a bright-yellow flame.

black market: A system of trade where goods are sold illegally, often for excessively inflated prices. This type of trade usually develops to avoid paying taxes or tariffs levied by the government, or to get around import or export restrictions on products.

bloodless coup: The sudden takeover of a country's government by hostile means but without killing anyone in the process.

boat people: Used to describe individuals (refugees) who attempt to flee their country by boat.

bog: Wet, soft, and spongy ground where the soil is composed mainly of decayed or decaying vegetable matter.

Bolshevik Revolution. A revolution in 1917 in Russia when a wing of the Russian Social Democratic party seized power. The Bolsheviks advocated the violent overthrow of capitalism.

bonded labor: Workers bound to service without pay; slaves.

border dispute: A disagreement between two countries as to the exact location or length of the dividing line between them.

Brahman: A member (by heredity) of the highest caste among the Hindus, usually assigned to the priesthood.

broadleaf forest: A forest composed mainly of broadleaf (deciduous) trees.

Buddhism: A religious system common in India and eastern Asia. Founded by and based upon the teachings of Siddhartha Gautama, Buddhism asserts that suffering is an inescapable part of life. Deliverance can only be achieved through the practice of charity, temperance, justice, honesty, and truth.

buffer state: A small country that lies between two larger, possibly hostile countries, considered to be a neutralizing force between them.

bureaucracy: A system of government that is characterized by division into bureaus of administration with their own divisional heads. Also refers to the inflexible procedures of such a system that often result in delay.

Byzantine Empire: An empire centered in the city of Byzantium, now Istanbul in present-day Turkey.

CACM *see* Central American Common Market.

candlewood: A name given to several species of trees and shrubs found in the British West Indies, northern Mexico, and the southwestern United States. The plants are characterized by a very resinous wood.

canton: A territory or small division or state within a country.

capital punishment: The ultimate act of punishment for a crime, the death penalty.

capitalism: An economic system in which goods and services and the means to produce and sell them are privately owned, and prices and wages are determined by market forces.

Caribbean Community and Common Market (CARICOM): Founded in 1973 and with its headquarters in Georgetown, Guyana, CARICOM seeks the establishment of a common trade policy and increased cooperation in the Caribbean region. Includes 13 English-speaking Caribbean nations: Antigua and Barbuda, the Bahamas, Barbados, Belize, Dominica, Grenada, Guyana, Jamaica, Montserrat, Saint Kitts-Nevis, Saint Lucia, St. Vincent/Grenadines, and Trinidad and Tobago.

CARICOM *see* Caribbean Community and Common Market.

carnivore: Flesh-eating animal or plant.

carob: The common English name for a plant that is similar to and sometimes used as a substitute for chocolate.

cartel: An organization of independent producers formed to regulate the production, pricing, or marketing practices of its members in order to limit competition and maximize their market power.

cash crop: A crop that is grown to be sold rather than kept for private use.

cassation: The reversal or annulling of a final judgment by the supreme authority.

cassava: The name of several species of stout herbs, extensively cultivated for food.

caste system: One of the artificial divisions or social classes into which the Hindus are rigidly separated according to the religious law of Brahmanism. Membership in a caste is hereditary, and the privileges and disabilities of each caste are transmitted by inheritance.

Caucasian: The white race of human beings, as determined by genealogy and physical features.

Caucasoid: Belonging to the racial group characterized by light skin pigmentation. Commonly called the "white race."

cease-fire: An official declaration of the end to the use of military force or active hostilities, even if only temporary.

CEMA *see* Council for Mutual Economic Assistance.

censorship: The practice of withholding certain items of news that may cast a country in an unfavorable light or give away secrets to the enemy.

census: An official counting of the inhabitants of a state or country with details of sex and age, family, occupation, possessions, etc.

Central American Common Market (CACM): Established in 1962, a trade alliance of five Central American nations. Participating are Costa Rica, El Salvador, Guatemala, Honduras, and Nicaragua.

Central Powers: In World War I, Germany and Austria-Hungary, and their allies, Turkey and Bulgaria.

centrally planned economy: An economic system all aspects of which are supervised and regulated by the government.

centrist position: Refers to opinions held by members of a moderate political group; that is, views that are somewhere in the middle of popular thought between conservative and liberal.

cession: Withdrawal from or yielding to physical force.

chancellor: A high-ranking government official. In some countries it is the prime minister.

cholera: An acute infectious disease characterized by severe diarrhea, vomiting, and, often, death.

Christianity: The religion founded by Jesus Christ, based on the Bible as holy scripture.

Church of England: The national and established church in England. The Church of England claims continuity with the branch of the Catholic Church that existed in England before the Reformation. Under Henry VIII, the spiritual supremacy and jurisdiction of the Pope were abolished, and the sovereign (king or queen) was declared head of the church.

circuit court: A court that convenes in two or more locations within its appointed district.

CIS *see* Commonwealth of Independent States

city-state: An independent state consisting of a city and its surrounding territory.

civil court: A court whose proceedings include determinations of rights of individual citizens, in contrast to criminal proceedings regarding individuals or the public.

civil jurisdiction: The authority to enforce the laws in civil matters brought before the court.

civil law: The law developed by a nation or state for the conduct of daily life of its own people.

civil rights: The privileges of all individuals to be treated as equals under the laws of their country; specifically, the rights given by certain amendments to the U.S. Constitution.

civil unrest: The feeling of uneasiness due to an unstable political climate, or actions taken as a result of it.

civil war: A war between groups of citizens of the same country who have different opinions or agendas. The Civil War of the United States was the conflict between the states of the North and South from 1861 to 1865.

climatic belt: A region or zone where a particular type of climate prevails.

Club du Sahel: The Club du Sahel is an informal coalition which seeks to reverse the effects of drought and the desertification in the eight Sahelian zone countries: Burkina Faso, Chad, Gambia, Mali, Mauritania, Niger, Senegal, and the Cape Verde Islands. Headquarters are in Ouagadougou, Burkina Faso.

CMEA *see* Council for Mutual Economic Assistance.

coalition government: A government combining differing factions within a country, usually temporary.

coastal belt: A coastal plain area of lowlands and somewhat higher ridges that run parallel to the coast.

coastal plain: A fairly level area of land along the coast of a land mass.

coca: A shrub native to South America, the leaves of which produce organic compounds that are used in the production of cocaine.

coke: The solid product of the carbonization of coal, bearing the same relation to coal that charcoal does to wood.

cold war: Refers to conflict over ideological differences that is carried on by words and diplomatic actions, not by military action. The term is usually used to refer to the tension that existed between the United States and the USSR from the 1950s until the breakup of the USSR in 1991.

collective bargaining: The negotiations between workers who are members of a union and their employer for the purpose of deciding work rules and policies regarding wages, hours, etc.

collective farm: A large farm formed from many small farms and supervised by the government; usually found in communist countries.

collective farming: The system of farming on a collective where all workers share in the income of the farm.

colloquial: Belonging to ordinary, everyday speech: often especially applied to common words and phrases which are not used in formal speech.

colonial period: The period of time when a country forms colonies in and extends control over a foreign area.

colonist: Any member of a colony or one who helps settle a new colony.

colony: A group of people who settle in a new area far from their original country, but still under the jurisdiction of that country. Also refers to the newly settled area itself.

COMECON *see* Council for Mutual Economic Assistance.

commerce: The trading of goods (buying and selling), especially on a large scale, between cities, states, and countries.

commercial catch: The amount of marketable fish, usually measured in tons, caught in a particular period of time.

commercial crop: Any marketable agricultural crop.

commission: A group of people designated to collectively do a job, including a government agency with certain law-making powers. Also, the power given to an individual or group to perform certain duties.

commodity: Any items, such as goods or services, that are bought or sold, or agricultural products that are traded or marketed.

common law: A legal system based on custom and decisions and opinions of the law courts. The basic system of law of England and the United States.

common market: An economic union among countries that is formed to remove trade barriers (tariffs) among those countries, increasing economic cooperation. The European Community is a notable example of a common market.

commonwealth: A commonwealth is a free association of sovereign independent states that has no charter, treaty, or constitution. The association promotes cooperation, consultation, and mutual assistance among members.

Commonwealth of Independent States: The CIS was established in December 1991 as an association of 11 republics of the former Soviet Union. The members include: Russia, Ukraine, Belarus (formerly Byelorussia), Moldova (formerly Moldavia), Armenia, Azerbaijan, Uzbekistan, Turkmenistan, Tajikistan, Kazakhstan, and Kirgizstan (formerly Kirghiziya). The Baltic states—Estonia, Latvia, and Lithuania—did not join. Georgia maintained observer status before joining the CIS in November 1993.

Commonwealth of Nations: Voluntary association of the United Kingdom and its present dependencies and associated states, as well as certain former dependencies and their dependent territories. The term was first used officially in 1926 and is embodied in the Statute of Westminster (1931). Within the Commonwealth, whose secretariat (established in 1965) is located in London, England, are numerous subgroups devoted to economic and technical cooperation.

commune: An organization of people living together in a community who share the ownership and use of property. Also refers to a small governmental district of a country, especially in Europe.

communism: A form of government whose system requires common ownership of property for the use of all citizens. All profits are to be equally distributed and prices on goods and services are usually set by the state. Also, communism refers directly to the official doctrine of the former U.S.S.R.

compulsory: Required by law or other regulation.

compulsory education: The mandatory requirement for children to attend school until they have reached a certain age or grade level.

conciliation: A process of bringing together opposing sides of a disagreement for the purpose of compromise. Or, a way of settling an international dispute in which the disagreement is submitted to an independent committee that will examine the facts and advise the participants of a possible solution.

concordat: An agreement, compact, or convention, especially between church and state.

confederation: An alliance or league formed for the purpose of promoting the common interests of its members.

Confucianism: The system of ethics and politics taught by the Chinese philosopher Confucius.

coniferous forest: A forest consisting mainly of pine, fir, and cypress trees.

conifers: Cone-bearing plants. Mostly evergreen trees and shrubs which produce cones.

conscription: To be required to join the military by law. Also known as the draft. Service personnel who join the military because of the legal requirement are called conscripts or draftees.

conservative party: A political group whose philosophy tends to be based on established traditions and not supportive of rapid change.

constituency: The registered voters in a governmental district, or a group of people that supports a position or a candidate.

constituent assembly: A group of people that has the power to determine the election of a political representative or create a constitution.

constitution: The written laws and basic rights of citizens of a country or members of an organized group.

constitutional monarchy: A system of government in which the hereditary sovereign (king or queen, usually) rules according to a written constitution.

constitutional republic: A system of government with an elected chief of state and elected representation, with a written constitution containing its governing principles. The United States is a constitutional republic.

consumer goods: Items that are bought to satisfy personal needs or wants of individuals.

continental climate: The climate of a part of the continent; the characteristics and peculiarities of the climate are a result of the land itself and its location.

continental shelf: A plain extending from the continental coast and varying in width that typically ends in a steep slope to the ocean floor.

copra: The dried meat of the coconut; it is frequently used as an ingredient of curry, and to produce coconut oil. Also written *cobra, coprah,* and *copperah.*

Coptic Christians: Members of the Coptic Church of Egypt, formerly of Ethiopia.

cordillera: A continuous ridge, range, or chain of mountains.

corvette: A small warship that is often used as an escort ship because it is easier to maneuver than larger ships like destroyers.

Council for Mutual Economic Assistance (CMEA): Also known as Comecon, the alliance of socialist economies was established on 25 January 1949 and abolished 1 January 1991. It included Afghanistan*, Albania, Angola*, Bulgaria, Cuba, Czechoslovakia, Ethiopia*, East Germany, Hungary, Laos*, Mongolia, Mozambique*, Nicaragua*, Poland, Romania, USSR, Vietnam, Yemen*, and Yugoslavia. Nations marked with an asterisk were observers only.

counterinsurgency operations: Organized military activity designed to stop rebellion against an established government.

county: A territorial division or administrative unit within a state or country.

coup d'ètat or coup: A sudden, violent overthrow of a government or its leader.

court of appeal: An appellate court, having the power of review after a case has been decided in a lower court.

court of first appeal: The next highest court to the court which has decided a case, to which that case may be presented for review.

court of last appeal: The highest court, in which a decision is not subject to review by any higher court. In the United States, it could be the Supreme Court of an individual state or the U.S. Supreme Court.

cricket (sport): A game played by two teams with a ball and bat, with two wickets (staked target) being defended by a batsman. Common in the United Kingdom and Commonwealth of Nations countries.

criminal law: The branch of law that deals primarily with crimes and their punishments.

crown colony: A colony established by a commonwealth over which the monarch has some control, as in colonies established by the United Kingdom's Commonwealth of Nations.

Crusades: Military expeditions by European Christian armies in the eleventh, twelfth, and thirteenth centuries to win land controlled by the Muslims in the middle east.

cultivable land: Land that can be prepared for the production of crops.

Cultural Revolution: An extreme reform movement in China from 1966 to 1976; its goal was to combat liberalization by restoring the ideas of Mao Zedong.

Cushitic language group: A group of Hamitic languages that are spoken in Ethiopia and other areas of eastern Africa.

customs union: An agreement between two or more countries to remove trade barriers with each other and to establish common tariff and nontariff policies with respect to imports from countries outside of the agreement.

cyclone: Any atmospheric movement, general or local, in which the wind blows spirally around and in towards a center. In the northern hemisphere, the cyclonic movement is usually counter-clockwise, and in the southern hemisphere, it is clockwise.

Cyrillic alphabet: An alphabet adopted by the Slavic people and invented by Cyril and Methodius in the ninth century as an alphabet that was easier for the copyist to write. The Russian alphabet is a slight modification of it.

decentralization: The redistribution of power in a government from one large central authority to a wider range of smaller local authorities.

deciduous species: Any species that sheds or casts off a part of itself after a definite period of time. More commonly used in reference to plants that shed their leaves on a yearly basis as opposed to those (evergreens) that retain them.

declaration of independence: A formal written document stating the intent of a group of persons to become fully self-governing.

deficit: The amount of money that is in excess between spending and income.

deficit spending: The process in which a government spends money on goods and services in excess of its income.

deforestation: The removal or clearing of a forest.

deity: A being with the attributes, nature, and essence of a god; a divinity.

delta: Triangular-shaped deposits of soil formed at the mouths of large rivers.

demarcate: To mark off from adjoining land or territory; set the limits or boundaries of.

demilitarized zone (DMZ): An area surrounded by a combat zone that has had military troops and weapons removed.

demobilize: To disband or discharge military troops.

democracy: A form of government in which the power lies in the hands of the people, who can govern directly, or can be governed indirectly by representatives elected by its citizens.

denationalize: To remove from government ownership or control.

deportation: To carry away or remove from one country to another, or to a distant place.

depression: A hollow; a surface that has sunken or fallen in.

deregulation: The act of reversing controls and restrictions on prices of goods, bank interest, and the like.

desalinization plant: A facility that produces freshwater by removing the salt from saltwater.

desegregation: The act of removing restrictions on people of a particular race that keep them socially, economically, and, sometimes, physically, separate from other groups.

desertification: The process of becoming a desert as a result of climatic changes, land mismanagement, or both.

détente: The official lessening of tension between countries in conflict.

devaluation: The official lowering of the value of a country's currency in relation to the value of gold or the currencies of other countries.

developed countries: Countries which have a high standard of living and a well-developed industrial base.

development assistance: Government programs intended to finance and promote the growth of new industries.

dialect: One of a number of regional or related modes of speech regarded as descending from a common origin.

dictatorship: A form of government in which all the power is retained by an absolute leader or tyrant. There are no rights granted to the people to elect their own representatives.

diplomatic relations: The relationship between countries as conducted by representatives of each government.

direct election: The process of selecting a representative to the government by balloting of the voting public, in contrast to selection by an elected representative of the people.

disarmament: The reduction or depletion of the number of weapons or the size of armed forces.

dissident: A person whose political opinions differ from the majority to the point of rejection.

dogma: A principle, maxim, or tenet held as being firmly established.

domain: The area of land governed by a particular ruler or government, sometimes referring to the ultimate control of that territory.

domestic spending: Money spent by a country's government on goods used, investments, running of the government, and exports and imports.

dominion: A self-governing nation that recognizes the British monarch as chief of state.

dormant volcano: A volcano that has not exhibited any signs of activity for an extended period of time.

dowry: The sum of the property or money that a bride brings to her groom at their marriage.

draft constitution: The preliminary written plans for the new constitution of a country forming a new government.

Druze: A member of a Muslim sect based in Syria, living chiefly in the mountain regions of Lebanon.

dual nationality: The status of an individual who can claim citizenship in two or more countries.

duchy: Any territory under the rule of a duke or duchess.

due process: In law, the application of the legal process to which every citizen has a right, which cannot be denied.

durable goods: Goods or products which are expected to last and perform for several years, such as cars and washing machines.

duty: A tax imposed on imports by the customs authority of a country. Duties are generally based on the value of the goods (*ad valorem* duties), some other factors such as weight or quantity (specific duties), or a combination of value and other factors (compound duties).

dyewoods: Any wood from which dye is extracted.

dynasty: A family line of sovereigns who rule in succession, and the time during which they reign.

earned income: The money paid to an individual in wages or salary.

Eastern Orthodox: The outgrowth of the original Eastern Church of the Eastern Roman Empire, consisting of eastern Europe, western Asia, and Egypt.

EC *see* European Community

ecclesiastical: Pertaining or relating to the church.

echidna: A spiny, toothless anteater of Australia, Tasmania, and New Guinea.

ecological balance: The condition of a healthy, well-functioning ecosystem, which includes all the plants and animals in a natural community together with their environment.

ecology: The branch of science that studies organisms in relationship to other organisms and to their environment.

economic depression: A prolonged period in which there is high unemployment, low production, falling prices, and general business failure.

economically active population: That portion of the people who are employed for wages and are consumers of goods and services.

ecotourism: Broad term that encompasses nature, adventure, and ethnic tourism; responsible or wilderness-sensitive tourism; soft-path or small-scale tourism; low-impact tourism; and sustainable tourism. Scientific, educational, or academic tourism (such as biotourism, archetourism, and geotourism) are also forms of ecotourism.

elected assembly: The persons that comprise a legislative body of a government who received their positions by direct election.

electoral system: A system of choosing government officials by votes cast by qualified citizens.

electoral vote: The votes of the members of the electoral college.

electorate: The people who are qualified to vote in an election.

emancipation: The freeing of persons from any kind of bondage or slavery.

embargo: A legal restriction on commercial ships to enter a country's ports, or any legal restriction of trade.

emigration: Moving from one country or region to another for the purpose of residence.

empire: A group of territories ruled by one sovereign or supreme ruler. Also, the period of time under that rule.

enclave: A territory belonging to one nation that is surrounded by that of another nation.

encroachment: The act of intruding, trespassing, or entering on the rights or possessions of another.

endangered species: A plant or animal species whose existence as a whole is threatened with extinction.

endemic: Anything that is peculiar to and characteristic of a locality or region.

Enlightenment: An intellectual movement of the late seventeenth and eighteenth centuries in which scientific thinking gained a strong foothold and old beliefs were challenged. The idea of absolute monarchy was questioned and people were gradually given more individual rights.

enteric disease: An intestinal disease.

epidemic: As applied to disease, any disease that is temporarily prevalent among people in one place at the same time.

Episcopal: Belonging to or vested in bishops or prelates; characteristic of or pertaining to a bishop or bishops.

ethnolinguistic group: A classification of related languages based on common ethnic origin.

EU *see* European Union

European Community: A regional organization created in 1958. Its purpose is to eliminate customs duties and other trade barriers in Europe. It promotes a common external tariff against other countries, a Common Agricultural Policy (CAP), and guarantees of free movement of labor and capital. The original six members were Belgium, France, West Germany, Italy, Luxembourg, and the Netherlands. Denmark, Ireland, and the United Kingdom became members in 1973; Greece joined in 1981; Spain and Portugal in 1986. Other nations continue to join.

European Union: The EU is an umbrella reference to the European Community (EC) and to two European integration efforts introduced by the Maastricht Treaty: Common Foreign and Security Policy (including defense) and Justice and Home Affairs (principally cooperation between police and other authorities on crime, terrorism, and immigration issues).

exports: Goods sold to foreign buyers.

external migration: The movement of people from their native country to another country, as opposed to internal migration, which is the movement of people from one area of a country to another in the same country.

fallout: The precipitation of particles from the atmosphere, often the result of a ground disturbance by volcanic activity or a nuclear explosion.

family planning: The use of birth control to determine the number of children a married couple will have.

Fascism: A political philosophy that holds the good of the nation as more important than the needs of the individual. Fascism also stands for a dictatorial leader and strong oppression of opposition or dissent.

federal: Pertaining to a union of states whose governments are subordinate to a central government.

federation: A union of states or other groups under the authority of a central government.

fetishism: The practice of worshipping a material object that is believed to have mysterious powers residing in it, or is the representation of a deity to which worship may be paid and from which supernatural aid is expected.

feudal estate: The property owned by a lord in medieval Europe under the feudal system.

feudal society: In medieval times, an economic and social structure in which persons could hold land given to them by a lord (nobleman) in return for service to that lord.

final jurisdiction: The final authority in the decision of a legal matter. In the United States, the Supreme Court would have final jurisdiction.

Finno-Ugric language group: A subfamily of languages spoken in northeastern Europe, including Finnish, Hungarian, Estonian, and Lapp.

fiscal year: The twelve months between the settling of financial accounts, not necessarily corresponding to a calendar year beginning on January 1.

fjord: A deep indentation of the land forming a comparatively narrow arm of the sea with more or less steep slopes or cliffs on each side.

fly: The part of a flag opposite and parallel to the one nearest the flagpole.

fodder: Food for cattle, horses, and sheep, such as hay, straw, and other kinds of vegetables.

folk religion: A religion with origins and traditions among the common people of a nation or region that is relevant to their particular life-style.

foreign exchange: Foreign currency that allows foreign countries to conduct financial transactions or settle debts with one another.

foreign policy: The course of action that one government chooses to adopt in relation to a foreign country.

Former Soviet Union: The FSU is a collective reference to republics comprising the former Soviet Union. The term, which has been used including and excluding the Baltic republics (Estonia, Latvia, and Lithuania), includes the other 12 republics: Russia, Ukraine, Belarus, Moldova, Armenia, Azerbaijan, Uzbekistan, Turkmenistan, Tajikistan, Kazakhstan, Kyrgizstan, and Georgia.

fossil fuels: Any mineral or mineral substance formed by the decomposition of organic matter buried beneath the earth's surface and used as a fuel.

free enterprise: The system of economics in which private business may be conducted with minimum interference by the government.

free-market economy: An economic system that relies on the market, as opposed to government planners, to set the prices for wages and products.

frigate. A medium-sized warship.

fundamentalist: A person who holds religious beliefs based on the complete acceptance of the words of the Bible or other holy scripture as the truth. For instance, a fundamentalist would believe the story of creation exactly as it is told in the Bible and would reject the idea of evolution.

game reserve: An area of land reserved for wild animals that are hunted for sport or for food.

GDP *see* gross domestic product.

Germanic language group: A large branch of the Indo-European family of languages including German itself, the Scandinavian languages, Dutch, Yiddish, Modern English, Modern Scottish, Afrikaans, and others. The group also includes extinct languages such as Gothic, Old High German, Old Saxon, Old English, Middle English, and the like.

glasnost: President Mikhail Gorbachev's frank revelations in the 1980s about the state of the economy and politics in the Soviet Union; his policy of openness.

global greenhouse gas emissions: Gases released into the atmosphere that contribute to the greenhouse effect, a condition in which the earth's excess heat cannot escape.

global warming: Also called the greenhouse effect. The theorized gradual warming of the earth's climate as a result of the burning of fossil fuels, the use of man-made chemicals, deforestation, etc.

GMT *see* Greenwich Mean Time.

GNP *see* gross national product.

grand duchy: A territory ruled by a nobleman, called a grand duke, who ranks just below a king.

Greek Catholic: A person who is a member of an Orthodox Eastern Church.

Greek Orthodox: The official church of Greece, a self-governing branch of the Orthodox Eastern Church.

Greenwich (Mean) Time: Mean solar time of the meridian at Greenwich, England, used as the basis for standard time throughout most of the world. The world is divided into 24 time zones, and all are related to the prime, or Greenwich mean, zone.

gross domestic product: A measure of the market value of all goods and services produced within the boundaries of a nation, regardless of asset ownership. Unlike gross national product, GDP excludes receipts from that nation's business operations in foreign countries.

gross national product: A measure of the market value of goods and services produced by the labor and property of a nation. Includes receipts from that nation's business operation in foreign countries

groundwater: Water located below the earth's surface, the source from which wells and springs draw their water.

guano: The excrement of seabirds and bats found in various areas around the world. Gathered commercially and sold as a fertilizer.

guerrilla: A member of a small radical military organization that uses unconventional tactics to take their enemies by surprise.

gymnasium: A secondary school, primarily in Europe, that prepares students for university.

hardwoods: The name given to deciduous trees, such as cherry, oak, maple, and mahogany.

harem: In a Muslim household, refers to the women (wives, concubines, and servants in ancient times) who live there and also to the area of the home they live in.

harmattan: An intensely dry, dusty wind felt along the coast of Africa between Cape Verde and Cape Lopez. It prevails at intervals during the months of December, January, and February.

heavy industry: Industries that use heavy or large machinery to produce goods, such as automobile manufacturing.

hoist: The part of a flag nearest the flagpole.

Holocaust: The mass slaughter of European civilians, the vast majority Jews, by the Nazis during World War II.

Holy Roman Empire: A kingdom consisting of a loose union of German and Italian territories that existed from around the ninth century until 1806.

home rule: The governing of a territory by the citizens who inhabit it.

homeland: A region or area set aside to be a state for a people of a particular national, cultural, or racial origin.

homogeneous: Of the same kind or nature, often used in reference to a whole.

Horn of Africa: The Horn of Africa comprises Djibouti, Eritrea, Ethiopia, Somalia, and Sudan.

housing starts: The initiation of new housing construction.

human rights activist: A person who vigorously pursues the attainment of basic rights for all people.

human rights issues: Any matters involving people's basic rights which are in question or thought to be abused.

humanist: A person who centers on human needs and values, and stresses dignity of the individual.

humanitarian aid: Money or supplies given to a persecuted group or people of a country at war, or those devastated by a natural disaster, to provide for basic human needs.

hydrocarbon: A compound of hydrogen and carbon, often occurring in organic substances or derivatives of organic substances such as coal, petroleum, natural gas, etc.

hydrocarbon emissions: Organic compounds containing only carbon and hydrogen, often occurring in petroleum, natural gas, coal, and bitumens, and which contribute to the greenhouse effect.

hydroelectric potential: The potential amount of electricity that can be produced hydroelectrically. Usually used in reference to a given area and how many hydroelectric power plants that area can sustain.

hydroelectric power plant: A factory that produces electrical power through the application of waterpower.

IBRD *see* World Bank.

illegal alien: Any foreign-born individual who has unlawfully entered another country.

immigration: The act or process of passing or entering into another country for the purpose of permanent residence.

imports: Goods purchased from foreign suppliers.

indigenous: Born or originating in a particular place or country; native to a particular region or area.

Indo-Aryan language group: The group that includes the languages of India; also called Indo-European language group.

Indo-European language family: The group that includes the languages of India and much of Europe and southwestern Asia.

industrialized nation: A nation whose economy is based on industry.

infanticide: The act of murdering a baby.

infidel: One who is without faith or belief; particularly, one who rejects the distinctive doctrines of a particular religion.

inflation: The general rise of prices, as measured by a consumer price index. Results in a fall in value of currency.

installed capacity: The maximum possible output of electric power at any given time.

insurgency: The state or condition in which one rises against lawful authority or established government; rebellion.

insurrectionist: One who participates in an unorganized revolt against an authority.

interim government: A temporary or provisional government.

interim president: One who is appointed to perform temporarily the duties of president during a transitional period in a government.

internal migration: Term used to describe the relocation of individuals from one region to another without leaving the confines of the country or of a specified area.

International Date Line: An arbitrary line at about the 180th meridian that designates where one day begins and another ends.

Islam: The religious system of Mohammed, practiced by Moslims and based on a belief in Allah as the supreme being and Mohammed as his prophet. The spelling variations, Muslim and Muhammed, are also used, primarily by Islamic people. Islam also refers to those nations in which it is the primary religion.

isthmus: A narrow strip of land bordered by water and connecting two larger bodies of land, such as two continents, a continent and a peninsula, or two parts of an island.

Judaism: The religious system of the Jews, based on the Old Testament as revealed to Moses and characterized by a belief in one God and adherence to the laws of scripture and rabbinic traditions.

Judeo-Christian: The dominant traditional religious makeup of the United States and other countries based on the worship of the Old and New Testaments of the Bible.

junta: A small military group in power of a country, especially after a coup.

khan: A sovereign, or ruler, in central Asia.

khanate: A kingdom ruled by a khan, or man of rank.

kwashiorkor: Severe malnutrition in infants and children caused by a diet high in carbohydrates and lacking in protein.

kwh: The abbreviation for kilowatt-hour.

labor force: The number of people in a population available for work, whether actually employed or not.

labor movement: A movement in the early to mid-1800s to organize workers in groups according to profession to give them certain rights as a group, including bargaining power for better wages, working conditions, and benefits.

land reforms: Steps taken to create a fair distribution of farmland, especially by governmental action.

landlocked country: A country that does not have direct access to the sea; it is completely surrounded by other countries.

least developed countries: A subgroup of the United Nations designation of "less developed countries;" these countries generally have no significant economic growth, low literacy rates, and per person gross national product of less than $500. Also known as undeveloped countries.

leeward: The direction identical to that of the wind. For example, a *leeward tide* is a tide that runs in the same direction that the wind blows.

leftist: A person with a liberal or radical political affiliation.

legislative branch: The branch of government which makes or enacts the laws.

leprosy: A disease that can effect the skin and/or the nerves and can cause ulcers of the skin, loss of feeling, or loss of fingers and toes.

less developed countries (LDC): Designated by the United Nations to include countries with low levels of output, living standards, and per person gross national product generally below $5,000.

literacy: The ability to read and write.

Maastricht Treaty: The Maastricht Treaty (named for the Dutch town in which the treaty was signed) is also known as the Treaty of European Union. The treaty creates a European Union by: (a) committing the member states of the European Economic Community to both European Monetary Union (EMU) and political union; (b) introducing a single currency (European Currency Unit, ECU); (c) establishing a European System of Central Banks (ESCB); (d) creating a European Central Bank (ECB); and (e) broadening EC integration by including both a common foreign and security policy (CFSP) and cooperation in justice and home affairs (CJHA). The treaty entered into force on November 1, 1993.

Maghreb states: The Maghreb states include the three nations of Algeria, Morocco, and Tunisia; sometimes includes Libya and Mauritania.

maize: Another name (Spanish or British) for corn or the color of ripe corn.

majority party: The party with the largest number of votes and the controlling political party in a government.

mangrove: A tree which abounds on tropical shores in both hemispheres. Characterized by its numerous roots which arch out from its trunk and descend from its branches, mangroves form thick, dense growths along the tidal muds, reaching lengths hundreds of miles long.

manioc: The cassava plant or its product. Manioc is a very important food-staple in tropical America.

maquis. Scrubby, thick underbrush found along the coast of the Mediterranean Sea.

marginal land: Land that could produce an economic profit, but is so poor that it is only used when better land is no longer available.

marine life: The life that exists in, or is formed by the sea.

maritime climate: The climate and weather conditions typical of areas bordering the sea.

maritime rights: The rights that protect navigation and shipping.

market access: Market access refers to the openness of a national market to foreign products. Market access reflects a government's willingness to permit imports to compete relatively unimpeded with similar domestically produced goods.

market economy: A form of society which runs by the law of supply and demand. Goods are produced by firms to be sold to consumers, who determine the demand for them. Price levels vary according to the demand for certain goods and how much of them is produced.

market price: The price a commodity will bring when sold on the open market. The price is determined by the amount of demand for the commodity by buyers.

Marshall Plan: Formally known as the European Recovery Program, a joint project between the United States and most Western European nations under which $12.5 billion in U.S. loans and grants was expended to aid European recovery after World War II.

Marxism *see* Marxist-Leninist principles.

Marxist-Leninist principles: The doctrines of Karl Marx, built upon by Nikolai Lenin, on which communism was founded. They predicted the fall of capitalism, due to its own internal faults and the resulting oppression of workers.

Marxist: A follower of Karl Marx, a German socialist and revolutionary leader of the late 1800s, who contributed to Marxist-Leninist principles.

massif: A central mountain-mass or the dominant part of a range of mountains.

matrilineal (descent): Descending from, or tracing descent through, the maternal, or mother's, family line.

Mayan language family: The languages of the Central American Indians, further divided into two subgroups: the Maya and the Huastek.

mean temperature: The air temperature unit measured by the National Weather Service by adding the maximum and minimum daily temperatures together and diving the sum by 2.

Mecca (Mekkah): A city in Saudi Arabia; a destination of pilgrims in the Islamic world.

Mediterranean climate: A wet-winter, dry-summer climate with a moderate annual temperature range.

mestizo: The offspring of a person of mixed blood; especially, a person of mixed Spanish and American Indian parentage.

migratory birds: Those birds whose instincts prompt them to move from one place to another at the regularly recurring changes of season.

migratory workers: Usually agricultural workers who move from place to place for employment depending on the growing and harvesting seasons of various crops.

military coup: A sudden, violent overthrow of a government by military forces.

military junta: The small military group in power in a country, especially after a coup.

military regime: Government conducted by a military force.

military takeover: The seizure of control of a government by the military forces.

militia: The group of citizens of a country who are either serving in the reserve military forces or are eligible to be called up in time of emergency.

millet: A cereal grass whose small grain is used for food in Europe and Asia.

minority party: The political group that comprises the smaller part of the large overall group it belongs to; the party that is not in control.

missionary: A person sent by authority of a church or religious organization to spread his religious faith in a community where his church has no self-supporting organization.

Mohammed (or Muhammedor Mahomet): An Arabian prophet, known as the "Prophet of Allah" who founded the religion of Islam in 622, and wrote *The Koran,* the scripture of Islam. Also commonly spelled Muhammed, especially by Islamic people.

monarchy: Government by a sovereign, such as a king or queen.

money economy: A system or stage of economic development in which money replaces barter in the exchange of goods and services.

Mongol: One of an Asiatic race chiefly resident in Mongolia, a region north of China proper and south of Siberia.

Mongoloid: Having physical characteristics like those of the typical Mongols (Chinese, Japanese, Turks, Eskimos, etc.).

Moors: One of the Arab tribes that conquered Spain in the eighth century.

Moslem (Muslim): A follower of Mohammed (spelled Muhammed by many Islamic people), in the religion of Islam.

mosque: An Islam place of worship and the organization with which it is connected.

mouflon: A type of wild sheep characterized by curling horns.

mujahideen (mujahedin or mujahedeen): Rebel fighters in Islamic countries, especially those supporting the cause of Islam.

mulatto: One who is the offspring of parents one of whom is white and the other is black.

municipality: A district such as a city or town having its own incorporated government.

Muslim: A frequently used variation of the spelling of Moslem, to describe a follower of the prophet Mohammed (also spelled Muhammed), the founder of the religion of Islam.

Muslim New Year: A Muslim holiday. Although in some countries 1 Muharram, which is the first month of the Islamic year, is observed as a holiday, in other places the new year is observed on Sha'ban, the eighth month of the year. This practice apparently stems from pagan Arab times. Shab-i-Bharat, a national holiday in Bangladesh on this day, is held by many to be the occasion when God ordains all actions in the coming year.

NAFTA (North American Free Trade Agreement): NAFTA, which entered into force in January 1994, is a free trade agreement between Canada, the United States, and Mexico. The agreement progressively eliminates almost all U.S.-Mexico tariffs over a 10–15 year period.

nationalism: National spirit or aspirations; desire for national unity, independence, or prosperity.

nationalization: To transfer the control or ownership of land or industries to the nation from private owners.

native tongue: One's natural language. The language that is indigenous to an area.

NATO *see* North Atlantic Treaty Organization

natural gas: A combustible gas formed naturally in the earth and generally obtained by boring a well. The chemical makeup of natural gas is principally methane, hydrogen, ethylene compounds, and nitrogen.

natural harbor: A protected portion of a sea or lake along the shore resulting from the natural formations of the land.

naturalize: To confer the rights and privileges of a native-born subject or citizen upon someone who lives in the country by choice.

nature preserve: An area where one or more species of plant and/or animal are protected from harm, injury, or destruction.

neutrality: The policy of not taking sides with any countries during a war or dispute among them.

Newly Independent States: The NIS is a collective reference to 12 republics of the former Soviet Union: Russia, Ukraine, Belarus (formerly Byelorussia), Moldova (formerly Moldavia), Armenia, Azerbaijan, Uzbekistan, Turkmenistan, Tajikistan, Kazakhstan, and Kirgizstan (formerly Kirghiziya), and Georgia. Following dissolution of the Soviet Union, the distinction between the NIS and the Commonwealth of Independent States (CIS) was that Georgia was not a member of the CIS. That distinction dissolved when Georgia joined the CIS in November 1993.

news censorship *see* censorship

Nonaligned Movement: The NAM is an alliance of third world states that aims to promote the political and economic interests of developing countries. NAM interests have included ending colonialism/neo-colonialism, supporting the integrity of independent countries, and seeking a new international economic order.

Nordic Council: The Nordic Council, established in 1952, is directed toward supporting cooperation among Nordic countries. Members include Denmark, Finland, Iceland, Norway, and Sweden. Headquarters are in Stockholm, Sweden.

North Atlantic Treaty Organization (NATO): A mutual defense organization. Members include Belgium, Canada, Denmark, France (which has only partial membership), Greece, Iceland, Italy, Luxembourg, Netherlands, Norway, Portugal, Spain, Turkey, United Kingdom, United States, and Germany.

nuclear power plant: A factory that produces electrical power through the application of the nuclear reaction known as nuclear fission.

nuclear reactor: A device used to control the rate of nuclear fission in uranium. Used in commercial applications, nuclear reactors can maintain temperatures high enough to generate sufficient quantities of steam which can then be used to produce electricity.

OAPEC (Organization of Arab Petroleum Exporting countries): OAPEC was created in 1968; members include: Algeria, Bahrain, Egypt, Iraq, Kuwait, Libya, Qatar, Saudi Arabia, Syria, and the United Arab Emirates. Headquarters are in Cairo, Egypt.

OAS (Organization of American States): The OAS (Spanish: Organizaciûn de los Estados Americanos, OEA), or the Pan American Union, is a regional organization which promotes Latin American economic and social development. Members include the United States, Mexico, and most Central American, South American, and Caribbean nations.

OAS *see* Organization of American States

oasis: Originally, a fertile spot in the Libyan desert where there is a natural spring or well and vegetation; now refers to any fertile tract in the midst of a wasteland.

occupied territory: A territory that has an enemy's military forces present.

official language: The language in which the business of a country and its government is conducted.

oligarchy: A form of government in which a few people possess the power to rule as opposed to a monarchy which is ruled by one.

OPEC *see* OAPEC

open economy: An economy that imports and exports goods.

open market: Open market operations are the actions of the central bank to influence or control the money supply by buying or selling government bonds.

opposition party: A minority political party that is opposed to the party in power.

Organization of Arab Petroleum Exporting Countries *see* OAPEC

organized labor: The body of workers who belong to labor unions.

Ottoman Empire: An Turkish empire founded by Osman I in about 1603, that variously controlled large areas of land around the Mediterranean, Black, and Caspian Seas until it was dissolved in 1918.

overfishing: To deplete the quantity of fish in an area by removing more fish than can be naturally replaced.

overgrazing: Allowing animals to graze in an area to the point that the ground vegetation is damaged or destroyed.

overseas dependencies: A distant and physically separate territory that belongs to another country and is subject to its laws and government.

Pacific Rim: The Pacific Rim, referring to countries and economies bordering the Pacific Ocean.

pact: An international agreement.

Paleolithic: The early period of the Stone Age, when rough, chipped stone implements were used.

panhandle: A long narrow strip of land projecting like the handle of a frying pan.

papyrus: The paper-reed or -rush which grows on marshy river banks in the southeastern area of the Mediterranean, but more notably in the Nile valley.

paramilitary group: A supplementary organization to the military.

parasitic diseases: A group of diseases caused by parasitic organisms which feed off the host organism.

parliamentary republic: A system of government in which a president and prime minister, plus other ministers of departments, constitute the executive branch of the government and the parliament constitutes the legislative branch.

parliamentary rule: Government by a legislative body similar to that of Great Britain, which is composed of two houses—one elected and one hereditary.

parochial: Refers to matters of a church parish or something within narrow limits.

patriarchal system: A social system in which the head of the family or tribe is the father or oldest male. Kinship is determined and traced through the male members of the tribe.

patrilineal (descent): Descending from, or tracing descent through, the paternal or father's line.

pellagra: A disease marked by skin, intestinal, and central nervous system disorders, caused by a diet deficient in niacin, one of the B vitamins.

per capita: Literally, per person; for each person counted.

perestroika: The reorganization of the political and economic structures of the Soviet Union by president Mikhail Gorbachev.

periodical: A publication whose issues appear at regular intervals, such as weekly, monthly, or yearly.

petrochemical: A chemical derived from petroleum or from natural gas.

pharmaceutical plants: Any plant that is used in the preparation of medicinal drugs.

plantain: The name of a common weed that has often been used for medicinal purposes, as a folk remedy and in modern medicine. *Plaintain* is also the name of a tropical plant producing a type of banana.

poaching: To intrude or encroach upon another's preserves for the purpose of stealing animals, especially wild game.

polar climate: Also called tundra climate. A humid, severely cold climate controlled by arctic air masses, with no warm or summer season.

political climate: The prevailing political attitude of a particular time or place.

political refugee: A person forced to flee his or her native country for political reasons.

potable water: Water that is safe for drinking.

pound sterling: The monetary unit of Great Britain, otherwise known as the pound.

prefect: An administrative official; in France, the head of a particular department.

prefecture: The territory over which a prefect has authority.

prime meridian: Zero degrees in longitude that runs through Greenwich, England, site of the Royal Observatory. All other longitudes are measured from this point.

prime minister: The premier or chief administrative official in certain countries.

private sector: The division of an economy in which production of goods and services is privately owned.

privatization: To change from public to private control or ownership.

protectorate: A state or territory controlled by a stronger state, or the relationship of the stronger country toward the lesser one it protects.

Protestant Reformation: In 1529, a Christian religious movement begun in Germany to deny the universal authority of the Pope, and to establish the Bible as the only source of truth. (*Also see* Protestant)

Protestant: A member or an adherent of one of those Christian bodies which descended from the Reformation of the sixteenth century. Originally applied to those who opposed or protested the Roman Catholic Church.

proved reserves: The quantity of a recoverable mineral resource (such as oil or natural gas) that is still in the ground.

province: An administrative territory of a country.

provisional government: A temporary government set up during time of unrest or transition in a country.

pulses: Beans, peas, or lentils.

purge: The act of ridding a society of "undesirable" or unloyal persons by banishment or murder.

Rastafarian: A member of a Jamaican cult begun in 1930 as a semi-religious, semi-political movement.

rate of literacy: The percentage of people in a society who can read and write.

recession. A period of reduced economic activity in a country or region.

referendum: The practice of submitting legislation directly to the people for a popular vote.

Reformation *see* Protestant Reformation.

refugee: One who flees to a refuge or shelter or place of safety. One who in times of persecution or political commotion flees to a foreign country for safety.

revolution: A complete change in a government or society, such as in an overthrow of the government by the people.

right-wing party: The more conservative political party.

Roman alphabet: The alphabet of the ancient Romans from which the alphabets of most modern western European languages, including English, are derived.

Roman Catholic Church: The designation of the church of which the pope or Bishop of Rome is the head, and that holds him as the successor of St. Peter and heir of his spiritual authority, privileges, and gifts.

romance language: The group of languages derived from Latin: French, Spanish, Italian, Portuguese, and other related languages.

roundwood: Timber used as poles or in similar ways without being sawn or shaped.

runoff election: A deciding election put to the voters in case of a tie between candidates.

Russian Orthodox: The arm of the Orthodox Eastern Church that was the official church of Russia under the czars.

sack: To strip of valuables, especially after capture.

Sahelian zone: Eight countries make up this dry desert zone in Africa: Burkina Faso, Chad, Gambia, Mali, Mauritania, Niger, Senegal, and the Cape Verde Islands. *Also see* Club du Sahel.

salinization: An accumulation of soluble salts in soil. This condition is common in desert climates, where water evaporates quickly in poorly drained soil due to high temperatures.

Samaritans: A native or an inhabitant of Samaria; specifically, one of a race settled in the cities of Samaria by the king of Assyria after the removal of the Israelites from the country.

savanna: A treeless or near treeless plain of a tropical or subtropical region dominated by drought-resistant grasses.

schistosomiasis: A tropical disease that is chronic and characterized by disorders of the liver, urinary bladder, lungs, or central nervous system.

secession: The act of withdrawal, such as a state withdrawing from the Union in the Civil War in the United States.

sect: A religious denomination or group, often a dissenting one with extreme views.

segregation: The enforced separation of a racial or religious group from other groups, compelling them to live and go to school separately from the rest of society.

seismic activity: Relating to or connected with an earthquake or earthquakes in general.

self-sufficient: Able to function alone without help.

separation of power: The division of power in the government among the executive, legislative, and judicial branches and the checks and balances employed to keep them separate and independent of each other.

separatism: The policy of dissenters withdrawing from a larger political or religious group.

serfdom: In the feudal system of the Middle Ages, the condition of being attached to the land owned by a lord and being transferable to a new owner.

Seventh-day Adventist: One who believes in the second coming of Christ to establish a personal reign upon the earth.

shamanism: A religion of some Asians and Amerindians in which shamans, who are priests or medicine men, are believed to influence good and evil spirits.

shantytown: An urban settlement of people in flimsy, inadequate houses.

Shia Muslim: Members of one of two great sects of Islam. Shia Muslims believe that Ali and the Imams are the rightful successors of Mohammed (also commonly spelled Muhammed). They also believe that the last recognized Imam will return as a messiah. Also known as Shiites. (*Also see* Sunnis.)

Shiites *see* Shia Muslims.

Shintoism: The system of nature- and hero-worship which forms the indigenous religion of Japan.

shoal: A place where the water of a stream, lake, or sea is of little depth. Especially, a sand-bank which shows at low water.

sierra: A chain of hills or mountains.

Sikh: A member of a politico-religious community of India, founded as a sect around 1500 and based on the principles of monotheism (belief in one god) and human brotherhood.

Sino-Tibetan language family: The family of languages spoken in eastern Asia, including China, Thailand, Tibet, and Burma.

slash-and-burn agriculture: A hasty and sometimes temporary way of clearing land to make it available for agriculture by cutting down trees and burning them.

slave trade: The transportation of black Africans beginning in the 1700s to other countries to be sold as slaves—people owned as property and compelled to work for their owners at no pay.

Slavic languages: A major subgroup of the Indo-European language family. It is further subdivided into West Slavic (including Polish, Czech, Slovak and Serbian), South Slavic (including Bulgarian, Serbo-Croatian, Slovene, and Old Church Slavonic), and East Slavic (including Russian Ukrainian and Byelorussian).

social insurance: A government plan to protect low-income people, such as health and accident insurance, pension plans, etc.

social security: A form of social insurance, including life, disability, and old-age pension for workers. It is paid for by employers, employees, and the government.

socialism: An economic system in which ownership of land and other property is distributed among the community as a whole, and every member of the community shares in the work and products of the work.

socialist: A person who advocates socialism.

softwoods: The coniferous trees, whose wood density as a whole is relatively softer than the wood of those trees referred to as hardwoods.

sorghum (also known as Syrian Grass): Plant grown in various parts of the world for its valuable uses, such as for grain, syrup, or fodder.

Southeast Asia: The region in Asia that consists of the Malay Archipelago, the Malay Peninsula, and Indochina.

staple crop: A crop that is the chief commodity or product of a place, and which has widespread and constant use or value.

state: The politically organized body of people living under one government or one of the territorial units that make up a federal government, such as in the United States.

steppe: A level tract of land more or less devoid of trees, in certain parts of European and Asiatic Russia.

student demonstration: A public gathering of students to express strong feelings about a certain situation, usually taking place near the location of the people in power to change the situation.

subarctic climate: A high latitude climate of two types: *continental subarctic*, which has very cold winters, short, cool summers, light precipitation and moist air; and *marine subarctic*, a coastal and island climate with polar air masses causing large precipitation and extreme cold.

subcontinent: A land mass of great size, but smaller than any of the continents; a large subdivision of a continent.

subsistence economy: The part of a national economy in which money plays little or no role, trade is by barter, and living standards are minimal.

subsistence farming: Farming that provides the minimum food goods necessary for the continuation of the farm family.

subtropical climate: A middle latitude climate dominated by humid, warm temperatures and heavy rainfall in summer, with cool winters and frequent cyclonic storms.

subversion: The act of attempting to overthrow or ruin a government or organization by stealthy or deceitful means.

Sudanic language group: A related group of languages spoken in various areas of northern Africa, including Yoruba, Mandingo, and Tshi.

suffrage: The right to vote.

Sufi: A Muslim mystic who believes that God alone exists, there can be no real difference between good and evil, that the soul exists within the body as in a cage, so death should be the chief object of desire, and sufism is the only true philosophy.

sultan: A king of a Muslim state.

Sunni Muslim: Members of one of two major sects of the religion of Islam. Sunni Muslims adhere to strict orthodox traditions, and believe that the four caliphs are the rightful successors to Mohammed, founder of Islam. (Mohammed is commonly spelled Muhammed, especially by Islamic people.) (*Also see* Shia Muslim.)

Taoism: The doctrine of Lao-Tzu, an ancient Chinese philosopher (about 500 B.C.) as laid down by him in the *Tao-te-ching*.

tariff: A tax assessed by a government on goods as they enter (or leave) a country. May be imposed to protect domestic industries from imported goods and/or to generate revenue.

temperate zone: The parts of the earth lying between the tropics and the polar circles. The *northern temperate zone* is the area between the tropic of Cancer and the Arctic Circle. The *southern temperate zone* is the area between the tropic of Capricorn and the Antarctic Circle.

terracing: A form of agriculture that involves cultivating crops in raised banks of earth.

terrorism: Systematic acts of violence designed to frighten or intimidate.

thermal power plant: A facility that produces electric energy from heat energy released by combustion of fuel or nuclear reactions.

Third World: A term used to describe less developed countries; as of the mid-1990s, it is being replaced by the United Nations designation Less Developed Countries, or LDC.

topography: The physical or natural features of the land.

torrid zone: The part of the earth's surface that lies between the tropics, so named for the character of its climate.

totalitarian party: The single political party in complete authoritarian control of a government or state.

trachoma: A contagious bacterial disease that affects the eye.

treaty: A negotiated agreement between two governments.

tribal system: A social community in which people are organized into groups or clans descended from common ancestors and sharing customs and languages.

tropical monsoon climate: One of the tropical rainy climates; it is sufficiently warm and rainy to produce tropical rainforest vegetation, but also has a winter dry season.

tsetse fly: Any of the several African insects which can transmit a variety of parasitic organisms through its bite. Some of these organisms can prove fatal to both human and animal victims.

tundra: A nearly level treeless area whose climate and vegetation are characteristically arctic due to its northern position; the subsoil is permanently frozen.

undeveloped countries *see* least developed countries.

unemployment rate: The overall unemployment rate is the percentage of the work force (both employed and unemployed) who claim to be unemployed.

UNICEF: An international fund set-up for children's emergency relief: United Nations Children's Fund (formerly United Nations International Children's Emergency Fund).

universal adult suffrage: The policy of giving every adult in a nation the right to vote.

untouchables: In India, members of the lowest caste in the caste system, a hereditary social class system. They were considered unworthy to touch members of higher castes.

urban guerrilla: A rebel fighter operating in an urban area.

urbanization: The process of changing from country to city.

USSR: An abbreviation of Union of Soviet Socialist Republics.

veldt: In South Africa, an unforested or thinly forested tract of land or region, a grassland.

Warsaw Pact: Agreement made 14 May 1955 (and dissolved 1 July 1991) to promote mutual defense between Albania, Bulgaria, Czechoslovakia, East Germany, Hungary, Poland, Romania, and the USSR.

Western nations: Blanket term used to describe mostly democratic, capitalist countries, including the United States, Canada, and western European countries.

wildlife sanctuary: An area of land set aside for the protection and preservation of animals and plants.

workers' compensation: A series of regular payments by an employer to a person injured on the job.

World Bank: The World Bank is a group of international institutions which provides financial and technical assistance to developing countries.

world oil crisis: The severe shortage of oil in the 1970s precipitated by the Arab oil embargo.

wormwood: A woody perennial herb native to Europe and Asiatic Russia, valued for its medicinal uses.

yaws: A tropical disease caused by a bacteria which produces raspberry-like sores on the skin.

yellow fever: A tropical viral disease caused by the bite of an infected mosquito, characterized by jaundice.

Zoroastrianism: The system of religious doctrine taught by Zoroaster and his followers in the Avesta; the religion prevalent in Persia until its overthrow by the Muslims in the seventh century.

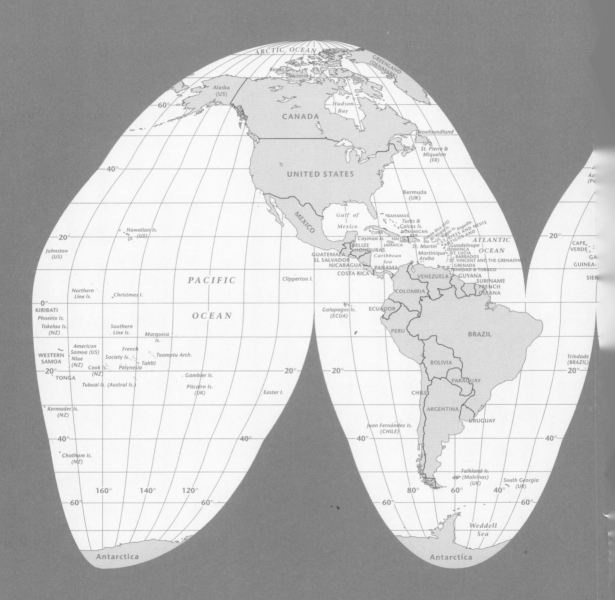